Developing Thinking

Approaches to children's cognitive development

edited by

SARA MEADOWS

METHUEN
LONDON AND NEW YORK

First published in 1983 by
Methuen & Co. Ltd
11 New Fetter Lane, London EC4P 4EE

Published in the USA by
Methuen & Co.
in association with Methuen, Inc.
733 Third Avenue, New York, NY 10017

Printed in Great Britain by
The Burlington Press (Cambridge) Ltd, Foxton, Cambridge.

British Library Cataloguing in Publication Data
Meadows, Sara
Developing thinking.–(Psychology in progress)
1. Cognition in children
I. Title II. Series
155.4'13 BF723.C5

ISBN 0-416-33030-4
ISBN 0-416-33040-1 Pbk

Library of Congress Cataloging in Publication Data
Developing thinking
(Psychology in progress)
Bibliography: p.
Includes indexes.
1. Cognition in children. 2. Child development.
I. Meadows, Sara. II. Series. [DNLM: 1. Cognition – In infancy and childhood. 2. Child development.
3. Thinking – In infancy and childhood. WS 105.5.C7 D489]
BF723.C5D47 1983 155.4'13 83-11381
ISBN 0-416-33030-4
ISBN 0-416-33040-1 Pbk

Psychology
in
Progress

General editor: Peter Herriot

Developing
Thinking

Psychology in Progress

Already available

Philosophical Problems in Psychology
edited by Neil Bolton

The Pathology and Psychology of Cognition
edited by Andrew Burton

Thinking in Perspective
Critical essays in the study of thought processes
edited by Andrew Burton and John Radford

The School Years
Current issues in the socialization of young people
edited by John C. Coleman

Applications of Conditioning Theory
edited by Graham Davey

Personality
Theory, measurement and research
edited by Fay Fransella

Aspects of Memory
edited by Michael M. Gruneberg and Peter Morris

Issues in Childhood Social Development
edited by Harry McGurk

Brain, Behaviour and Evolution
edited by David A. Oakley and H. C. Plotkin

Small Groups and Personal Change
edited by Peter B. Smith

Contents

Notes on the contributors

Charles J. Brainerd is Henry Marshall Tory Professor of Social Science, University of Alberta. He is the author of numerous papers and book chapters on cognitive development and of *Piaget's Theory of Intelligence* (Prentice-Hall, 1978). He is the general editor of the Springer-Verlag series on cognitive development. His current research interests include working-memory theories of cognitive development and developmental analysis of learning.

Elaine Funnell initially qualified as a teacher, and subsequently took a degree in Psychology at the University of Reading. Her research interests include aspects of cognitive development and language processing, especially after brain damage.

Paul Light is a lecturer in Psychology at the University of Southampton. He has researched and published on social and cognitive development, including *The Development of Social Sensitivity* (Cambridge University Press, 1979) and (as co-editor with George Butterworth) *Social Cognition: Studies of the Development of Understanding* (Harvester, 1982). His current research interests include language remediation for non-speaking autistic and mentally retarded children, and the study of children's drawings.

Ingrid Lunt is an educational psychologist working for the Inner London Education Authority. Before becoming an educational psychologist she taught for five years in a London comprehensive school. She is the co-author (with Kathy Sylva) of *Child Development: A First Course* (Grant McIntyre, 1982).

Sara Meadows is a lecturer in the School of Education of the University of Bristol, where she teaches developmental psychology to teachers. She works on motivational aspects of cognitive development and early childhood education, and her current interests are reflected in her selection of chapters for this book.

Maggie Mills is an honorary lecturer in Psychology at Bedford College, University of London, and previously lectured at the University of Reading. Her current research is on individual differences in mothering style, funded by the Medical Research Council, and on developmental dyslexia. She is also a member of the British Board of Film Censors.

David R. Olson is a professor in the Department of Applied Psychology in the Ontario Institute for Studies in Education. He has published widely on cognitive development and literacy, including (as editor) *The Social Foundations of Language and Thought: Essays in Honor of Jerome S. Bruner* (Norton, 1980).

Elizabeth Robinson is a research fellow in the School of Education of the University of Bristol. Among her publications are *The Invention and Discovery of Reality* (published under her maiden name of Peill, Wiley, 1975) and a number of papers on children's understanding of communication. Her current research interests are in this area and in problems of communication between doctors and patients.

Andrew Sutton trained as an educational psychologist and now works largely in the field of child care. He has an honorary lectureship at the Faculty of Education of the University of Birmingham, and has studied Soviet psychology for the last ten years. He has published on children's rights, forensic psychology and the sociology of professional practice as well as on Soviet developmental psychology.

Nancy G. Torrance is a research associate of the Centre for Applied Cognitive Science at the Ontario Institute for Studies in Education. Her interests are in cognitive development and literacy.

Editor's introduction

This book on cognitive development in children takes its place in a series on psychology in progress. The period over which it was planned, written and produced was unquestionably one of tremendous activity in the study of children's thinking, and to my mind one of progress perhaps amounting to what Kuhn (1962) has called a 'paradigm shift'. There have been for the last few years new answers, new questions, new ideas, new frames of reference and new applications. One purpose of this book is to illustrate what they are, to document a lively area of psychology.

It is clear that cognitive development is complex, mysterious and important. Cognition, traditionally one of the main characteristics distinguishing 'humanness' from 'animality' and, perhaps as a consequence, highly esteemed, has been in and out of fashion as a subject for psychological study as successive attempts to describe and measure it ran into problems. Introspectionism's difficulties were followed by the behaviourists' preference for ignoring the cognition that came between stimulus and response, and this strategy was followed in turn by attempts to specify the structures and processes that made up the 'mediating responses' which had to be postulated to make sense of observed S-R links. The contemporaneous development of sophisticated computers contributed to this renaissance of the psychology of cognition both as a source of metaphors and as a means of testing models, and in certain areas, memory being perhaps the most notable, there has been impressive achievement. Recently, attempts have been made to extend this approach to the study of children's thought (Wallace, 1980), and this would seem likely to be a useful enterprise. The largest component of cognitive development theory has, however, had a rather different history. Piaget, isolated from behaviourist-dominated English-language psychology, constructed a model of the nature of children's thinking which, when it eventually became known in

Britain and America, had an overwhelming impact on psychological research. For at least twenty years the majority of work on cognitive development involved reference to Piaget. It is no accident that the first chapter of this book is on the Piagetian model, and that every other chapter shows signs of his ideas. It is worth noting that Piaget's material influenced work on information-processing in children, and his own interest shifted towards the end of his life from structures of knowledge to the processes of knowing, so these two approaches to cognitive development co-exist. Analysis in detail of the processes children use in thinking, both in the carefully-defined experimental situations of information-processing and post-Piagetian work and, increasingly, in more 'natural' settings such as school maths lessons or conflicts within the family, is one of the most important and exciting areas of the psychology of cognitive development, and a major focus of this book.

There are, of course, other bodies of relevant work. Language development is close to cognitive development, perhaps ultimately inseparable from it, and its psychology has undergone very similar changes. Psychometrics has made some slight use of cognitive-development theory but has not yet contributed much to our understanding of cognitive development (see Chapter 4). Indeed, it has rather tended to assume that ontogenetic changes in cognition, changes from childish to adult ways of thinking, are relatively unimportant. Sociobiology is just beginning to move into the field of cognition (Lumsden and Wilson, 1981), postulating epigenetic rules which direct the assembly of mind and culture. In so doing, it is beginning to show some realization that human sociobiology must become more discreet and more sophisticated than it has been, since 'the mind of the human being intervenes to impose an immense new realm of order and process between learning and explicit behaviour' (ibid., p. 251). The strongest example so far of universal biological processes constraining human behaviour into a very limited range of cognition, despite environmental and cultural diversity, is the basic classification of colours (ibid., p. 43ff.). Highly selective use of evidence allows them to make a case for a more obvious sociobiological favourite, maternal instinct, but necessitates recognition of the overwhelming importance of mind and culture, which may have a reciprocal effect on genes. This approach is too new to have made much contribution to cognitive development yet, though it is in many ways reminiscent of the Piaget of *Biology and*

Knowledge (Piaget, 1971). I would suggest that here, too, the shift of emphasis (or of paradigm) which is changing the psychology of cognitive development should be encouraged.

My very brief description of the different approaches that have contributed to the study of cognitive development, although it verges on caricature, does something to demonstrate the complexity of the question of cognition. It is a question which has been central and problematic in psychology and philosopy for centuries. What do we know about our own knowing, or about our conspecifics'? How are we to understand our, or our children's, understanding? Are there different sorts of knowledge in different cultures or at different historical periods, or in different areas of intellectual activity (perhaps scientific knowledge differs from religious knowledge, for example); or, returning to a focus on cognitive development, is knowledge different at different ages in the same individual? If it is, how does it change, and why? And, there being an important educational component to human life, what, if anything, ought we to do about it?

These are not rhetorical questions, although it is very hard to provide adequate answers to them. The possible paradigm shift that we may discern in recent work on cognitive development, and which unites the chapters of this book, centres on the epistemological issue of the nature of the knower and of the sources of knowledge. The traditional conception in English-language psychology, and a major strand in the philosophy of epistemology, has been predominantly one drawn in a Cartesian framework (Markova, 1982). The knower is primarily an isolated individual, constructing his understanding apart from any social context, his consciousness also rather separate from the outside world which he contemplates rather than acts on; knowledge comes from intuition and deduction applied to the stimuli which impinge on the relatively passive knower from outside; thought is described and assessed for adequacy in terms of formal systems such as truth-functional logic; the dominant metaphor for the knower is a machine, and parts of his activities are studied in isolation from the whole. Markova argues that most of these fundamental assumptions are misleading, have placed constraints on psychology which are making it unproductive, and should be replaced by a shift of paradigm into a Hegelian framework. This would entail recognition of the knower as someone who develops his knowledge inextricably in and with a social context, whose mind is active in the selection and alteration of information and in the construction and use of knowledge, whose thought may be pragmatic as much as logical, who revises his theories and so transforms his consciousness; and who, importantly for research methods in psychology, does this even when acting as subject (or experimenter) in psychological experiments.

Psychology as in progress at the moment has not developed the unanimity or the courage needed to make so great a shift of paradigm as this, and it is not clear whether it will or indeed should. However, the developments in the recent study of children's thinking which are described in this book do show changes in emphasis towards a more Hegelian position. The chapters by Paul Light and Elizabeth Robinson, for example, show the current emphasis on social interaction as a source of cognitive development, and the importance of consciousness of thought is clear from David Olson and Nancy Torrance's chapter as well as Elizabeth Robinson's. Charles Brainerd and Ingrid Lunt both spell out the importance of this shift in position for practice in education and assessment. Maggie Mills and Elaine Funnell, linking a number of approaches, illustrate both how cognitive development is naturally embedded in social situations and how rewarding efforts to analyse cognitive processing in detail can be. This last point is implicit throughout the book: it is essential to work out exactly what children do in thinking, understanding and problem-solving, and to consider carefully why they do what they do, separating cognition and affectivity as little as possible.

What follows, then, is a collection of papers on some of the areas of work on developing thinking that seemed to the editor at the beginning of the 1980s particularly exciting, coherent or important. A great deal is omitted; there is virtually nothing on babies or adolescents, or on handicapped children, who deserve a book to themselves. The focus is psychological, but a psychology that concerns itself with the other biological and social sciences, and in particular with education, which is a professional preoccupation of most of the contributors. This focus is one which we share with our predecessors; notably with Bruner and, as Andrew Sutton describes in the last chapter, with Soviet developmental psychologists.

'Developing thinking' is of course a phrase with more than one meaning. In one sense, 'developing' is something that 'thinking' does, as in the phrase 'flying ducks' the primary meaning is that the ducks fly. Our preoccupation here is in describing the developing and the thinking, a preoccupation we would share with Piaget. In another sense, 'developing thinking' is something we do, like 'flying kites', and could perhaps do better. The preoccupation here is on how we can make thinking develop, or on how we can encourage it to develop, if we are horticulturalists rather than interventionists. These two senses of course are likely to interact, ideally to inform each other, as they do in the work of Bruner or the Soviet developmental psychologists, and both can apply to ourselves as to other people. But there is a further sense, worth pointing out in the light of what is said later in the book about the importance of metacognition and metalanguage. I have emphasized that the way we think about thinking is changing: I have suggested (with ambivalence and with awareness of how very much is owed to earlier work) that it is changing for the better. An exact title for this book might be 'Developing Thinking about Developing Thinking'. The contents are accounts of research in action and debate in progress, not definitive answers in terms of Cartesian absolute truth. Here too we are Hegelian (or Popperian); our successive accounts of phenomena are asymptotic to the 'true' account, and efforts at understanding involve transformations not just of the phenomena but of the understander. If this last is the case, of course, it may explain my feeling that the chapters of this book cohere and that they represent, with certain other writing (see, e.g., Beveridge, 1982; Olson, 1980; Sants, 1980) in current developmental psychology, progress towards a paradigm shift. Readers must ask their own questions, examine their own assumptions, and decide for themselves.

It remains for me to thank the contributors for their enthusiasm and professionalism, Peter Herriot and Mary Ann Kernan of Methuen for support and good advice, Maureen Harvey and colleagues for their patient productive efforts, Philip Meadows for help with indexing, and too many friends, colleagues, students and teachers to name individually for comments, questions, insights, criticisms and interest.

SARA MEADOWS

References

Beveridge, M. (1982) *Children Thinking Through Language*. London: Edward Arnold.

Kuhn. T. S. (1962) *The Structure of Scientific Revolutions*. Chicago: Chicago University Press.

Lumsden, C. J. and Wilson, E. O. (1981) *Genes, Mind and Culture: The Coevolutionary Process*. Cambridge, Mass.: Harvard University Press.

Markova, I. (1982) *Paradigms, Thought and Language*. Chichester: Wiley.

Olson, D. R. (ed.) (1980) *The Social Foundations of Language and Thought: Essays in Honor of Jerome S. Bruner*. New York: W. W. Norton.

Piaget, J. (1971) *Biology and Knowledge*. Edinburgh: Edinburgh University Press.

Sants, J. (ed.) (1980) *Developmental Psychology and Society*. London: Macmillan.

Wallace, J. G. (1980) The nature of educational competence. In J. Sants (ed.) *Developmental Psychology and Society*. London: Macmillan.

1 An assessment of Piaget's theory of cognitive development

Sara Meadows

Jean Piaget was by far the most important single figure of all those who have ever studied cognitive development. His work is a most impressive achievement. His productivity was very high, over a working life of around seventy years, and few have read all or even most of his books and papers. Fundamental ideas appear very early, and were repeatedly reworked and rephrased so that he was his own main revisionist. Although he did not regard himself as either a psychologist or an educationalist, he has had a most marked influence on both disciplines, and many textbooks discussing the development of children's thought hardly get beyond an elementary exposition of Piagetian theory. Other chapters in this book describe and discuss some of the other approaches to cognitive development, less well known and mostly less well developed: in this first chapter I outline some of the achievements and some of the pitfalls of the Piagetian theory of intelligence.[1] Fuller accounts of Piaget's work can be found in Flavell (1963, 1977) and Vuyk (1981).

A two-part caution is needed as a preliminary. Because of the size and scope of his work, because of the wide range of intellectual disciplines which it touches on, and because of the enthusiasm of his followers (and his opponents), discussion of the merits of Piaget's ideas and data can resemble the exegesis of Biblical texts by religious fanatics. Some critics regard their non-Piagetian findings on phenomenon A as refuting all Piaget's work on phenomena B to Z, and on the other hand better-founded criticisms which turn out to hold difficulties for the faithful have been dismissed by some

Piagetians as misunderstandings, more or less ignorant or wilful. Perhaps inevitably in so much work, variably translated, texts can be found which support or refute opposed understandings. Misquotation, both of Piaget and of his critics, can unfortunately also be found in the literature. Similarly, what is seen by a psychologist as a stunning intellectual insight may appear crude to a philosopher and banal to a biologist: cognitive systems which are described in terms of an elegant logic may be decried by empiricist psychologists who can find no evidence of them in behaviour. Specialists from different fields require different things from theory. The relationship between science and knowledge is itself under dispute (see e.g. Mischel, 1971 and Garfield, 1981). Thus it must be borne in mind while reading this chapter that there is no one universally acceptable evaluation of Piagetian theory, and what follows is merely an attempt to point out 'insights' and 'illusions' which are respectively valuable and dangerous to psychologists' study of cognitive development. The terminology, 'insights' and 'illusions', is taken incidentally from Piaget's *Insights and Illusions of Philosophy* (Piaget, 1971c).

A first tremendously important merit of Piaget's work is that he was throughout his career much more interested in, and explicit about, his basic assumptions than is generally the case for students of cognitive development. He thus considered and elaborately stated the position he took on a number of important issues about the nature of knowledge and the knower, and related his position to, for example, biological and philosophical considerations. There are dangers in this, as I shall discuss, but it is far more dangerous to ignore altogether issues raised by other disciplines, and to leave one's own assumptions completely unexamined.

One elementary assumption he spelled out, claiming to have found a 'tertium quid' between rationalism and empiricism, is that the knower, both child and adult, is an active constructor of his knowledge, neither the passive recipient of outside experience or information (which was a common position in psychology) nor the passive vehicle of innate ideas. I am not going to discuss the philosophical arguments involved in this basic issue (see for example Hamlyn, 1978, 1982; Russell, 1978), though I will later discuss some of the difficulties of Piaget's elaboration of the constructivist position. I will just say here that although some 'knowledge' may be substantially innate (a possible example is, perhaps, that something heard may be expected to be visible) and some the result of a passive reception of experience (as in some rote learning experiments), most learning and knowing will involve activity of some sort on the part of the learner or knower. This is particularly true in the developing child.

A consequence of this position was that there must be more than one 'propellant' of cognitive development. Piaget listed four general factors in his 'summing-up of our work in child psychology' (Piaget and Inhelder, 1969, pp. 154–7). The first is organic growth, especially the maturation of the nervous system, which he calls 'necessary' and 'indispensable' but 'only one factor among several'. This is probably both correct and uncontroversial and I say 'probably' only because we know so little about the relationship between cognition and the brain either in adults or in children. The second is 'the role of exercise and of acquired experience in the actions performed upon objects', including both direct physical experience and indirect logico-mathematical experience. Both involve constructive activity in that they involve logico-mathematical structures. Piaget elaborated this second factor much more than he did maturation; I will come back to the question of the nature of 'logico-mathematical structures', later. The third factor listed is 'social interaction and transmission', which like maturation is 'necessary', 'essential', and 'insufficient by itself', and like physical and logico-mathematical experience involves the child's activity and 'operatory structures'. Piaget did not entirely neglect the child's social experience, as has sometimes been wrongly claimed, but he did underemphasize it. He was wrong to belittle social transmission, as several chapters of this book show, and he also overlooked the importance of social interaction where it was crucial to his work, in his method of examining the child (see below). He was no doubt right to say that social experience is actively organized, interpreted and understood by the child, and it is a pity he failed to recognize how much this active social understanding might affect behaviour in ostensibly non-social areas.

The fourth and final factor, the co-ordinator of the disparate first three factors into the simple and regular sequence of stages which Piaget saw cognitive development as being, is 'equilibration'. This is perhaps the central concept in Piaget's work. It is also amongst its most controversial. I propose to consider it at some length, since the origins of the concept illustrate some of the dilemmas of Piagetian theory, and its ramifications both cause and justify some of the forms the theory took. I have used as my main source Piaget's most detailed and latest treatment of equilibration (Piaget, 1978), with a more general and earlier account (Piaget, 1968) and *Biology and Knowledge* (Piaget, 1971a) as the main secondary sources.

Recapitulating briefly the elementary assumptions that have already been described, knowing consists of the active construction of knowledge, and it develops because of maturation, action on physical and logico-mathematical objects and relations, and social interaction and transmission. It proceeds relatively smoothly and predictably despite its diverse causes. The need to explain this smoothness, the acceptance of constructivism, and perhaps a recollection of the finite though large human brain, suggest that knowledge is organized by the knower who seeks to avoid incoherence and inefficiency, this organization being the final and perhaps most important factor in development. Some such organization would probably be assumed by most theorists (and is certainly hoped for by most educationalists!), but as Piaget moves to the details of 'what', 'why' and 'how' things become more controversial. For him, the central mechanism is equilibration, and the development of knowledge in the individual (and in such groups as scientific communities) consists of a sequence of successively improving forms of equilibrium ('equilibrium' being something on the lines of a coherent system of knowledge, here), each achieved because new problems made the preceding equilibrium inadequate, and each to be superseded in due course by a better. This is said to be the pattern of all development of knowledge, and when Piaget turns his attention to evolutionary biology, of evolution too.

Discussion of Piaget's treatment of 'equilibration' would seem to require a precise definition of the concept as a first step. This is difficult to provide, since while it was central to his theory from the beginning to the end of his career, there were many changes in his descriptions and terminology, and a continuing elaboration of the model. In general terms, equilibration is the process of adaptive integration which maintains a biological (or intellectual) system through the structural self-development which enables it to cope with new external demands. It might not be too misleading to regard it as like the self-regulatory processes which keep missiles on target despite changes in the world outside such as the movement of their prey. At a late stage (Piaget, 1978) he differentiated three levels: first between the subject's mental schemes and external objects, e.g. between the mental scheme of grasping and the physical characteristics of the object to be grasped; second between the mental subschemes coordinated into an overall scheme e.g. the coordination of looking and grasping; and, third, the differentiation and integration of schemes or systems into a total system of knowledge qualitatively different from the parts and opening up new possibilities of action and understanding, e.g. the construction of a conceptual model or theory such as gravitation (or equilibration!). This third level was elaborated late in Piaget's career, and the most accessible account of it in English is Rita Vuyk's (Vuyk, 1981, vol. 1, ch. 10 particularly).

Considering its wide explanatory scope, it is perhaps appropriate that the concept of equilibration has roots in both logic and biology. It relates to the coherence, closure and self-structuring properties of logico-mathematical systems (see e.g. Hofstadter, 1979; Boden, 1981, pp. 236–61), but also more crucially to biological self-regulating systems, such as mammalian blood temperature. (Piaget was insistent that human cognition was an instance of general biological adaptation. As I shall show, his development of this position had its dangers, but the opposite pole, that of separating human cognition categorically from other biological phenomena, is worse. See Midgley (1979) for a brilliant discussion of the effects of such a separation.) There are various physiological systems which use self-regulating mechanisms so as to maintain a constant internal environment in equilibrium, and make the organism relatively independent of the outside world. Piaget saw cognition as just such a constant internal structure, maintained in equilibrium by an interaction of assimilation (relating new external information to pre-existing structures), accommodation (developing old structures into new ones at the behest of new external problems) and organization. Its difference from the maintenance of blood temperature would be that the successive equilibria were progressively improving rather than identical. For both cognitive and physiological systems there is a strong need for maximally stable equilibria: 'Durable disequilibria constitute pathological organic or mental states.' (Piaget, 1968, p. 102.)

A 'need' for equilibrium is well documented in physiological systems like blood temperature and blood sugar level, but it is rather more problematic in cognition. It might perhaps be frivolous to cite Lewis Carroll's Red Queen, or Zen Buddhism, in support of the position that human beings are quite happy with conflicting cognitive contents; Boden (1982) states that 'work in artificial intelligence has suggested that knowledge may be modular, with limited opportunities of co-ordination between the various modules, and that potential contradictions can exist within a knowledge system without prejudicing its functioning'. Certainly, as far as cognition is concerned, how we recognize disequilibria is unclear, and their resolution into equilibria is not as simple and mechanical as the restoration of blood temperature. Piaget recognizes this, but his comments are formal and abstract rather than translatable into types of observable behaviour. The 'need' for equilibrium 'is the expression of a scheme's momentary non-functioning' (Piaget, 1978, p. 84): 'non balance . . . alone can force a subject . . . to seek new equilibriums' (op. cit., p. 12): 'nevertheless it cannot succeed in giving rise to the content required for specific re-equilibrations' (op. cit., p. 12). Thus a momentary non-functioning is the sole motivator of advance towards new cognitive equilibria, but it cannot indicate what has caused the non-functioning or what should be done to resolve the problem.

It must not be assumed, as indeed Piaget warned, that all cognitive conflict will lead to cognitive progress. He regarded contradictions in the formal systems of thought (operational structures) as more germane to cognitive development than are momentary conflicts due to historical accident. However in order to resolve disequilibrium in the direction of cognitive growth, you must be able to recognize the disequilibrium (which as Rotman (1977) points out is not unproblematic); you must recognize at least approximately what has caused it; you must *want* to resolve it, rather than deciding to live with the contradiction; and you must be capable of achieving a new and better equilibrium. I would also suggest that in the case of many contradictions, even in extremely clearly articulated formal systems, there may be disequilibria incapable of resolution or alternative equilibria of equal validity. (Hofstadter (1979) makes an entertaining *tour de force* of discussing these paradoxes.) Piaget did not, to my knowledge, discuss with any thoroughness which disequilibria will be resolved, or why cognitive development consists, as he claimed, of a uniform order of equilibrated stages, not, like evolution, a branching and differentiation. The succession of equilibrated stages is characterized by an improvement in their quality – later stages are 'better' equilibria than earlier ones; that is, they are enlarged in the number of elements or dimensions they can cope with; they are both more differentiated and more integrated; they co-ordinate and complete earlier equilibria; etc. (Piaget, 1978, pp. 30–8, 194). On a general level, this sort of description seems well fitted to cognitive development, but it does not translate very easily into behavioural terms. It is not sufficiently precise about the 'how' of equilibration (see also Boden, 1982), it does not touch on the possibility of alternative forms of equilibria, and it does not account for the prevalence of 'lower' forms of cognition (or in the evolutionary context for the even more conspicuous prevalence of lower forms of life; it is far from clear that amoeba, for example, are truly less equilibrated than humans).

Insistence on cognitive development as a single invariant sequence of stages left Piaget open to accusations of preformationism. He was anxious to avoid them. 'The [cognitive structures] are all contructed and the construction – this I find to be the great mystery of the stages – becomes more and more necessary with time. The necessity is at the end of development, not at the point of departure' (Piaget, 1971b). At about the same time as this relatively informal paper, however, he was drawing attention in *Biology and Knowledge* (Piaget, 1971a) to the similarity between his own work on cognitive development and that of biologists such as Waddington who demonstrated that much of embryological development and physical growth is heavily preprogrammed, even if not totally predetermined, in such a way that if environment or experience force a deviation from the normal course of growth, development will return to the normal path as soon as the deviating force is removed. Piaget's emphasis on cognitive development as governed internally by the intrinsic and universal laws of equilibration, with maturation as first of the other factors and more emphasis on physical and logico-mathematical experience, which would appear to be the more universal, than on social experience and cultural transmission, would seem to have a pronounced predeterminist and teleological tinge. (Various papers in Mischel (1971) touch on this issue.)

Until we have a great deal more information on the nature and mechanisms of genetic programming (and, it should not be overlooked, on the nature and mechanisms of the effects of life experiences, which are no better understood and no less complex) it would be foolish to pronounce on how far cognitive development is predetermined. Some of its universal features may relate to genetic programming, some to the unvarying existence of the physical world, but I will predict with some confidence that some of cognitive development's consistency, as well as much of its variation, will be found to be related to social consistencies. In other words, social or cultural phenomena will have not just a facilitating but a determining effect on cognition. This is a possibility that Piaget would not have been happy with. Even the social interaction and transmission which he underemphasized were seen as working through the individual's reconstruction. His concern was overwhelmingly with knowledge developing through the individual, and its development is only the same from person to person because they all use the same principles of 'reflective abstraction', assimilation and accommodation. These principles give rise to mental structures which exist inside the heads of individuals who have 'grown' them themselves through equilibration, maturation and experience. Other people are acknowledged as important as sources of conflict which force the individual out of his early egocentrism, and to a very grudging extent as providers of readymade ways of representing reality, such as language. These readymade systems of symbols are however assimilated by the individual to his current cognitive structures, and are themselves the product of individuals' cognitive development. The child is seen as recreating mathematics, for example, facilitated rather than determined by influence from society or culture, or language.

Other chapters in this book make it abundantly clear that this view of knowledge developing inside the individual and his status as a member of a social community having little effect on the course of his knowledge is seriously misconceived, and I shall not go into detail on the evidence here. Piaget's paradigm of knowledge as individualistic (and of the scientific community as an aggregate of individualistic knowers) is one of the parts of his theory adversely affected by his emphasis on equilibration, and by his description of knowledge in terms of structures. It is to some aspects of Piaget's use of 'structures' that I now turn.

It would be hard to deny that human thought, at least after infancy, is in some senses structured. It has rules, legitimate procedures and hierarchies of concepts. We are not completely bound by these structures, we may not be aware of them, and we do not, on the whole, have adequate descriptions of them, but generally we work within their system. So far, this is commonplace, a very vague description applicable to language, Piaget's formulations, number systems and even the extreme behaviourists' associative networks (Feldman and Toulmin, 1976). As we become more detailed, problems start to arise, and I want to discuss the forms some of these take in Piaget's work (see particularly Piaget, 1970, 1971d).

The first problem is that of the ontological nature of 'structures', what sort of existence they have. The slightest sort of existence would be that of theoretical construct: thus we make no claims about whether there are such structures in the child but we describe his thinking in terms of organizations and properties which exist only in our theoretical analysis. If we keep to it, this is a fairly safe position, though it may look trivial – but it is all too easy to forget that the 'structures' are in our description not in the child's thought, and be carried away by our metaphor. Locating the structures in the child reifies them a degree beyond descriptive constructs, and serious problems arise. One is the question of *where* they are in the child, thinking, mind or brain all being possibilities. There are too many controversies about the relationship between these three to go into; Piaget's position was ultimately reductionist, that thinking is firmly centred in a neuro-physiological base, but also that it must have an abstract description, the two levels being isomorphic. His description of the earliest stage of thought was primarily biological, that of the later stages primarily abstract and in terms of formal logic. This general position is a reasonable avoidance of the dilemma, though what the isomorphisms are remains unknown. A second problem is that we do not directly observe thinking or other cognitive processes, we infer them from observable behaviour. Inhelder and Piaget (1980), discussing the relationship between procedures and structures, reiterate that the best evidence for the existence of structures in the child's mind is 'what the child considers possible, impossible, or necessary' (p. 23), and some very interesting and ingenious research is being done in this area (see e.g. Russell, 1981, 1982). However, unless we are extremely careful, clever and scrupulous, we may make the wrong inferences, and this is particularly likely when we are studying people different from ourselves or comparing groups different in say age, class or culture. Cole and Means (1981) discuss this question very thoroughly. Their strictures apply to much of Piaget's account of the inadequacies of young children's thought, which we will come back to. Piaget's formulation, which slides (often almost within a chapter) between structures which are in the theorist's description and identical or virtually identical structures which are in the child, was inadequate.

There is one further possible sort of existence for structures of thought, not incompatible with those already described. This is that they exist in some sense outside the individual, as in what Popper calls 'World 3' (Popper, 1972; Popper and Eccles, 1977). I know of no comment by Piaget on this idea, but it would not seem to be a part of his formulation of cognitive development.

Piaget was, then, not so precise as one could wish about the ontological status of structures, and his position was fraught with similar difficulties over his treatment of the relation he believed there to be between 'structures' and observable behaviour. It is often difficult to be sound about the transition from performance to competence, but Piaget's treatment of the problem has seemed to many psychologists to be peculiarly unsatisfactory. Behaviour is an important source of data for the theory, but it has to be *interpreted* before its degree of support for his theoretical claims can be assessed. This was clearly his procedure in most of his published 'experiments': a deliberately artificial situation is presented to the child and his thinking about it is probed and then interpreted by the experimenter – this 'thinking' being manifested primarily in the child's talk about the situation and secondarily in his manipulations of the material. The theory arises from the interpretations, not from the overt behaviour; and the behaviour is reported, selectively, as supporting illustration of the theory. Thus it can be for the reader a matter of considerable doubt and difficulty to relate what the child can be observed to do or, very often, say, and the abstract formal mental structures that are said to explain the child's activities, and this I will come back to when I discuss some questions of the empirical validity of Piagetian structures. It was, presumably, not a problem for Piaget, but then he was neither a psychologist nor an empiricist. The elucidation of thought by the examination of language does not seem to have struck him as particularly problematic. He believed that language was unable to convey what was not already established in thought. This would seem to imply that language is, at least slightly, retarded compared with thinking. Unless the lag is very small, this would mean that there would be occasions when the child's language was too undeveloped to express the greater sophistication of his thinking. Using language to diagnose thought would in these cases give rise to false diagnoses of immature thinking; and there are indeed many demonstrations of 'failures of thinking' which appear to be due primarily to language difficulties (e.g. Donaldson, 1978). Nor is the interpretation of children's language necessarily unproblematic.

There is one further central problem in Piaget's use of structures, which we must deal with before discussing the empirical validity of his work. This is two characteristics of structures which appeared very early in his work on them (Piaget, 1952) and which relate to both his biologism and his description of structures in formal and abstract terms. Cognitive structures tend to form structured wholes (*structures-d'ensemble*), and this is what, once they are fully established, the concrete operational stage, the formal operational stage and other logico-mathematical systems consist of. 'Stages' are periods of relative equilibrium in the development of the child's thought, which is said to resemble the development of thought in the human species (this resemblance being one reason for Piaget's interest in children's thought, it being impossible to investigate the thought of, say, Australopithecus or Neanderthalers).[2] There are a number of points here which need a brief comment on a theoretical level: some we will return to as they raise empirically answerable questions.

Both '*structure-d'ensemble*' and 'stage' imply the existence of a fairly tight relationship amongst a set of cognitive structures. On the whole, we would expect the structures which form a *structure-d'ensemble* to develop and appear together, and to react one upon the other. Piaget's theory also suggests that they form at each stage qualitatively different structures, being not just bigger but better (in terms of coherence, complexity and field of application, as we said earlier). Again, at a very general level this would appear really rather likely, but the detail of Piaget's models of *structures-d'ensemble* turns out to be unsatisfactory. Both concrete operations and formal operations are described in terms of logical systems which logicians regard as of poor quality (see e.g. Boden, 1979, pp. 80–6; Ennis, 1978), and which are inferred from behavioural (largely verbal) data in ways that turn out, at least in the case of formal operations, to be quite simply wrong (Bynum *et al.*, 1972).

In addition to these difficulties Piaget's model of stages has changed with development. The earlier model implied a stage sequence where transitions from stage to stage are the disequilibrated periods and are relatively brief, so that there are fairly abrupt changes from stage to stage. It is this model of clearly contrasted stages that dominates most popular accounts of Piagetian theory. In the later model there is a considerably less step-like development, and the preparation, achievement, consolidation and superseding of, say, concrete operations flow into one another smoothly and cover a period of several years. If this is the better picture (and, as I describe below, the empirical evidence is for the later more complex model not for the earlier one) the descriptive value of stage and *structure-d'ensemble* concepts begins to look very slight indeed. There are indications that psychologists studying cognitive development are moving away from their use (e.g. Flavell, 1977, p. 249). One might perhaps hope educationalists soon will too.

I will discuss a little later some of the empirical work which looks at single cognitive operations: I want here to make some brief comments on some work that sought to investigate questions about the concurrence or sequencing of operations which Piaget's structural description suggests belong together. The operations in question belong to the concrete operations stage, which is generally the best studied. There is not, however, much relevant work, and there are good practical reasons for this. In the first place, different versions of the description of the development of concrete operations imply different degrees of concurrence of operations. In the second, making an accurate judgement of concurrence or sequence requires perfect diagnostic tests (Flavell, 1977, pp. 220–31 discusses this quite thoroughly) and, remembering what I have said already about the relationship between operations and behaviour, it will be appreciated that these are not easily found or employed. Surprisingly, even 'Piaget systematized' (Voyat, 1982) does not solve this problem.

However, in general there is little evidence that concrete operations are achieved either rapidly (as their basis in logical structures might suggest) or co-ordinatedly (as one might expect of a *structure-d'ensemble*). My own study in this area (Meadows, 1975) began in a sincere and scrupulous admiration of Piaget's work and found nothing that would be well represented by his groupings model of concrete operations. Most factor-analytic studies have similarly found non-Piagetian patterns (e.g. Klausmeier and Sipple, 1982). To my knowledge no one has yet found behavioural evidence supporting it; though there are an enormous number of replications of most of Piaget's sets of data on such things as conservation and classifications there are very few indications of how they fit together. It seems unlikely that there really are *structures-d'ensemble*.

It is still, of course, possible to describe thought in terms of logical operations, even if the operations do not fit together as tightly as Piaget sometimes implied, and I would maintain that this may be sensible and useful. One habit of Piaget's which, however, I do regret was to account for immature performances and failures by saying they were due to logical failures or incapacities. Thus the young child who has compared two member pairs of a seriated set, A bigger than B, and B bigger than C, but does not know the relative sizes of A and C, is at a loss (or wrong) because of a failure to make the necessary logical inference; or the young child who says that there are more of a subordinate class A than a superordinate B made up of A and a smaller set A′ (more daisies than flowers, in a mixed bunch of tulips and daisies) gets it wrong because he cannot hold in mind together subordinate and superordinate classes and make the necessary comparisons. The 'wrong' answers of young children on these and other tests are not disputed; what is questioned is the cause.

The general point is that Piaget was too quick to postulate logical inadequacies, and more detailed task analyses have drawn our attention to features of his test situations which make substantial contributions to children's apparently operational failures (and successes). Failure to compare A and C correctly, for example, in the transitive inference test, may be due to failure of memory not of logic (Bryant and Trabasso, 1971; and see also Mills and Funnell, Chapter 7); and it may well be that some cases of successful comparison of A and C in older children and adults may be due not to logical operations but to memorizing and reading-off an image of the seriated set (Trabasso, 1975). This latter possibility is worth taking seriously in conjunction with the substantial body of work that suggests even logically trained adults tend to use infra-logical processes in solving logical problems (see Wason and Johnson-Laird, 1972, for examples). Adults and children seem to find much the same logic problems easy and difficult (Ennis, 1978), and development is not simply from poor to good reasoning. Indeed Matthews (1980) suggests, though with anecdotal evidence only, that young children may be better at philosophizing than adults!

Piaget, then, probably over-emphasized both the illogicality of small children and the logical competence of adults. I want to mention briefly two other features of his testing and analysis which recent work shows as needing more caution than he used. The first is the question of language. His 'clinical method' of testing was highly dependent on language both in the tester's presentation of test and questions, and in the child's response. A large number of experiments have now shown details of language use to be crucially important in 'success' and 'failure' on a wide range of tests: question form influences the justification of conservation responses, for example (Goodnow, 1973); a phrase or single additional word for the superordinate class makes class inclusion easier (Donaldson, 1978; Markman, 1973); and an indirect question may be easier than a direct one, as in the class inclusion variant (Siegel *et al.*, 1978) where children who answered incorrectly the standard class inclusion question 'Are there more candies or more smarties?' chose (except for a few who were explicitly altruistic or choosey about their confectionery) the larger set, when asked 'Do you want to eat the candies or the smarties?'

The other feature of the test situation which Piaget did not sufficiently take into account is that it is irretrievably a social one. If you ask a captive young child a question he cannot manage easily he may respond with the answer to a different question, as some of my subjects did in the class-inclusion test (Meadows, 1977). Or he may be much concerned with why the experimenter asked it (e.g. Donaldson, 1982). Or he may reiterate an answer that seemed satisfactory on a previous occasion, as in the co-ordination of perspectives test where the child is much more likely to give 'egocentric' answers proposing his own view as visible from all directions if he has been asked first about his own view than if he has not (Garner and Plant, 1972; Cox, 1980). Or on hearing a question repeated he may believe that the repetition indicates that his first answer was wrong, as may happen in conservation tests (Rose and Blank, 1974). Similarly, if the standard Piagetian test is redesigned to make 'human sense' children often, but not always (Miller, 1982), perform in a much more adult way, as in Hughes' co-ordination of perspectives task (Donaldson, 1978; Hughes and Donaldson, 1979) and Light's conservation of liquid task where the ostensible reason for the pouring of liquid from the standard glass to another is the 'discovery' of a 'dangerous' chip in the standard glass (Light *et al.*, 1979). The psychological experiment is often socially problematic (Neilson and Dockrell, 1982), but the importance of remembering this is particularly acute when working with children and most of all, perhaps, when seeking to draw conclusions about cognition. Others beside Piaget have believed that what they have elicited is universal truth, when it may be much more nearly 'strange behaviours in strange places' (Bronfenbrenner, 1979).

It remains to summarize the points made so far, and I would repeat my caution that specialist opinion on each varies somewhat. First, and briefly, the criticisms.

The data on which the theory rests, while not much disputed in themselves, are seen as, variously: capable of explanation in other terms than Piaget's, that is he failed to rule out other possible explanations (e.g. transitive inferences); not sufficiently rigorously related to the theory, that is the theory derives more from high-level theoretical considerations than from the data (e.g. formal operations); simply missing, that is there is little or no evidence to support the theory (e.g. *structures-d'ensemble*); or they are the result of inadequate test methods (linguistically or socially) as well as of the qualities of children's thought. Among remedies for all these faults are rigorous analysis of the demands of a task, better testing methods, more cautious generalization with more consideration of variations between paradigms or within subjects, and, of course, better theories. As a consequence of Piaget's work, advances on these lines are being made.

The theory remains a more impressive achievement than any other in the field. Among reasons for being cautious about it are, however, the following: its tenuous base in good data; its over-emphasis on failures or successes of logical structure as explanations of behaviour; its insistence on the individual nature of knowledge and thought and its underemphasis of the possibility that much of knowledge is socially constructed and transmitted; and above all, perhaps, its central tenet of equilibration, which is inadequately modelled as a mechanism, unevidenced as a process and at present vacuous as an explanation. Enthusiasts have derived from the theory recommendations for which Piaget should not, perhaps, be held primarily responsible: the worst of these, as is often the case, are prominent in educational recommendations, and I have not discussed them because Charles Brainerd does so in Chapter 2.

The last two paragraphs may seem to suggest that Piagetian theory is 'mad, bad and dangerous to know'. I would assert that 'mad' and 'bad' are absolutely inapplicable, and 'dangerous to know' applies only to those who can only conceive of dogmatic total acceptance or dogmatic total rejection. There is a middle course, and realization of the historical perspective of the study of cognitive development supports a more subtle assessment. Piaget is important and irreplaceable because he asked important questions and tried to answer them. This was pioneering work done from a relatively isolated position, and its insights are often amazingly ahead of its time. If we are able to make well-founded criticisms of his work and identify his 'illusions' it is only because we have profited from his insights. I want to end with two quotations which indicate my judgement of his achievement. The first is from Rotman, with a minor change of emphasis:

> Piaget has dominated [the study of cognitive development] for half a century. A dominion achieved by taking [it] . . . more seriously, more coherently, articulately and systematically, with more conceptual gravitas, and with greater variety, ingenuity and brilliance of experiment than any has ever done. (1977, p. 182)

The second is from W. H. Auden's epitaph poem on Freud.

> If often he was wrong, and at times absurd,
> To us he is no more a person
> Now but a whole climate of opinion
> Under whom we conduct our differing lives.

Notes

[1] Piaget did important work on various other subjects which have received less attention generally and regrettably get none here. Some of the criticisms that Hotopf (1977) makes of Piaget's theory of perception are bolder versions of comments I make here on his theory of intelligence.

[2] While it is a point more relevant to the history of science than to the assessment of Piagetian theory, the belief that the development of the individual recapitulates the development of the species, that ontogeny recapitulates phylogeny, is not now taken as literally as it was at the turn of the century, when it was extremely pervasive and influential. It was one source of Freud's description of psychosexual stages, to mention another body of work that has, like Piaget's, greatly influenced psychological ideas (see Sulloway, 1979).

References

Auden, W. H. (1940) In memory of Sigmund Freud. *Another Time*. London: Faber.

Boden, M. A. (1979) *Piaget*. London: Fontana.

Boden, M. A. (1981) *Minds and Mechanisms: Philosophical Psychology and Computational Models*. Brighton: The Harvester Press.

Boden, M. A. (1982) Is equilibration important? A view from artificial intelligence. *British Journal of Psychology* **73**: 165–73.

Bronfennbrenner, U. (1979) *The Ecology of Human Development*. Cambridge, Mass.: Harvard University Press.

Bryant, P. E. and Trabasso, T. (1971) Transitive inferences and memory in young children. *Nature* **232**: 456–8.

Bynum, T. W., Thomas, J. A. and Weitz, L. J. (1972) Truth-functional logic in formal operational thinking. *Developmental Psychology* **7**: 129–32.

Cole, M. and Means, B. (1981) *Comparative Studies of How People Think*. Cambridge, Mass.: Harvard University Press.

Cox, M. V. (ed.) (1980) *Are Young Children Egocentric?* London: Batsford.

Donaldson, M. (1978) *Children's Minds*. London: Fontana.

Donaldson, M. (1982) Conservation: what is the question? *British Journal of Psychology* **73**: 199–207.

Ennis, R. H. (1978) Conceptualization of children's logical competence: Piaget's propositional logic and an alternative proposal. In L. S. Siegel and C. J. Brainerd (eds) *Alternatives of Piaget*. New York: Academic Press.

Feldman, C. F. and Toulmin, S. (1976) Logic and the theory of mind. *Nebraska Symposium on Motivation, 1975*. Lincoln: University of Nebraska Press.

Flavell, J. H. (1963) *The Developmental Psychology of Jean Piaget*. Princeton, NJ: Van Nostrand.

Flavell, J. H. (1977) *Cognitive Development*. Englewood Cliffs, NJ: Prentice-Hall.

Garfield, M. J. (1981) Piaget – Possible worlds or real worlds? Paper given at conference: Jean Piaget: A British Tribute, May 1981, Brighton Polytechnic.

Garner, J. and Plant, E. L. (1972) On the measurement of egocentrism: a replication and extension of Aebli's findings. *British Journal of Educational Psychology* **42**: 79–83.

Goodnow, J. J. (1973) Compensation arguments on conservation tasks. *Developmental Psychology* **8** (1): 140.

Hamlyn, D. W. (1978) *Experience and the Growth of Understanding*. London: Routledge & Kegan Paul.

Hamlyn, D. W. (1982) What exactly is social about the origins of understanding? In G. Butterworth and P. Light (eds) *Social Cognition: Studies of the Development of Understanding*. Brighton: The Harvester Press.

Hofstadter, D. R. (1979) *Gödel, Escher, Bach: an Eternal Golden Braid*. Harmondsworth: Penguin Books.

Hotopf, W. H. N. (1977) An examination of Piaget's theory of perception. In B. A. Geber (ed.) *Piaget and Knowing: Studies in Genetic Epistemology*. London: Routledge & Kegan Paul.

Hughes, M. and Donaldson, M. (1979) The use of hiding games for studying the co-ordination of viewpoints. *Educational Review* **31**: 133–40.

Inhelder, B. and Piaget, J. (1980) Procedures and structures. In D. R. Olson (ed.) *The Social Foundations of Language and Thought: Essays in Honor of Jerome S. Bruner*. New York: W. W. Norton.

Klausmeier, H. J. and Sipple, T. S. (1982) Factor structure of the Piagetian stage of concrete operations. *Contemporary Educational Psychology* **7**: 161–80.

Light, P. H., Buckingham, N. and Robbins, A. H. (1979) The conservation task as an interactional setting. *British Journal of Educational Psychology* **49** (3): 304–10.

Markman, E. (1973) The facilitation of part–whole comparisons by use of the collective noun 'family'. *Child Development* **44**: 837–40.

Matthews, G. B. (1980) *Philosophy and the Young Child*. Cambridge, Mass.: Harvard University Press.

Meadows, S. A. C. (1975) *The Development of Concrete Operations: A Short-term Longitudinal Study*. Ph.D. thesis, University of London.

Meadows, S. (1977) An experimental investigation of Piaget's analysis of class inclusion. *British Journal of Psychology* **68** (2): 229–37.

Midgley, M. (1979) *Beast and Man: The Roots of Human Nature*. Brighton: The Harvester Press.

Miller, S. A. (1982) On the generalizability of conservation: a comparison of different kinds of transformation. *British Journal of Psychology* **73**: 221–30.

Mischel, T. (ed.) (1971) *Cognitive Development and Epistemology*. New York and London: Academic Press.

Neilson, I. and Dockrell, J. (1982) Cognitive tasks as interactional settings. In G. Butterworth and P. Light (eds) *Social Cognition: Studies of the Development of Understanding*. Brighton: The Harvester Press.

Piaget, J. (1952) Autobiography. In E. G. Boring *et al.* (eds) *History of Psychology in Autobiography*, vol. 4.

Piaget, J. (1968) *Six Psychological Studies*. London: University of London Press.

Piaget, J. (1970) *Genetic Epistemology*. New York: Columbia University Press.

Piaget, J. (1971a) *Biology and Knowledge*. Edinburgh: Edinburgh University Press.

Piaget, J. (1971b) The theory of stages in cognitive development. In D. R. Green, M. P. Ford and G. B. Flanner (eds) *Measurement and Piaget*. New York: McGraw Hill.

Piaget, J. (1971c) *Insights and Illusions of Philosophy*. London: Routledge & Kegan Paul.

Piaget, J. (1971d) *Structuralism*. London: Routledge & Kegan Paul.

Piaget, J. (1978) *The Development of Thought: Equilibration of Cognitive Structures*. Oxford: Blackwell.

Piaget, J. and Inhelder, B. (1969) *The Psychology of the Child*. London: Routledge & Kegan Paul.

Popper, K. R. (1972) *Objective Knowledge: An Evolutionary Approach*. London: Oxford University Press.

Popper, K. R. and Eccles, J. C. (1977) *The Self and its Brain*. Berlin: Springer.

Rose, S. A. and Blank, M. (1974) The potency of context in children's cognition: an illustration through conservation. *Child Development* **45**: 499–502.

Rotman, B. (1977) *Jean Piaget: Psychologist of the Real*. Brighton: The Harvester Press.

Russell, J. (1978) *The Acquisition of Knowledge*. London: Macmillan.

Russell, J. (1981) Propositional attitudes. In M. Beveridge (ed.) *Children's Thinking Through Language*. London: Edward Arnold.

Russell, J. (1982) The child's appreciation of the necessary truth and necessary falseness of propositions. *British Journal of Psychology* **73**: 253–66.

Siegel, L. S., McCabe, A. E. and Matthews, J. (1978) Evidence for the understanding of class inclusion in pre-school children: linguistic factors and training effects. *Child Development* **49**: 688–93.

Sulloway, F. J. (1979) *Freud, Biologist of the Mind*. London: Burnett Books.

Trabasso, T. (1975) Representation, memory and reasoning: how do we make transitive inferences? In A. D. Pick (ed.) *Minnesota Symposium on Child Psychology*, vol. 9.

Voyat, G. (1982) *Piaget Systematized*. Hillsdale, NJ: Lawrence Erlbaum Associates.

Vuyk, R. (1981) *Overview and Critique of Piaget's Genetic Epistemology, 1965–1980*, vols 1 and 2. London: Academic Press.

Wason, P. C. and Johnson-Laird, P. N. (1972) *The Psychology of Reasoning*. London: Batsford.

2 Modifiability of cognitive development[1]

Charles J. Brainerd

A perennial question about human intelligence, one that has befuddled educators and developmental researchers alike, concerns the extent to which the normal course of intellectual development can be altered by appropriate learning experiences. There are two opposing doctrines, which are sometimes called the *interventionist* position and the *horticulturalist* position.

Extreme interventionists believe that cognitive development is largely controlled by learning. In everyday life, we are all familiar with newspaper accounts of parents who read great works of literature to newborn infants in the belief that it will foster genius. In modern psychology, behaviorism is usually taken as the textbook illustration of an interventionist theory, though behaviorists themselves are inclined to reject this interpretation (e.g. Skinner, 1974). Interventionism's philosophical roots are in the British empiricist and utilitarian traditions.

Extreme horticulturalists believe that learning can modify cognitive development in only minor respects and that attempts at such modification, though well intentioned, may do more harm than good. An everyday illustration of horticulturalism is provided by parents who avoid any direct teaching of basic skills such as bladder control, walking, speech, etc. to their offspring and, instead, wait for such skills to emerge 'spontaneously'. Philosophically horticulturalism is easily recognizable as a Rousseauian doctrine (e.g. Brainerd, 1978a, 1978b). Piaget's stage model of cognitive development (e.g. Piaget, 1970a; Piaget and Inhelder, 1969) is the standard example of a horticulturalist theory in psychology, though Piagetians, like behaviorists, are inclined to disagree (e.g. Sinclair, 1973).

We know, of course, that neither extreme interventionism nor extreme horticulturalism is correct. Research has shown that there are maturational limits on what can be taught to children of given ages, which argues against interventionism. For example, bladder and bowel control cannot be trained until certain areas of the motor cortex have been myelinated (McGraw, 1940). But research has also shown that the effects of learning on cognitive development are far from trivial, which argues against horticulturalism. Here, the most compelling illustrations come from cross-cultural studies, wherein subjects from cultures with different levels of literacy tend to perform very differently on standardized cognitive tests (Cole and Scribner, 1974).

Although interventionism and horticulturalism, in their pure forms, are wrong, a question of considerable scientific interest lies between these poles, namely, what are the exact constraints under which learning operates during cognitive development? Historically, developmental researchers have studied this question in many ways. For the past two decades, however, such research has been closely connected to Piaget's theory. In particular, there are two topics which are especially relevant to the problem of just how modifiable cognitive development is. The first is the series of laboratory-style learning experiments in which investigators have sought to teach conceptual skills from Piaget's stages to children who do not yet possess them. The second is a group of experimental preschool curricula in which early-childhood educators have attempted to implement Piaget's ideas about the relationship between learning and development.

These two themes form the core of this chapter. In the first section below, I review some of the things that we have discovered from learning experiments with Piagetian concepts. In addition to summarizing some of the principal findings from such research, the general stance that Piagetian theory takes on the relationship between learning and development is adumbrated. In the second section, Piaget-based preschool programs are reviewed. The programs are divided into two groups, those developed in the late-1960s to mid-1970s, for which some evaluation data are available, and those developed more recently, for which evaluation data are as yet sparse.

Teaching Piagetian concepts in the laboratory

As everyone knows, Piaget proposed that cognitive development consists of four global stages – the sensorimotor stage (roughly birth to 2 years), the preoperational stage (roughly 2 to 7 years), the concrete-operational stage (roughly 7 to 11 years), and the formal-operational stage (roughly 11 years and beyond). During each stage, there is a fundamental control program, or underlying competence system, which Piaget called 'cognitive structures'. The cognitive structures of a stage, which are comprised of mental entities called 'operations', define the basic characteristics of intelligence during that stage and are supposed to set certain constraints on learning (see Inhelder, Sinclair and Bovet, 1974; Inhelder and Sinclair, 1969; Piaget, 1970a). This section of the chapter is concerned with research on these constraints.

Most of the pertinent literature deals with how children learn a particular class of concepts, namely, the conservation concepts of the concrete-operational and formal-operational stages. To avoid repetition, therefore, I begin with a brief precis of the main varieties of conservation. Next, the specific constraints on learning that Piaget's theory imposes are considered. Finally, research bearing on the reality of these constraints is reviewed. For convenience, the research is partitioned into early experiments published between 1959 and 1971 and experiments published after 1971.

Conservation concepts

The cognitive skills that are most often associated with Piaget's theory are the well-known conservation concepts. According to the theory, most types of conservation appear during the concrete-operational stage, though some complex versions of it do not emerge until the formal-operational stage. Broadly speaking, conservation refers to children's understanding that quantitative relationships among objects remain invariant (are 'conserved') across changes in irrelevant perceptual aspects of the objects. A particular conservation concept (say, conservation of number) refers to children's understanding that some specific quantitative property (number in this case) remains invariant in the face of some specific type of perceptual transformation (changes in length in this case).

The standard paradigm for assessing a conservation concept involves presenting the child with two familiar objects. Depending on the particular concept that is being measured, the objects are such things as rows of plastic chips, clay balls, glasses of water, lengths of string, etc. Following the terminology in an early paper by Elkind (1967), one of the objects in the pair is called the *standard stimulus* (*S*) and the other object is called the *variable stimulus* (*V*). This emphasizes the fact that one object, *S*, will remain unchanged throughout the assessment, whereas the other object, *V*, will undergo certain perceptual deformations. After the variable stimulus has been deformed in some way, it is then denoted V' rather than *V*.

At the start of a conservation problem, *S* and *V* are perceptually identical. The assessment begins by establishing to the child's satisfaction that *S* and *V* are also equal with respect to some familiar quantitative dimension (e.g. length, height, number, weight, mass). Next, the experimenter transforms *V* in such a way that the perceptual identity is destroyed but the quantitative equivalence is preserved. The experimenter then asks one or more questions that are designed to determine whether the child understands that $S = V'$ despite the fact that they no longer look the same. For example, suppose that it is number conservation that is being measured. The first step would be to construct two parallel rows of familiar objects (e.g. poker chips) which (a) contain the same number of items and (b) are of exactly the same length. After the subject has agreed that the two rows have the same number, the experimenter destroys the perceptual identity by lengthening or shortening one of the rows. The experimenter then poses questions such as, 'Do the two rows still have the same number of chips, or does one of them have more chips now?' Remarkably, children younger than about 5 or 6 are strongly inclined to say that the longer row has more (Piaget, 1952).

Although there are as many forms of conservation as there are dimensions of quantitative variation, the types that have been studied in most conservation-learning experiments are number conservation, length conservation, mass conservation, quantity conservation, and weight conservation. For the sake of clarity, the assessment procedures for these five concepts are summarized in Table 2.1.

Table 2.1 Five types of conservation that have frequently been studied in learning experiments.

Length conservation	Two wooden or metal rods of the same length	(1) The experimenter places the rods close together so the child can see that they are the same length. (2) The experimenter places one of the rods so that it is perpendicular to the other rod. (3) The experimenter poses questions of the form, 'Are the two rods still the same length or is one of them longer now?'
Mass conservation	Two clay balls of the same size	(1) The experimenter presents the two clay balls so the child can see that they have the same amount of clay. (2) The experimenter flattens one of the clay balls into a 'pancake'. (3) The experimenter poses questions of the form, 'Do the ball and the pancake have the same amount of clay or does one of them have more?'
Number conservation	Some red and blue poker chips	(1) The experimenter builds a row of blue chips and a row of red chips side-by-side so the child can see that they contain the same number of chips. (2) The experimenter lengthens one of the rows. (3) The experimenter poses questions of the form, 'Is there still the same number of red and blue chips, or does one of the rows have more now?'
Quantity conservation	Two identical glasses, plus a third glass that is taller and thinner than the other two	(1) The experimenter fills the two identical glasses with water in such a way that they contain the same amount of water. (2) The experimenter pours the contents of one of the identical glasses into the tall, thin glass. (3) The experimenter poses questions of the form, 'Is there the same amount of water in the two glasses now, or does one of them have more?'

There is an extensive data base on the normative course of development of conservation concepts in Western children. At least three conclusions appear to be unarguable. First, the earliest conservation concepts do not spontaneously appear in most children's thinking until about age 6 or so. Second, there appears to be a definite sequence in the emergence of some of them. For example, number conservation is usually the first form of conservation for most children. Length conservation normally appears sometime after number, while concepts such as quantity and weight conservation are later still. Third, the development of conservation takes quite a long time. Although the normative data show that the average 7- or 8-year-old child understands number and length conservation (e.g. Brainerd and Brainerd, 1972), these same data show that concepts such as volume conservation, density conservation, and area conservation are not understood by the average junior high school (12–14 years old) student (e.g. Brainerd, 1971; Brainerd and Allen, 1971b).

The Piagetian view of learning

Piaget (e.g. 1970a) proposed that children's ability to learn the concepts from his stages via programs of direct instruction is constrained in two general ways. First, whether or not learning occurs hinges on children's current stages of cognitive development. Second, it also depends on the teaching methods that we use. To set the stage for the discussion of experimental findings, I summarize what the theory has to say on each of these matters.

The when of learning

The key idea here is that learning, in the sense of coming to understand a concept such as conservation as a consequence of direct instruction, is under the control of development. It is because of this idea that Piagetian theory is often consigned to the horticultural end of the interventionist-horticulturalist dimension.

To begin with, a general process called 'cognitive development' is posited in the theory, and this process is said to be governed by its own special laws and principles (e.g. assimilation, accommodation, equilibration, decentration). It is cognitive development that supposedly determines when and under what conditions an instructional program will be effective: 'Learning is no more than a sector of cognitive development which is facilitated by experience' (Piaget, 1970a, p. 714). The rule of thumb is that children's capacity to profit from learning experiences will be 'subject to the general constraints of the current developmental stage' (Piaget, 1970a, p. 713). If a group of children is trained on a concept from one of Piaget's stages, the amount of learning that is obtained in individual children is expected to 'vary very significantly as a function of the initial cognitive levels of the children' (Piaget, 1970a, p. 715). Other things being equal, the higher a child's current stage of cognitive development, the better his or her learning is likely to be. From statements such as these, it is obvious that the Piagetian view of learning is a classical readiness doctrine.

To see why Piaget made such statements, it is necessary to delve into the infrastructure of his theory. Cognitive development is described as a stage-like process in the theory. As I have mentioned, each of these stages is defined by its own unique set of cognitive structures. The concepts that are associated with a given stage are thought to be 'deduced' from these structures or 'generated' by them in a manner that is vaguely analogous to the way in which a logician deduces or generates theorems from a small set of axioms (see Brainerd, 1978c). According to the theory, a target concept (say, conservation) cannot be expressed by a child unless the relevant structures for that concept (in this case, the so-called grouping structures of the concrete-operational stage) have been laid in. These structures are acquired as a by-product of the process of cognitive development, not as a consequence of learning. Therefore, learning experiences designed to induce a particular concept can only be effective to the extent that the structures which are necessary for the expression of that concept *have already developed*. This means that training will not be successful whenever the child's current stage is far below the one at which the pertinent structures appear. Successful training requires that the current stage be the same as or very near to the one at which the target concept 'spontaneously' appears. These claims were aptly summarized in Piaget's statement that 'teaching children concepts that they have not acquired in their spontaneous development . . . is completely useless' (Piaget, 1970b, p. 30).

At first glance, it would not seem difficult to test the validity of such proposals. Naively, we should only have to conduct a learning experiment in which, first, we train children at various stages of cognitive development on some given concept and, second, we determine whether or not learning is better in children who are at more advanced stages. For example, imagine a hypothetical experiment in which we attempt to train the concept of number conservation in a group of children who do not yet possess it. Suppose that the children in our experiment are of two types, concrete-operational children (i.e the stage at which conservation 'spontaneously' develops) and preoperational children (i.e. the stage preceding the emergence of conservation). Suppose that we assign each child to one of two conditions, a training condition in which the child receives some sort of direct instruction that should enhance conservation knowledge and a no-training control group. In other words, our experiment is a simple 2 × 2 factorial design, with the two factors being stage of cognitive development (concrete-operational or preoperational) and amount of training (some or none). It is obvious what Piagetian theory anticipates in this situation: there should be a large stage × training interaction. Specifically, the training procedure should produce larger improvements in conservation knowledge among the concrete-operational children than among the preoperational children.

Unfortunately, it is impossible to conduct experiments of this sort. The reason is that one of the two factors in the design, stage of cognitive development, cannot be measured. Although Piaget and his collaborators have often spoken of stages as though they were objective characteristics of children (e.g. Inhelder, 1956; Piaget, 1960), they are not. Unlike height, weight, eye color, gender, and so forth, we do not have any way of telling exactly what a child's 'current stage of cognitive development' is. This is because stages are not objective things at all but, rather, they are what theoreticians call *hypothetical constructs* or *intervening variables* (cf. Brainerd, 1981, 1982a and b). That is, they are *assumptions* that Piaget introduced in the hope of explaining certain kinds of data, not things that he actually measured in children's behavior. Hence, our simple 2 × 2 experiment cannot be conducted because we have no way of knowing precisely which children are preoperational and which are concrete-operational.

Assuming that we still wish to investigate Piaget's views on learning after discovering this problem, the only solution is to seek other, objective variables in terms of which children can be classified and which should be related to stage of cognitive development in a sensible way. Ideally, we should rely on variables that can be assumed to be *monotonically related* to stage of cognitive development –

i.e. children who have more of the variable are always at higher stages than children who have less of it. To date, two such variables have been used in attempts to evaluate the hypothesis that children's concept learning depends on their stages of cognitive development: (a) levels of pretraining performance on tests for the to-be-trained concept and (b) chronological age.

Concerning (a), suppose that all the children in our hypothetical experiment received an extensive battery of tests for conservation concepts before they participated in the training phase of the research. When performance on these pre-tests is inspected, suppose that we find that the children tend to fall into two groups, namely, those who fail all the tests across the board and those who pass some tests while failing others. In other words, some children appear to know nothing about conservation, whereas others have some slight grasp of it. We still do not know which of these children are preoperational and which are concrete-operational. However, Piaget did tell us this much: conservation concepts first develop during the concrete-operational stage, which means that children in the second group are more likely to be a concrete-operational than children in the first group. Therefore, we can conduct a 2 × 2 experiment in which the factors are level of pretraining performance (none or some) and amount of training (some or none). In this study, level of pretraining performance substitutes for stage of cognitive development in the original design.

In such an experiment, there are two findings that would tend to support the hypothesis that concept learning is constrained by stage of cognitive development. First, since the hypothesis anticipated a stage × training interaction in the original design, it anticipates a pretraining performance × training interaction here such that children who show some understanding of conservation learn better than children who show none. Second, since children who fail conservation pre-tests across the board should be primarily preoperational, this group should be especially difficult to train (because preoperational children do not yet possess the cognitive structures whereby conservation is expressed).

Concerning (b), the standard age norms given for the preoperational and concrete-operational stages are 2 to 7 and 7 to 11, respectively. Although these are said to be only averages, they can be used to divide children into groups that are more likely to be at a given stage than other groups. For example, suppose we selected a group of normal children, all of whom were in the 4- to 5-year-old age range (i.e. older preschoolers and kindergarteners). All of these children come from the nominal age range for the preoperational stage. Hence, except for an occasional precocious child, the age norms indicate that this is a preoperational sample. If we were to attempt to train concrete-operational concepts with such children, the theory tells us that we should fail. In short, chronological age can be used to test the hypothesis that concept learning is constrained by cognitive development as follows. First, use the age norms for the stages to select a sample that, by and large, can be assumed to be operating at a given stage. Second, attempt to train concepts from some more advanced stage, with poor learning being the expected outcome.

The how of learning

The other type of constraint that cognitive development is said to impose on learning is concerned with the nature of the learning experiences themselves. Suppose, for the sake of discussion, that we obey the first constraint and select a sample of children whom we have reason to suppose have attained a stage that is appropriate for whatever it is that we wish to teach. The theory now tells us that not just any training procedure will work. Instead, our training must take account of what happens in everyday cognitive development to be effective. For example, Inhelder, Sinclair and Bovet (1974) explain the rationale for the training methods used in Genevan learning research as follows: 'We started with the idea that under certain conditions an acceleration of cognitive development would be possible, but that this could only occur if the training resembled the kind of situations in which progress takes place outside the experimental set-up' (p. 24). In connection with the same research, Inhelder and Sinclair (1969) observed that 'The choice of exercise items has been dictated by what we know of the spontaneous (that is, outside the laboratory) acquisition of the operations or concepts in question' (p. 5), and Sinclair (1973) remarked that 'in learning – that is, in situations specifically constructed so that the subject has active encounters with the environment – the same mechanisms as in development are at work to make progress' (p. 58).

The specific type of learning experiences that Piagetians favor are those that involve *active self-discovery* of the concept that is being trained. These methods are usually contrasted in Genevan writings with procedures that involve *passive reception of information*, which are not supposed to work very well (e.g. Sinclair, 1973). For example, Inhelder and Sinclair (1969) described Genevan learning methods by noting that 'in all of them we avoid imposing definite strategies on the child . . . the child is encouraged to make his own coordinations . . . the child is asked to anticipate the likely outcome of certain transformations and then to observe the actual outcome of the transformation. . . . In other cases, we aim at a step-by-step circumscription of the problem destined to make the child aware of contradictions in his arguments' (pp. 4 and 5). Later, Sinclair (1973) stated that all Genevan learning methods are guided by the assumption that 'the subject himself is the mainspring of his development, in that it is his own activity on the environment or his own active reactions that make progress' (p. 58).

To see why active self-discovery learning is favored by Piagetians, it is necessary to delve into the theory's infrastructure again. The general principle that is supposed to govern cognitive development in everyday life is called *construction*. According to this principle, it is children's active manipulations of their environments (building things, tearing them down, transforming things) that produce cognitive growth. Of course, we all know that children, especially young children, spend considerable time in such activity. Piaget believed that children's active manipulation of things in their environments leads to cognitive changes via a disequilibrium/equilibrium process. The general idea is that the child's current stage of cognitive development leads him or her to anticipate that a manipulation will produce certain results. When results do not conform to expectations, the child's cognitive structures are thrown into a state of disequilibrium. Ultimately, the disequilibrium is resolved by acquiring new cognitive structures which will make correct predictions about the results of manipulations.

A standard illustration (e.g. Piaget, 1970c) of these assumptions is provided by the concept of number conservation. Preoperational children believe that the number of elements in a set is affected by their spatial arrangement. They fail the usual tests for number conservation because they maintain that a set whose members are more widely dispersed (e.g. the longer of two parallel rows of objects) contains more elements than a set whose members are close together (e.g. the shorter of two parallel rows of objects). Suppose that a preoperational child is playing with a collection of six marbles. The child, being preoperational, naturally expects that the spatial proximity of the marbles effects their numerosity. Thus, spreading them far apart should give some number greater than six, and bunching them close together should give some number less than six. But if the marbles are counted before and after each such transformation, the child will soon discover that numerosity is invariant. Discoveries of this sort eventually lead to the emergence of new cognitive structures (in this case, concrete-operational structures) that will correctly anticipate the invariance of number under spatial transformation.

Following earlier terminology (Brainerd, 1978a), I shall refer to the active, manipulative training experiences emphasized by Piagetians as *self-discovery* training and to the passive-reception procedures that they eschew as *tutorial* training. Common illustrations of tutorial instruction include: (a) observational learning, where children who lack a certain concept observe the performance of children or adults who possess the concept (e.g. Rosenthal and Zimmerman, 1978); (b) rule instruction, where children who lack a certain concept are taught a rule or rules that are critical to correct performance (e.g. Beilin, 1965; Goldschmid, 1968; Hamel and Riksen, 1973); (c) corrective feedback, where children who lack a certain concept are given direct training on the correct answers to the items on tests for that concept (e.g. Brainerd, 1972a and b; Bucher and Schneider, 1973). Generally speaking, Piagetians claim that self-discovery training is successful and tutorial training is not. The reason, naturally, is that the former mirrors the principle of construction but the latter does not.

It is much easier to evaluate these proposals about the 'how' of children's learning than it is to evaluate the earlier proposals about the dependence of learning on stage of cognitive development. This is because our training methods are objective variables that we can control and measure, not hypothetical constructs as stages are. If we conduct learning experiments in which the type of training that children receive is varied, then there are several results that bear on the claim that training must reflect the construction principle if it is to be effective. To begin with, children should be able to learn concepts such as conservation via self-discovery, but they should not show much improvement as a result of tutorial training. Second, suppose that we conducted experiments in which specific varieties of self-discovery training were compared to specific varieties of tutorial training. We would expect consistently better learning with the former. Finally, suppose that we conducted experiments in which subjects received several types of training, with training procedures differing in the amount of self-discovery that they incorporate. Here, we would expect some sort of monotonic increase in amount of learning as the amount of self-discovery in a training method increases. All these predictions presuppose that we have taken account of the first constraint and have selected groups of children who can be assumed to have attained whatever stage is required for the concepts being trained.

Experimental findings

Now that Piaget's basic proposals about learning have been considered, we can turn to what research has shown about their validity. As mentioned, the bulk of this research consists of experiments in which investigators have attempted to train one or more conservation concepts. However, at the time of this writing learning experiments have also been reported on several other concepts from the concrete-operational and formal-operational stages. Examples from the concrete-operational stage include seriation (e.g. Bingham-Newman and Hooper, 1974; Coxford, 1964), identity (e.g. Hamel and Riksen, 1973; Litrownik, Franzini, Livingston and Harvey, 1978), class inclusion (e.g. Kuhn, 1972; Youniss, 1971), transitivity (e.g. Brainerd, 1973, 1974a), classification (e.g. Denney and Actio, 1974; McLaughlin and Brinley, 1973), subjective morality (e.g. Arbuthnot, 1975; Jensen and Larm, 1970), perspective taking (e.g. Burns and Brainerd, 1979; Iannotti, 1978), and ordinal and cardinal number (e.g. Brainerd, 1974b; Brainerd and Howe, 1979). Examples from the formal-operational stage include isolation of variables (e.g. Case, 1974; Siegler, Liebert and Liebert, 1973), density (e.g. Brainerd and Allen, 1971b), and proportionality (e.g. Brainerd, 1971).

In this section, I summarize some of the findings from this literature that are pertinent to Piaget's claims about learning. To make the review more concrete, I begin by describing the prototypical design of most experiments. I then consider some selected results from experiments published between 1959 and 1971. Next, selected results from experiments published between 1972 and the present are reviewed.

Basic design

Most experiments have involved three steps, namely, a pre-test phase, a training phase, and a post-test phase. During the pre-test phase, tests are administered for one or more concepts from some Piagetian stage (e.g. tests for certain conservation concepts). A decision as to whether a given child is to continue to the second phase is rendered on the basis of his or her performance on these pre-tests. In some experiments, only children who fail all the pre-tests are retained for training. In other experiments, children are permitted to pass some minimum proportion of items (say, up to 50 per cent). In all instances, however, subjects who pass all or nearly all the items are discarded.

At the beginning of the training phase, the remaining children are assigned to treatment groups. The minimum design consists of two conditions, a treatment group whose members all receive the same type of training and a control group whose members receive no training. More elaborate designs involve multiple treatment groups, with the members of each group receiving different types of training, plus a control condition. The subjects who are assigned to a given treatment condition may either receive a fixed amount of training or they may be trained until they reach a performance criterion of some sort (criterion training).

The post-test phase begins sometime after the subject has completed training. There are two important post-test variables, namely, the types of post-tests that are administered and the time interval between the completion of training and the beginning of the post-tests. On the former point, Piaget and his collaborators have emphasized that 'true learning' of a concept demands that the improvements produced by training should generalize across variations in the way that a concept is measured. For example, if we conducted a conservation-learning experiment in which we attempted to train *number* conservation during the second phase, we would probably administer post-tests for both number conservation and some other types of conservation (e.g. length, weight). On the latter point, Piaget and his collaborators have also emphasized that 'true learning' has occurred only if improvements are retained for a long time after training. Thus, in the experiment just mentioned, we would probably administer conservation post-tests immediately after training and a week or two later as well. We might even administer conservation post-tests several months later (see Gelman, 1969; Goldschmid, 1968).

Early findings: 1959–71

It is convenient to divide Piagetian learning research into two historical periods, an early period running from 1959 to 1971 and a recent period running from 1972 to the present. As we shall see, the questions investigators have been concerned with during these periods have been somewhat different.

The nominal starting point for the early period was the publication of two pilot experiments conducted in Geneva (Smedslund, 1959; Wohlwill, 1959), though the investigators themselves were not Genevans. The early period concluded with the publication within a few months of each other of three independent reviews of experiments that had been reported through 1970 (Beilin, 1971; Brainerd and Allen, 1971a; Goldschmid, 1971). The main question throughout this period was whether it was possible to produce *any* learning of Piagetian concepts, especially conservation. It was widely believed at this time that Piagetian theory simply predicted no learning. Although we have already seen that this interpretation is not accurate, the results of some of the earliest experiments appeared to support it.

In Smedslund's (1959) and Wohlwill's (1959) original pilot studies, Wohlwill attempted to train conservation of number and Smedslund attempted to train quantity conservation. Wohlwill subsequently replicated his study with a larger sample (Wohlwill and Lowe, 1962), and Smedslund expanded his study into a series of experiments (Smedslund, 1961a, b, c, d, e and f). In the Wohlwill and Lowe (1962) experiment, children were trained on number conservation with three different procedures: corrective feedback, rule instruction, and perceptual-set training. The key result was no evidence of learning – i.e. the post-test conservation performance of the children in each of these conditions was not measurably better than that of the children in the no-treatment condition. In the initial experiments in the Smedslund series, children were trained on weight conservation with three different techniques: training of weighing operations (Smedslund, 1961b), teaching an addition-subtraction rule (Smedslund, 1961b), and perceptual-set training (Smedslund, 1961d). Like Wohlwill, Smedslund found no significant improvement in conservation as a consequence of such training.

At the time, these findings, together with some other negative results that had been reported earlier (Churchill, 1958a and b; Harker, 1960) were thought to show that Piagetian concepts are extremely difficult for children to learn, a conclusion that obviously favors the theory's claim that learning is sharply limited by development. For example, Flavell's (1963) early book on Piaget's theory contains the following commentary:

> What can be concluded from all these experiments? Perhaps the most certain conclusion is that it can be a surprisingly difficult undertaking to manufacture Piagetian concepts in the laboratory. Almost all the training methods reported impress one as sound and reasonable and well-suited to the educative job at hand. And yet most of them have had remarkably little success in producing cognitive change. It is not easy to convey the sense of disbelief that creeps over one in reading these experiments . . . there is more than a suspicion from present evidence that when one does succeed in inducing some behavioral change through this or that training procedure, it may not cut very deep. (p. 377)

Investigators outside Geneva, primarily in North America, did not allow this conclusion to go unchallenged. During the next few years, several experiments were reported in which various tutorial methods were used to train concrete-operational concepts. Priority for the first successful experiment following Flavell's book goes to Wallach and Sprott (1964). They reported a study in which number conservation was trained by giving children instruction on a reversibility rule. On number conservation post-tests, trained children performed much better than controls. In subsequent experiments, various other tutorial procedures produced large differences in the post-test conservation performance of trained and untrained children. Examples include rule instruction via perceptual demonstration (e.g. Brison, 1966; Wallach, Wall and Anderson, 1967), rule instruction via verbal statement (e.g. Beilin, 1965; Smith, 1968), observation of skilled models (e.g. Sullivan, 1967), extinction of non-conservers, dependency on irrelevant visual cues (e.g. Emrick, 1967; Gelman, 1969), learning-set training (e.g. Kingsley and Hall, 1967), and Asch-type conformity training (e.g. Murray, 1968).

Although some unsuccessful experiments were also reported after 1963 (e.g. Mermelstein and Meyer, 1969), by 1970 most of the basic varieties of conservation had been successfully trained in more than one experiment. Further, successful learning experiments had been reported for some other Piagetian concepts (e.g. Coxford, 1964). These facts were noted in the three literature reviews mentioned earlier. The authors of these reviews differed somewhat in their theoretical interpretations, especially as regards the degree of support conferred by the experiments on Piaget's theory of learning. However, it was clear from all three reviews, first, that laboratory-style learning experiments could produce large improvements in certain concrete-operational and formal-operational concepts; second, that the tutorial-type training which Piagetians criticize actually works rather well; and third, that the same tutorial procedures that appeared to fail in the early Smedslund and Wohlwill studies could be made to succeed (Hatano, 1971; Hatano and Suga, 1969). By 1971, therefore, there appeared to be some consensus that it was not necessarily a 'difficult undertaking to manufacture Piagetian concepts in the laboratory'. However, many questions remained to be answered about the limits of children's susceptibility to training.

Although the issue of whether Piagetian concepts are, in principle, trainable dominated early research, we have already seen that the theory does not actually predict untrainability. Instead, it merely restricts learning in two general ways. The early literature, perhaps because of its emphasis on mere trainability, did not provide definitive evidence on either of these limitations.

Concerning the first limitation (learning depends on stage of cognitive development), some data appeared to favor this assumption and others argued against it. I noted earlier that there have been three experimental strategies for investigating the hypothesis that stage constrains concept learning. The first strategy (determine the relationship between pretraining knowledge of a concept and susceptibility to training) was adopted in conservation-learning experiments by Beilin (1965) and by Strauss and Langer (1970). These investigators classified children as being either preoperational or in transition between the preoperational and concrete-operational stages on the basis of conservation pre-tests. Following training, the subjects were reclassified as preoperational, transitional, or concrete-operational. A correlation was observed between the children's pre-training and post-training stage classification. In line with Piagetian theory, Beilin interpreted this result as showing that 'the group most likely to profit from training is that group whose members have at least some . . . conservation ability' (1965, p. 335).

The second strategy (determine the trainability of children who fail pre-tests across the board) was adopted in several experiments. In fact, most of the conservation-learning experiments reported between 1964 and 1970 were concerned with children who showed no pre-training knowledge of conservation. In contrast to the results from the first strategy, most of these experiments produced clear evidence of learning, a result which suggests that preoperational children can learn concrete-operational concepts. Finally, data from experiments involving the third strategy (determine trainability of very young children), like those from experiments involving the first strategy, seemed to favor Piagetian theory. Except for a study by Emrick (1967), conservation-learning experiments with preschool children that were published up to 1970 were consistently unsuccessful (e.g. Bruner, 1964; Halford, 1970; Mermelstein and Meyer, 1969).

Concerning the second constraint on learning (self-discovery training is best), the early literature also presented a mixed picture. On the one hand, the fact that procedures such as observational learning, rule instruction, and corrective feedback had proved effective in teaching children Piagetian concepts made the hypothesis that tutorial procedures do not work untenable. On the other hand, virtually nothing was known about the effects of self-discovery training. Genevan investigators (e.g. Inhelder and Sinclair, 1969; Inhelder, Sinclair, Bovet and Smock, 1966) had reported some pilot studies with small numbers of children in which self-discovery procedures were used to train conservation. Although these results suggested that self-discovery training might be effective, the data were too thin to conclude that such training was actually successful and, more important, to assess the relative effectiveness of self-discovery and tutorial training.

Recent findings: 1972 – present

Fortunately, subsequent experimentation has delivered reasonably unambiguous answers to the questions that were left open in the early literature. In particular, studies published after 1971 provide rather strong disconfirmation of both of the constraints that Piaget imposed on learning. I summarize the data bearing on each constraint separately.

Does learning depend on stage of cognitive development? It has been noted that early studies which adopted either the first or third approach to this question produced data that seemed favorable to the theory, whereas those that adopted the second strategy produced unfavorable data. In later studies, however, both the first and third strategies produced unfavorable data.

With respect to the first strategy, a fairly large number of experiments accumulated during the early 1970s in which children with differing pre-test levels of conservation knowledge received conservation training. This literature included several experiments conducted in Geneva by three of Piaget's collaborators (Inhelder, Sinclair and Bovet, 1974). Those experiments that had been published as of 1977 were reviewed with a view toward deciding whether or not they supported the hypothesis that concept learning improves as pre-test knowledge of trained concepts increases (Brainerd, 1977). Most of these experiments followed Beilin's (1965) design in the sense that subjects were classified as preoperational or transitional on the basis of pre-tests, were then trained, and finally were reclassified as preoperational, transitional, or concrete-operational on the basis of post-tests. As in Beilin's (1965) and Strauss and Langer's (1970) original studies, it was generally found that the pre- and post-test stage classifications correlated with each other. In particular, children classified as preoperational on the pre-test tended to be classified either preoperational or transitional on the post-test, whereas children classified as transitional on the pre-test tended to be classified either transitional or concrete-operational on the post-test. This datum was usually interpreted as supporting the hypothesis that stage constrains learning. For example: 'the nature and extent of the subjects' progress was always, in fact strikingly so, dependent on their initial developmental level' (Inhelder *et al.*, 1974, p. 244). In fact, however, this conclusion does not follow. As long as the pre- and post-tests on which the stage classifications are based are reliable, a positive correlation between pre- and post-test classifications is virtually guaranteed. What we really need to know is whether *the amount of pre- to post-test improvement* in performance (i.e. the amount of learning) is different for children with different stage classifications. What we anticipate, of course, is that the amount of pre- to post-test improvement should be smaller for children with a preoperational classification than for children with a transitional classification. However, when the amount of improvement was calculated for studies published up to 1977, it turned out that conservation training produced just as much improvement in preoperational children as in transitional children (see Brainerd, 1977, Table 1). This finding has been replicated in later experiments (e.g. Brainerd, 1979). It has even been found that under some conditions, children who know less about a concept learn *more* than children who know more about that concept (Brainerd, 1982a)!

Turning to the third strategy, although early experiments generally failed to produce learning in preschoolers, several successful experiments with preschool samples have been reported since 1971. As usual, most of them were concerned with conservation learning, and all of them relied on forms of training that Piagetians would regard as tutorial. So far, the particular techniques that have proved to be effective with preschoolers are attentional training (Emrick, 1967), verbal rule instruction (Denney, Zeytinoglu and Selzer, 1977; Field, 1981), observation of skilled models (Rosenthal and Zimmerman, 1972; Zimmerman and Lanaro, 1974), behavior modification (Bucher and Schneider, 1973), and corrective feedback (Brainerd, 1974a). In most studies, the amount of learning obtained with a given method is smaller for preschoolers than for elementary schoolers. However, it is clear that it is possible to produce substantial pre- to post-test improvements with preschoolers, that these learning effects will generalize to untrained concepts (e.g. Denney *et al.*, 1974), and that they are stable for several months following training (e.g. Field, 1981).

Is self-discovery training best? We saw that the early literature left some doubt as to whether self-discovery training is an effective approach to training Piagetian concepts, and if it is, whether self-discovery training is more effective than tutorial training. The subsequent literature indicates that although self-discovery training can produce learning, it is generally *less* effective than tutorial training.

Concerning the ability of self-discovery training to produce learning, Inhelder *et al.* (1974) reported a series of experiments in which conservation and class inclusion were trained with self-discovery methods. In these experiments, the children were encouraged to manipulate various types of apparatus that were designed to lead them to discover a certain rule that is critical to the concept being trained. As an illustration, consider the first experiment that they reported. The object was to train liquid quantity conservation. In the liquid quantity task (see Table 2.1), non-conservers think that the amount of liquid in a glass depends on its height: when confronted with two glasses of liquid of different heights, they claim that the taller column of liquid is more than the shorter column, regardless of the true quantities involved. One problem that such children appear to have is that they do not understand that heights and widths are compensatory. Hence, Inhelder *et al.* (1974, Chapter 1) devised an apparatus consisting of different-size beakers. Non-conservers of liquid quantity were encouraged to pour a fixed amount of liquid from one beaker to another in the hope that they would notice, much like the child with the marbles discussed earlier, that the amount of liquid stays the same regardless of the beaker in which it is contained. The fact that this procedure, and analogous methods, produced improved performance on tests for concrete-operational concepts suggests that children can benefit from self-discovery instruction. Similar findings have been obtained in experiments conducted outside Geneva (e.g. Cantor, Dunlap and Rettie, 1982).

On the other hand, there is no evidence that self-discovery training works better than tutorial training and, in fact, the weight of evidence favors the opposite conclusion. It has been pointed out elsewhere (Brainerd, 1978a) that the size of improvements observed in Genevan self-discovery experiments has been smaller than those observed in tutorial experiments. Also, the subjects in Genevan self-discovery experiments were older (7 years and above) than those in most tutorial experiments (kindergarteners and preschoolers). Last, Inhelder *et al.* (1974) found very little evidence of learning in children who showed no knowledge of the target concept during the pre-test phase. As we have seen, however, various types of tutorial training are known to produce learning in children who fail pre-tests across the board.

There have also been a few experiments in which a given type of tutorial training was compared to a given type of self-discovery training. To date, the outcome has either been no difference in relative effectiveness (e.g. Botvin and Murray, 1975) or a difference in favor of tutorial training (Cantor, Dunlap and Rettie, 1982). All of these findings argue against the view that self-discovery training is the royal road to learning Piagetian concepts.

Synopsis

To sum up the implications of this section of the chapter, two decades of research, most of it on concrete-operational concepts, has failed to provide any definitive support for the two developmental constraints that Piagetian theory imposes on learning. With respect to the first constraint (learning depends on pretraining stage of cognitive development), there is converging evidence from three experimental strategies, and each type of evidence says the same thing, namely, that there do not seem to be strong stage limits on learning. With respect to the second constraint (self-discovery training works best), there is overwhelming evidence that tutorial procedures are effective, even with preschool children. In addition, there is growing evidence that the amount of learning produced by self-discovery learning is normally smaller than that produced by comparable tutorial methods.

Cognitive development and the preschool

I turn now to the other topic of this chapter, the implementation of Piaget's theory in the classroom. To many readers, it may seem odd that a theory whose predictions about the relationship between learning and development fare so poorly should prove influential in education. Nevertheless, it has. The chief reason for the anomaly is that the researchers who have conducted learning experiments and the educators who have devised Piaget-based curricula have not been the same people. Hence, curriculum development has tended to proceed in isolation from basic research on children's concept learning.

During the 1970s, Piagetian theory was at the center of what has come to be known as the 'cognitive curriculum movement' in North America. A number of pilot and experimental curricula were developed during this period which sought to translate the theory into educational practice. Nearly all of these curricula were in the area of early-childhood (preschool) education rather than elementary or secondary education. Reviews of much of this work can be found in sources such as Hooper and DeFrain (1980), Johnson and Hooper (1982), and Lawton and Hooper (1978).

My concern in this section of the chapter is to discuss some of the principal features of Piaget-inspired curricula in early-childhood education. I begin by considering certain prescriptions and proscriptions about instruction that, according to most educators, follow from the theory. I then consider illustrative Piagetian curricula. The discussion of curricula is subdivided into early programs developed during the late 1960s/early 1970s and more recent programs.

Global recommendations about instruction

Piaget wrote many papers on education during his life, some of them as early as the 1930s. From these articles, as well as from the theory itself, educators have isolated several recommendations that might be implemented in a variety of ways. In some cases, there has been controversy over whether or not some particular recommendation actually follows from the theory. To avoid becoming mired in ethereal disputes, I concentrate on the specific recommendations that most educators regard as uncontroversial. For convenience, they are discussed under three headings: (a) readiness recommendations; (b) recommendations about what to teach; and (c) recommendations about teaching methods.

Readiness

We have previously seen that Piaget's view of learning is what is usually called a readiness doctrine – i.e. he believed that children cannot and should not be taught concepts until they are developmentally prepared to learn them. This leads to four specific proposals about when children should be taught target concepts. We have already encountered one of them: do not teach children things that exceed their current stage of cognitive development. With preschoolers, it is the preoperational and concrete-operational stages that we are concerned with. The age range in most preschools is roughly $2\frac{1}{2}$–$5\frac{1}{2}$ years. Thus, the children in the lower half of this range will be almost entirely preoperational, whereas those in the upper half of the range will be a mixture of preoperational and concrete-operational children. According to the first proposal, instruction should focus on preoperational concepts (e.g. identity, topology) with the former children and blend in some concrete-operational concepts (e.g. classification, seriation) with the latter.

The second readiness proposal is concerned with the *rate* at which instruction proceeds. Because learning must await development, Piagetians tend to oppose fast-paced instruction designed to accelerate children's progress through curriculum material. To Piagetians, such programs smack of trying to speed up the 'natural' rate of cognitive development. In place of acceleration, they favor what is usually called *mastery learning*. Here, instruction follows a more leisurely pace wherein each topic or concept must be thoroughly mastered before proceeding to the next one: 'if we want learning to be permanent and solid enough to permit cognitive development throughout the child's life, we must (1) let the child go from one stage after another of being "wrong" rather than expect him to reason logically like an adult, and (2) allow for a certain slowness in the developmental progress' (Kamii, 1973a, p. 225).

The next readiness proposal deals with the order in which things are taught to children. In all of Piaget's research on cognitive development, much attention was given to describing the exact sequences in which children acquire concepts in everyday life. Much of the early Piaget replication research conducted by researchers outside Geneva focused on whether particular sequences that he had reported could be confirmed (for reviews, see Flavell, 1970; Hooper, Goldman, Storck and Burke, 1971). In line with the notion that learning should mirror spontaneous development as much as possible, the third proposal is that we should teach children concepts in exactly the same order in which they acquire them naturally. We saw earlier, for example, that most children understand number conservation before length conservation, and that they understand length conservation before quantity conservation. Thus, if we sought to teach these three concepts to children, introducing them in the order number → length → quantity would be 'developmentally correct', but any other ordering would be 'developmentally wrong'.

The last readiness proposal follows from the first three. If we seek to teach only concepts that are in accord with the current stage (first proposal), to avoid acceleration (second proposal), and to teach things in the correct sequence (third proposal), it is obvious that we shall have to know a great deal about each child's state of conceptual knowledge: implementing the first proposal requires that we have sufficient information to decide whether a given child is concrete operational or preoperational; implementing the second proposal requires that we know just how completely a given child has learned the material that is currently being taught; implementing the third proposal requires that we know which concepts in a sequence are already understood by a given child and which are not. All this means that Piagetian instruction is always a two-step process of *cognitive diagnosis followed by instruction*. Instruction should only proceed when extensive diagnostic information is available for a child. Of course, the diagnostic instruments are the usual Piaget tests for logical concepts, spatial concepts, arithmetical concepts, and so forth.

This last readiness proposal is not easy to carry out. The problem is that having sufficient diagnostic information available on a child means that teachers must spend large amounts of time in one-on-one testing. If the instruction of other children is not to suffer as a consequence, there must be other teachers available. In other words, the teacher-pupil ratio must be very low to put the diagnostic recommendation into practice, much lower than is typical in preschools. Because the first three proposals all hinge on being able to do detailed diagnostic work-ups for individual children, the fact that it is rarely possible to do such work-ups means that it is difficult to incorporate any of the Piagetian readiness recommendations in most preschools.

What to teach

First, we return again to the fact that most preschool classes will consist of a mixture of preoperational and concrete-operational children, with the latter predominating. Hence, the proper content of a Piaget-based early-childhood curriculum will be whatever concepts and skills are deemed to be essential to these stages. The concepts in question fall into the general areas of logic (e.g. transitive inference), mathematics (e.g. number), science (e.g. conservation), and space (e.g. Euclidean geometry). Thus, the most general recommendation about what to teach is that the key concepts of the preoperational stage are all fair game for children who have been diagnosed as preoperational, and the key concepts of the concrete-operational stage are all fair game for children who have been diagnosed as concrete operational. But some rather more explicit recommendations about curriculum content are also possible.

One of the most interesting of these is in the area of geometry. Historically, instruction in the initial elementary grades concentrated on two areas, namely, language (including reading and writing) and mathematics. With respect to the latter, the focus was chiefly on arithmetic. Geometry was usually left until high school. However, Genevan research on spatial development (Piaget and Inhelder, 1956; Piaget, Inhelder and Szeminska, 1960) suggests that concepts of topological geometry are acquired during the preoperational stage, while concepts of Euclidean and projective geometry are acquired during the concrete-operational stage. Thus, by the time most children have reached the second or third grade, the theory says that they are developmentally prepared for instruction in most forms of geometry. For this reason, Piaget-based curricula often include some exposure to geometrical concepts.

A second proposal about curriculum content is concerned with the physical medium that teachers use to transmit knowledge to children. From the earlier discussion of self-discovery learning, it should not be surprising that Piagetians favor the use of instructional materials that consist of *concrete objects* of some sort that can easily be *manipulated* by children. With respect to concreteness, Piaget believed that children cannot understand concepts at an abstract, linguistic level until they have reached the formal-operational stage. When teaching preoperational and concrete-operational children, therefore, instruction that relies entirely on language (e.g. teachers lecturing to children) is destined to fail. Rather than simply explaining ideas to children verbally, teachers must demonstrate them using concrete objects. Also, since learning is ostensibly an active self-discovery process, the objects should be things that children can manipulate in such a way that they can demonstrate concepts *to themselves*. Here, it may be useful to recall the earlier illustration of the child with the marbles.

An interesting implication of this emphasis on manipulability of materials is that not all concrete methods of demonstrating concepts are equally good. In fact, some may not be very good at all if they involve passive reception of information by children. Two obvious examples that are mainstays of most classrooms are films and textbooks. Films are very concrete, involving as they do pictures and sound, and textbooks can be made concrete with the inclusion of pictures and illustrations. But children do not *do* anything to either of these media. They merely sit and observe in both cases. Consequently, they should not be especially effective as learning aids. It is worth reiterating here that this claim does not square with the learning research considered earlier.

How to teach

Last, I consider three recommendations about 'styles' of instruction that most educators believe to be endorsed by the theory. The first is our old friend self-discovery learning: 'Good pedagogy must involve presenting the child with situations in which he himself experiments, in the broadest sense of the term – trying things out to see what happens, manipulating symbols, posing questions, and seeking his own answers, reconciling what he finds one time with what he finds at another, comparing his findings with those of other children . . .' (Duckworth, 1964, p. 2). As the available learning research does not support Genevan claims about self-discovery, I shall not belabor this point.

The second teaching strategy grows out of the previously discussed construction principle. Recall here that according to this principle, cognitive progress occurs through a disequilibrium/equilibrium process in which, broadly speaking, children attempt to reconcile their current beliefs about how the world works with discrepant information. Educators interpret this principle to mean that teaching strategies which promote this sort of disagreement between objective reality and what children currently believe should be especially effective.

This proposal has lead to an interesting line of learning research by Murray and his associates (e.g. Botvin and Murray, 1975; Murray, 1968, 1972). In these experiments, a group of children is first selected that show little or no understanding of some target concept, usually conservation. These subjects are then exposed to older children who do possess the concept. The basic idea is to produce cognitive conflict ('disequilibrium') in the subjects by making them aware that their current beliefs are not the same as those of other children. The standard procedure is to form groups comprised of one child who does not understand the to-be-learned concept and two children who do understand it. Tests for the concept are then administered to the group. The children are encouraged to debate their answers and to formulate a consensual response. This method, which is called conflict training, has proved to be quite effective.

The third strategy, peer teaching, has its origins in some of Piaget's earliest work. In his first book on cognitive development, *The Language and Thought of the Child*, he concluded that a child's peers play a major role in his or her cognitive development. In particular, a child's social interactions with other children, normally through the medium of some sort of play, was said to be the main force in cognitive growth: 'Piaget believed strongly that for intellectual development the cooperation among children is as important as the child's cooperation with adults. . . . Other children at similar cognitive levels can often help the child more than the adult can to move out of his egocentricity' (Kamii, 1973a, p. 200).

As the most natural mechanism of peer interaction among young children is play, this has led to an emphasis on play-based instruction in Piagetian curricula. In some of the most recently developed programs, attempts have been made to base the entire curriculum on activities such as constructive play or dramatic play (e.g. Forman and Hill, 1980). One technique is to have certain locations within the preschool classroom designated as play centers. These areas are equipped with materials that are appropriate to certain types of themes (e.g. going to the post office, cooking dinner). While they are in these areas, children are encouraged to engage in forms of play that are appropriate to the themes. The themes themselves are selected with regard to their potential value in transmitting certain concepts and interpersonal skills.

Illustrative Piagetian preschool programs

As has been mentioned, extant Piaget-based curricula can be conveniently divided into those that were developed during an initial spate of educational enthusiasm for the theory in the late 1960s/early 1970s and those that have been developed more recently. I discuss two influential representatives from each category.

Early programs

Of the various Piagetian curricula that were piloted during the late 1960s/early 1970s, the two that had the greatest impact were the Early Childhood Curriculum and the Open Framework Program. The former was developed by the late Celia Lavatelli (1970, 1971) at the University of Illinois, and the latter was developed by David Weikart (1973; Weikart, Rogers, Adcock and McClelland, 1974) in Ypsilanti, Michigan.

The principal distinguishing feature of Lavatelli's Early Childhood Curriculum is that it was the first program to bring systematic instruction in Piagetian concepts into the preschool. We have already seen that an important difficulty with Piaget-based curricula is the requirement of extensive diagnosis and testing of children's current states of knowledge. To deal with this problem, Lavatelli developed a battery of tests for various concrete-operational concepts that was subsequently made available to preschool teachers as a kit. The kit incorporated tests for concepts from five categories, namely, classification, measurement, number, seriation, and space.

By administering the various tests in the Lavatelli kit, it is possible, at least in principle, to obtain a reasonably clear fix on children's current stages of cognitive development: children who perform poorly in all five areas would obviously be regarded as pre-operational by the theory; children who perform well in all five areas would be regarded as concrete-operational; and other children would be regarded as transitional.

When it comes to instruction, the emphasis is squarely on learning concepts by having children manipulate concrete objects. Lavatelli (1970) gave the following illustration about learning number conservation, which is reminiscent of the child with the marbles: 'Using toys and pennies, for example, a child may on a perceptual level state that there are more toys in a long row than there are pennies to buy these toys when an identical amount of pennies is placed in a pile near the row of toys. Moving the pennies one-to-one beside each toy may cause the child to reconsider; now there is one penny for each toy. . . . His thinking has been challenged by operating on real materials in an enjoyable activity' (p. 4).

Peer interaction is also stressed in the Early Childhood Curriculum. The main strategy for promoting such interactions is what might be called 'committee work'. Teachers are encouraged to organize children into small working groups of about five children each. The working groups then carry out the manipulative activities that are designed to teach concrete-operational concepts, and presumably, assist each other in learning the concepts.

A final, important feature of the Early Childhood Curriculum is that the teacher, not the children, plays the dominant role in organizing each day's activities. It is the teacher who assigns children to working groups and who selects exercises for each group. Teachers are told to select specific exercises that emphasize the correct features of concrete-operational concepts, and they are discouraged from selecting exercises that might lead children to make errors. Specific examples of 'right' and 'wrong' exercises are given in Lavatelli's books.

Turning to the Open Framework Program, its principal distinguishing feature is that it is focused on only a single area of concrete-operational thinking, namely, classification concepts. The reason for this emphasis is Weikart's interpretation of some of Piaget and Inhelder's writings, according to which classification concepts are fundamental to most of the things that children will later be taught in the elementary grades (e.g. arithmetic and reading). Hence, the Open Framework Program consists of a series of exercises that are designed to transmit simple classificatory skills, as well as more complex classification concepts such as class inclusion. There are multiple exercises for each classification concept that Weikart deemed important. One of the readiness proposals mentioned earlier, sequentiality, is also emphasized. The order in which the exercises are introduced for individual classificatory concepts is roughly the same as the order in which children acquire these concepts in everyday life.

As in the Early Childhood Curriculum, the Open Framework teacher controls the curriculum. The teacher is instructed to select the specific exercise items, especially during the initial phases of instruction on a given concept, and explicit guidelines are provided as to which exercises should be introduced in which order. Also, the Open Framework teacher is told to observe children's performance and to ask them questions during the course of exercises.

Some evaluation data are available on both the Lavatelli and Weikart programs. When evaluating any preschool curriculum, the main question is, do children who are exposed to the curriculum show improved intellectual performance relative to children who did not attend any preschool, or relative to children who were exposed to some other preschool curriculum? Lavatelli examined this question by administering standardized intelligence tests, plus tests for certain concrete-operational concepts, to children both before they entered the program and one year later. The scores that children achieved on such tests were usually higher on the second administration than on the first, a datum that Lavatelli interpreted as showing that her curriculum was effective. Unfortunately, this conclusion does not necessarily follow. The difficulty is that Lavatelli failed to test a comparison sample of control children who were not exposed to the Early Childhood Curriculum. Normative data show that children's scores on tests of the sort that Lavatelli administered, especially the concrete-operational tests, will almost always be better after one year. For example, if we administered conservation tests to children on their fourth birthday and one year later on their fifth birthday, the latter scores will be much higher than the former. In short, without data on a control sample of children, we do not know how much of the improvement that Lavatelli observed in her children was due to the curriculum and how much was due to the spontaneous improvements that take place as children become older.

More thorough evaluation data are available on the Open Framework Program (Weikart, 1973). A sample of 3- and 4-year-old children attended an Open Framework classroom for several months. They attended five half-day sessions per week, and they also received a special tutorial session once a week in their homes. There were two comparison samples. The children in one of these groups, who were also 3- and 4-year-old retardates, received a comparable amount of instruction in a reinforcement-oriented curriculum (token economy) based on operant principles. The children in the other group received comparable exposure to a curriculum that stressed children's social and personality development rather than the acquisition of cognitive abilities.

After completion of their respective programs, three measures of curriculum impact were gathered for all three groups, namely, scores on standardized intelligence tests, teacher ratings of the children, and ratings of the children by outside experts. The surprising result was that although the three curricula were radically different, they did not differ in effectiveness; the three groups performed similarly on the three types of measures. This led Weikart to conclude that the *content* of a preschool curriculum is probably far less crucial to its effectiveness than the interest, commitment, and competence of the teachers.

Recent programs

Another round of Piagetian curriculum development began in the mid 1970s. The impetus for these second generation programs was certain conceptual criticisms of the early programs. Essentially, curricula such as the Lavatelli and Weikart programs were criticized for insufficient obeisance to the authority of Piagetian theory. They were accused, more particularly, of taking unacceptable liberties with the theory and, as a result, of not being 'truly Piagetian'.

Three of the more prominent illustrations of such criticisms are these. First, recall that both the Early Childhood Curriculum and the Open Framework Program consist of detailed instruction in concrete-operational concepts. Orthodox Piagetians are inclined to interpret this as violating the first and second readiness recommendations discussed earlier. That is, such instruction is said to involve teaching concepts that are clearly beyond preschoolers' current stage of cognitive development, and it amounts to speeding up the 'natural' rate of cognitive development. Second, recall that Early Childhood teachers and Open Framework teachers take active control of the curriculum. To orthodox Piagetians, this violates the maxim that children should learn through active self-discovery of concepts. Third, recall that Open Framework teachers comment on children's activities and help them learn by posing questions about exercises. Orthodox Piagetians believe that this violates the proscription that early-childhood instruction should not be language-based.

Criticisms such as these have led, naturally, to curricula in which the authors have sought to be as faithful as possible to Piagetian theory. The two most influential examples of such curricula are the Piagetian Preschool Education Program (Lawton, Hooper, Saunders and Roth, 1978; Bingham-Newman, 1974; Ershler, McAllister and Saunders, 1977; Saunders, 1976) and the Piaget for Early Education program (Kamii, 1973a and b; Kamii and DeVries, 1977, 1978).

The Piagetian Preschool Education Program was developed by F. H. Hooper and several collaborators at the University of Wisconsin. When the project began, the aim was simply to determine whether it was possible to design an orthodox Piagetian curriculum. During this phase, an extensive list of recommendations was culled from Piaget's writings (see Bingham-Newman, 1974). Next, a curriculum was designed around this list, and the curriculum was eventually introduced in the University of Wisconsin's experimental preschool. The content of the curriculum was superficially similar to Lavatelli's (1970, 1971) in that it emphasized several categories of concrete-operational concepts (classification, measurement, number, seriation, space, and time). But teachers' instructional strategies were quite different.

Briefly, teachers in the Piagetian Preschool Education Program are strongly discouraged from undertaking any sort of instruction that involves direct transmission of concepts to children. Instead, they are provided with a series of classroom activities that are designed to promote self-discovery of concepts by children. As might be expected, these exercises involve the active manipulation of concrete objects by children, *but not on instructions from the teachers*. Children are free to select whatever activities they wish and, importantly, teachers are discouraged from helping children to avoid 'wrong' exercises.

Evaluation data on the Piagetian Preschool Education Program are available. The principal source of evidence consists of scores on two standardized tests of intelligence (Peabody Picture Vocabulary and Raven's Progressive Matrices) and scores on tests for various concrete-operational concepts. These tests were administered before and after children had completed two years in the program. The same tests were administered to children who had been attending preschools using non-Piagetian curricula for the same period. The results were very similar to Weikart's. On the one hand, children performed much better on all tests after two years of preschool than at the outset. However, as in the case of Lavatelli's (1970, 1971) research, it is unclear how much of this improvement is attributable to the curriculum and how much is due to spontaneous age improvements. On the other hand, there were no differences in the performance of Piagetian and non-Piagetian pupils on either the standardized measures or the concrete-operational tests.

The second example of a recent and more orthodox Piagetian curriculum is the Piaget for Early Education program. Although this curriculum has been in operation for a few years, its developers, Kamii and DeVries, have not been very specific about its content in their writings. Perhaps the most accurate thing that can be said is that the curriculum is highly unstructured in comparison to those that we have already considered. Kamii was a member of the original group that developed the Open Framework Program, and the Piaget for Early Education program was an attempt to correct what Kamii believed were misinterpretations of Piagetian theory by Weikart.

The core of the Piaget for Early Education curriculum is a list of seven guiding principles of instruction (e.g. encourage children to be independent and curious, encourage children to interact with their peers, encourage children to learn in the context of play activities). These principles resemble the list developed during the initial phase of the Wisconsin program, and there are many points of overlap. Unlike the Wisconsin program, however, the list is not translated into a 'cookbook' curriculum complete with specific exercises for specific concepts.

Essentially, no evaluation data are available on this program. Although such data could easily be gathered, they have not been for reasons that are primarily philosophical. The type of evaluation data discussed for the other three programs are what educators call *summative* evaluation. But there is another type of evaluation called *formative* evaluation. Formative evaluation is purely conceptual. It is concerned with the degree of conformity of a program to the theory that inspired it. A program receives a high formative evaluation score if it adheres closely to the parent theory and a low formative evaluation score if it takes liberties with the theory. According to Kamii, summative evaluation is distinctly unPiagetian; the proper method of evaluating a Piagetian preschool program is formative (cf. Johnson and Hooper, 1982).

To many readers, this elevation of subjective, 'construct validity' methods of evaluation over hard data may seem like a cynical avoidance of educational responsibilities, especially in view of the lack of support for Piagetian hypotheses in the literature on children's concept learning. A more charitable interpretation, one that I favor, will be familiar to students of the history of science. Experience has taught us that skepticism is the proper attitude to adopt in connection with any theory. If one is committed to the fundamental truth of some theory, it becomes possible to justify all manner of far-fetched research procedures on the ground that they produce findings that agree with the theory. More to the point, one is inclined to ignore findings that disagree with theory, as well as the procedures that produce them, in the belief that they cannot possibly be correct. Unfortunately, Piaget's work, like Freud's before him, has given birth to a circle of acolytes, particularly within education, who appear to be deeply committed to the truth of the theory. The Piaget for Early Education curriculum is only one symptom of this problem. Many others could be given.

Synopsis

In this second section of the chapter, I have reviewed some aspects of how Piaget's theory has been put into practice in education, at least in North America. As we have seen, there appear to be a fairly substantial list of instructional dos and don'ts that can be derived from the theory. Some of these recommendations find support in basic research on cognitive development, but others are either poorly supported by basic research or are contradicted by it. I have also reviewed four examples of Piaget-inspired preschool curricula.

These programs vary considerably in their content and in their degree of adherence to theory.

Finally, I should like to stress that the development and testing of Piagetian preschool curricula remains an active area of educational research. In addition to the two illustrations of recent curricula that were considered, there are other still more recent programs. New themes are continuing to emerge. For example, the trend away from anything resembling formal instruction that is apparent in Piaget for Early Education seems to be accelerating, and there seems to be a growing emphasis on play (cf. Johnson and Hooper, 1982). But this is essentially crystal ball gazing. It will not be possible to comment authoritatively on this matter until such trends have become more firmly established in the literature.

Note

Preparation of this chapter was supported by Grant No. A0668 from the Natural Sciences and Engineering Research Council of Canada.

References

Arbuthnot, J. (1975) Modifications of moral judgment through role playing. *Developmental Psychology* **11**: 319–24.

Beilin, H. (1965) Learning and operational convergence in logical thought development. *Journal of Experimental Child Psychology* **2**: 317–39.

Beilin, J. (1971) The training and acquisition of logical operations. In M. F. Rosskopf, L. P. Steffe and S. Taback (eds) *Piagetian Cognitive-Developmental Research and Mathematics Education*. Washington, DC: National Council of Teachers of Mathematics.

Bingham-Newman, A. M. (1974) *Development of Logical Operations Ability in Early Childhood: A Longitudinal Comparison of the Effects of Two Preschool Settings*. Unpublished doctoral dissertation, University of Wisconsin.

Bingham-Newman, A. M. and Hooper, F. H. (1974) Classification and seriation instruction and logical task performance in the preschool. *American Educational Research Journal* **11**: 379–94.

Botvin, G. J. and Murray, F. H. (1975) The efficacy of peer modeling and social conflict in the acquisition of conservation. *Child Development* **46**: 796–9.

Brainerd, C. J. (1971) The development of the proportionality scheme in children and adolescents. *Developmental Psychology* **5**: 469–76.

Brainerd, C. J. (1972a) Reinforcement and reversibility in quantity conservation acquisition. *Psychonomic Science* **27**: 114–16.

Brainerd, C. J. (1972b) The age-stage issue in conservation acquisition. *Psychonomic Science* **27**: 115–17.

Brainerd, C. J. (1973) The origins of number concepts. *Scientific American* **228**(3): 101–9.

Brainerd, C. J. (1974a) Training and transfer of transitivity, conservation, and class inclusion of length. *Child Development* **45**: 324–34.

Brainerd, C. J. (1974b) Inducing ordinal and cardinal representations of the first five natural numbers. *Journal of Experimental Child Psychology* **18**: 524–34.

Brainerd, C. J. (1977) Cognitive development and concept learning: an interpretative review. *Psychological Bulletin* **84**: 919–39.

Brainerd, C. J. (1978a) Learning research and Piagetian theory. In L. S. Siegel and C. J. Brainerd (eds), *Alternatives to Piaget: Critical Essays on the Theory*. New York: Academic Press.

Brainerd, C. J. (1978b) Cognitive development and instructional theory. *Contemporary Educational Psychology* **3**: 37–50.

Brainerd, C. J. (1978c) *Piaget's Theory of Intelligence.* Englewood Cliffs, NJ: Prentice-Hall.

Brainerd, C. J. (1979) Concept learning and developmental stage. In H. J. Klausmeier *et al. Cognitive Learning and Development: Piagetian and Information-Processing Perspectives*. Cambridge, Mass.: Ballinger.

Brainerd, C. J. (1981) Stages II. *Developmental Review* **1**: 63–81.

Brainerd, C. J. (1982a) Children's concept learning as rule-sampling systems with Markovian properties. In C. J. Brainerd (ed.) *Children's Logical and Mathematical Cognition: Progress in Cognitive Development Research*. New York: Springer.

Brainerd, C. J. (1982b) The stage-learning hypothesis: strategies for instructional design. *Contemporary Educational Psychology*, 238–56.

Brainerd, C. J. and Allen, T. W. (1971a) Experimental inductions of the conservation of 'first-order' quantitative invariants. *Psychological Bulletin* **75**: 128–44.

Brainerd, C. J. and Allen, T. W. (1971b) Training and transfer of density conservation. *Child Development* **42**: 693–704.

Brainerd, C. J. and Brainerd, S. H. (1972) Order of acquisition of number and liquid quantity conservation. *Child Development* **43**: 1401–5.

Brainerd, C. J. and Howe, M. L. (1979) An attentional analysis of small cardinal number concepts in 5-year-olds. *Canadian Journal of Behavioural Science* **11**: 112–23.

Brison, D. W. (1966) Acceleration of conservation of substance. *Journal of Genetic Psychology* **109**: 311–22.

Bruner, J. S. (1964) The course of cognitive growth. *American Psychologist* **18**: 1–15.

Bucher, B. and Schneider, R. E. (1973) Acquisition and generalization of conservation by pre-schoolers using operant training. *Journal of Experimental Child Psychology* **16**: 187–204.

Burns, S. M. and Brainerd, C. J. (1979) Effects of constructive and dramatic play on perspective taking in very young children. *Developmental Psychology* **15**: 512–21.

Cantor, G. N., Dunlap, L. L. and Rettie, C. S. (1982) Effects of reception and discovery instruction on kindergarteners' performance on probability tasks. *American Educational Research Journal*, in press.

Case, R. (1974) Structures and strictures: some functional limitations on the course of cognitive growth. *Cognitive Psychology* **6**: 544–73.

Churchill, E. (1958a) The number concepts of the young child (part 1). *Researches and Studies* **17**: 34–9 (Leeds University).

Churchill, E. (1958b) The number of concepts of the young child (part 2). *Researches and Studies* **18**: 28–46 (Leeds University).

Cole, M. and Scribner, S. (1974) *Culture and Thought*. New York: Wiley.

Coxford, A. F. (1964) The effects of instruction on the age placement of children in Piaget's seriation experiments. *Arithmetic Teacher* **10**: 4–9.

Denney, N. W. and Actio, M. A. (1974) Classification training in 2- and 3-year-old children. *Journal of Experimental Child Psychology* **17**: 37–48.

Denney, N. W., Zeytinoglu, S. and Selzer, S. C. (1977) Conservation training in 4-year-olds. *Journal of Experimental Child Psychology* **24**: 129–46.

Duckworth, E. (1964) Piaget rediscovered. In R. E. Ripple and V. N. Rockcastle (eds), *Piaget Rediscovered*. Ithaca, NY: Cornell University Press.

Elkind, D. (1967) Piaget's conservation problems. *Child Development* **38**, 15–27.

Emrick, J. A. (1967) *The Acquisition and Transfer of Conservation Skills by 4-year-old Children*. Unpublished doctoral dissertation, University of California at Los Angeles.

Erschler, J., McAllister, A. and Saunders, R. A. (1977) *The Piagetian Derived Curriculum: Theoretical Framework, Preschool Objectives, and Program Description*. Working Paper No. 205, Wisconsin Research and Development Center for Cognitive Learning, University of Wisconsin.

Field, D. (1981) Can preschool children really learn to conserve? *Child Development* **52**: 326–34.

Flavell, J. H. (1963) *The Developmental Psychology of Jean Piaget*. Princeton, NJ: Van Nostrand.

Flavell, J. H. (1970) Concept development. In P. H. Mussen (ed.) *Carmichael's Manual of Child Psychology*. New York: Wiley.

Forman, G. E. and Hill, F. (1980) *Constructive Play: Applying Piaget in the Preschool*. Monterey, Calif.: Brooks/Cole.

Gelman, R. (1969) Conservation acquisition: a problem of learning to attend to relevant attributes. *Journal of Experimental Child Psychology* **7**: 167–87.

Goldschmid, M. L. (1968) Role of experience in the acquisition of conservation. *Proceedings of the American Psychological Association* **76**: 361–2.

Goldschmid, M. L. (1971) Role of experience in the rate and sequence of cognitive development. In D. R. Green, M. P. Ford and G. B. Flamer (eds) *Measurement and Piaget*. New York: McGraw-Hill.

Halford, G. S. (1970) A classification learning set which is a possible model for conservation of quantity. *Australian Journal of Psychology* **22**: 11–19.

Hamel, B. R. and Riksen, B. O. M. (1973) Identity, reversibility, verbal rule instruction and conservation. *Developmental Psychology* **9**: 66–72.

Harker, W. H. (1960) *Children's Number Concepts: Ordination and Cardination*. Unpublished master's thesis, Queen's University.

Hatano, G. (1971) A developmental approach to concept formation: a review of neo-Piagetian learning experiments. *Dokkyo University Bulletin of Liberal Arts and Education* **5**: 66–72.

Hatano, G. and Suga, Y. (1969) Equilibration and external reinforcement in the acquisition of number conservation. *Japanese Psychological Research* **11**: 17–31.

Hooper, F. H. and DeFrain, J. D. (1980) On delineating distinctly Piagetian contributions to education. *Genetic Psychology Monographs* **101**: 134–81.

Hooper, F. H., Goldman, J. A., Storck, P. A. and Burke, A. M. (1971) Stage sequence and correspondence in Piagetian theory: a review of the middle-childhood period. In *Research Relating to Children,* Bulletin No. 28. Washington, DC: US Printing Office.

Iannotti, R. J. (1978) Effects of role-taking experiences on role taking, empathy, altruism and aggression. *Developmental Psychology* **14**: 119–24.

Inhelder, B. (1956) Criteria of the stages of mental development. In J. M. Tanner and B. Inhelder (eds), *Discussions on Child Development*, vol. I. London: Tavistock.

Inhelder, B. and Sinclair, H. (1969) Learning cognitive structures. In P. H. Mussen, J. Langer and M. Covington (eds) *Trends and Issues in Developmental Psychology.* New York: Holt, Rinehart & Winston.

Inhelder, B., Sinclair, H. and Bovet, M. (1974) *Learning and the Development of Cognition.* Cambridge, Mass.: Harvard University Press.

Inhelder, B., Sinclair, H., Bovet, M. and Smock, C. (1966) On cognitive development. *American Psychologist* **21**: 160–4.

Jensen, L. C. and Larm, C. (1970) Effects of two training procedures on intentionality in moral judgment among children. *Developmental Psychology* **2**: 310.

Johnson, J. E. and Hooper, F. H. (1982) Piagetian structuralism and learning: reflections on two decades of educational application. *Contemporary Educational Psychology*, in press.

Kamii, C. (1973a) Pedagogical principles derived from Piaget's theory: relevance for educational practice. In M. Schwebel and J. Raph (eds) *Piaget in the Classroom.* New York: Basic Books.

Kamii, C. (1973b) Piaget's interactionism and the process of teaching young children. In M. Schwebel and J. Raph (eds) *Piaget in the Classroom.* New York: Basic Books.

Kamii, C. and DeVries, R. (1977) Piaget for early education. In M. C. Day and R. Parker (eds) *The Preschool in Action* (2nd edn). Boston: Allyn & Bacon.

Kamii, C. and DeVries, R. (1978) *Physical Knowledge in Preschool Education: Implications of Piagetian Theory.* Englewood Cliffs, NJ: Prentice-Hall.

Kingsley, R. C. and Hall, V. C. (1967) Training of conservation through the use of learning sets. *Child Development* **38**: 1111–26.

Kuhn, D. (1972) Mechanisms of change in the development of cognitive structures. *Child Development* **43**: 833–44.

Lavatelli, C. S. (1970) *Early Childhood Curriculum, A Piagetian Program.* Boston: American Science and Engineering.

Lavatelli, C. S. (1971) *Piaget's Theory Applied to an Early Childhood Curriculum.*

Boston: American Science and Engineering.

Lawton, J. T. and Hooper, F. H. (178) Developmental theory in the early childhood classroom: an analysis of Piagetian inspired principles and programs. In L. S. Siegel and C. J. Brainerd (eds) *Alternatives to Piaget: Critical Essays on the Theory*. New York: Academic Press.

Lawton, J. T., Hooper, F. H., Saunders, R. A. and Roth, P. (1978) *A Comparison of Three Early Childhood Instructional Programs*. Technical Report No. 462, Wisconsin Research and Development Center for Cognitive Learning, University of Wisconsin.

Litrownik, A. J., Franzini, L. R., Livingston, M. K. and Harvey, S. (1978) Developmental priority of identity conservation: acceleration of identity and equivalence in normal and moderately retarded children. *Child Development* **49**: 201–8.

McGraw, M. B. (1940) Neural maturation as exemplified in achievement of bladder control. *Journal of Pediatrics* **16**, 580–9.

McLaughlin, L. J. and Brinley, J. F. (1973) Age and observational learning of a multiple classification task. *Developmental Psychology* **9**: 9–15.

Mermelstein, E. and Meyer, E. (1969) Conservation training techniques and their effects on different populations. *Child Development* **40**: 471–90.

Murray, F. B. (1968) Cognitive conflict and reversibility training in the acquisition of length conservation. *Journal of Educational Psychology* **59**: 82–7.

Murray, F. B. (1972) Acquisition of conservation through social interaction. *Developmental Psychology* **6**: 1–6.

Piaget, J. (1952) *The Child's Conception of Number*. New York: Humanities Press.

Piaget, J. (1960) The general problems of the psychobiological development of the child. In J. M. Tanner and B. Inhelder (eds) *Discussions on Child Development*, vol. 4. London: Tavistock.

Piaget, J. (1970a) Piaget's theory. In P. H. Mussen (ed.) *Carmichael's Manual of Child Psychology*. New York: Wiley.

Piaget, J. (1970b) A conversation with Jean Piaget. *Psychology Today* **3** (12): 25–32.

Piaget, J. (1970c) *Genetic Epistemology*. New York: Columbia University Press.

Piaget, J. and Inhelder, B. (1956) *The Child's Conception of Space*. London: Routledge & Kegan Paul.

Piaget, J. and Inhelder, B. (1969) *The Psychology of the Child*. New York: Basic Books.

Piaget, J., Inhelder, B. and Szeminska, A. (1960) *The Child's Conception of Space*. New York: Harper.

Rosenthal, T. L. and Zimmerman, B. J. (1972) Modeling by exemplification and instruction in training conservation. *Developmental Psychology* **6**: 392–401.

Rosenthal, T. L. and Zimmerman, B. J. (1978) *Social Learning and Cognition*. New York: Academic Press.

Saunders, R. Q. (1976) *Classification Abilities in Young Children: Longitudinal Effects of a Piagetian Approach to a Preschool Program and to Teacher Education.*

Unpublished doctoral dissertation, University of Wisconsin.

Siegler, R. S., Liebert, D. E. and Liebert, R. M. (1973) Inhelder and Piaget's pendulum problem: teaching children to act as scientists. *Developmental Psychology* **9**: 97–101.

Sinclair, H. (1973) Recent Piagetian research in learning studies. In M. Schwebel and J. Raph (eds) *Piaget in the Classroom.* New York: Basic Books.

Skinner, B. F. (1974) *About Behaviorism.* New York: Knopf.

Smedslund, J. (1959) Apprentissage des notions de la conservation et de la transitivite du poids. *Etudes d'Epistemologie Genetique* **9**: 3–13.

Smedslund, J. (1961a) The acquisition of conservation of substance and weight in children. I: Introduction. *Scandinavian Journal of Psychology* **2**: 11–20.

Smedslund, J. (1961b) The acquisition of conservation of substance and weight in children. II: External reinforcement of conservation of weight and of the operations of addition and subtraction. *Scandinavian Journal of Psychology* **2**: 71–84.

Smedslund, J. (1961c) The acquisition of conservation of substance and weight in children. III: Extinction of conservation of weight acquired 'normally' and by means of empirical controls on a balance scale. *Scandinavian Journal of Psychology* **2**: 85–7.

Smedslund, J. (1961d) The acquisition of conservation of substance and weight in children. IV: An attempt at extinction of the visual components of the weight concept. *Scandinavian Journal of Psychology* **2**: 154–5.

Smedslund, J. (1961e) The acquisition of conservation of substance and wieght in children. V: Practice in conflict situations without reinforcement. *Scandinavian Journal of Psychology* **2**: 156–60.

Smedslund, J. (1961f) The acquisition of conservation of substance and weight in children. VI: Practice on continuous versus discontinuous material in conflict situations without external reinforcement. *Scandinavian Journal of Psychology* **2**: 203–10.

Smith, I. D. (1968) The effects of training procedures on the acquisition of conservation of weight. *Child Development* **39**: 515–26.

Strauss, S. and Langer, J. (1970) Operational thought inducement. *Child Development* **41**: 163–75.

Sullivan, E. (1967) Acquisition of conservation of substance through film modeling techniques. In D. W. Brison and E. Sullivan (eds) *Recent Research on the Acquisition of Substance.* Toronto, Canada: Ontario Institute for Studies in Education.

Wallach, L. and Sprott, R. L. (1964) Inducing number conservation in children. *Child Development* **35**: 1057–71.

Wallach, L., Wall, A. J. and Anderson, L. (1967) Number conservation: the roles of reversibility, addition/subtraction and misleading perceptual cues. *Child Development* **38**: 425–42.

Weikart, D. P. (1973) Development of effective preschool programs: a report on the results of the High/Scope-Ypsilanti preschool projects. Paper presented at High/Scope Educational Research Foundation Conference, Ann Arbor, Michigan.

Weikart, D. P., Rogers, L., Adcock, C. and McClelland, D. (1971) *The Cognitively Oriented Curriculum: A Framework for Preschool Teachers*. Urbana, Ill.: University of Illinois Press.

Wohlwill, J. F. (1959) Un essai d'apprentissage dans le domaine de la conservation du nombre. *Etudes d'Epistemologie Genetique* **9**: 125–35.

Wohlwill, J. F. and Lowe, R. C. (1962) An experimental analysis of the conservation of number. *Child Development* **33**: 153–67.

Youniss, J. (1971) Classificatory schemes in relation to class inclusion before and after training. *Human Development* **14**: 171–83.

Zimmerman, B. J. and Lanaro, P. (1974) Acquiring and retaining conservation of length through modeling and reversibility cues. *Merrill-Palmer Quarterly* **20**: 145–61.

3 Social interaction and cognitive development: a review of post-Piagetian research

Paul Light

Introduction

The no-man's-land between cognitive-developmental and social psychology has recently been transformed into a very busy place. The emergence of the label 'social cognition' marks a real convergence of interests. Much of the contemporary research identified by this label is concerned with the interpretation of social behaviour in cognitive terms. However, some interesting strands of social cognition research run in the opposite direction, investigating the extent to which individual cognitive development is itself a social process. The present chapter is intended to provide an introduction to recent research on this latter topic.

Do social interactions play an important part in the child's cognitive development? If so, what kinds of interactions have what kinds of effects on cognitive development, and what psychological mechanisms are involved? These are rather large questions, and no attempt will be made to provide comprehensive answers to them. Instead, this chapter will offer a review of some selected areas where research is in progress, in the hope that this will give some sense of the character and direction of contemporary work.

One area which will receive extensive coverage concerns the role of peer (child-child) interaction in facilitating individual cognitive development. Piaget's (1932) early emphasis on the importance of this kind of interaction, combined with the fact that this is at present a particularly lively research area, makes it a suitable starting point. A fairly detailed consideration of recent research will serve to bring out some conceptual issues which are relevant to any attempt to understand the significance of social interactions for cognitive growth. Central amongst these is the distinction between, on the one hand viewing social interaction as providing the child simply with a potent source of cognitive *conflict*, and on the other hand viewing it as providing the child with access to the 'right answer', or at least to the right way of understanding the question.

Any conceptualization of social interaction as giving the child access to knowledge possessed by others in his social milieu brings the role of language to the fore. Piaget's essentially negative treatment of language in relation to the genesis of operational thought has been subjected to much criticism. Recent research on adult-child interaction in the context of Piaget's cognitive testing situations has demonstrated that the child's understanding and use of language in such situations is highly sensitive to context. Recognition of this flexible and dynamic quality of the child's language use necessitates reconsideration of the part language may play in the development of the child's understanding. We shall take a brief look at some of this research before going on to review some other recent work which bears on the language training studies which Piaget adduced to support his position. Here again it will be argued that the focus needs to be shifted from language as a static collection of symbols to language as a means of discourse. What proves to be effective is not telling the child the right answer, but guiding him or her towards the right considerations.

With this in mind we shall next take a look at parent-child interaction as a potential source of the child's cognitive growth. The methodological problems of research in this area are considerable, but some studies based on interview data suggest that advanced development in the child is associated with a relatively personal, symmetrical relationship between child and parent. A more direct approach involving observation of mothers teaching their children to solve problems or complete puzzles has highlighted the importance of the *contingency* of the mother's behaviour upon that of her child. One way and another there is now a good deal of evidence which implicates the effectiveness of communication between parent and child as a significant factor in the child's cognitive development.

The studies concerned with characterizing mother-child

relationships through the use of teaching tasks have thrown some light on the nature of effective instruction in general. Teacher-child interactions in the classroom have rarely been studied in the context of cognitive developmental research, but this seems likely to be a major 'growth area' in the near future. The classroom provides not only another research setting in which we may learn about the effects of social interactions on cognitive development, but also a setting in which our increased understanding of these effects may eventually find its most useful application.

The focus of the chapter thus shifts from child-child to adult-child interaction, and within the latter from parent-child to teacher-child interaction. In all these areas, Piaget's theory of cognitive development forms the backdrop against which recent developments must be viewed, so we shall preface consideration of these developments with some brief remarks on Piaget's position regarding the role of social interaction in cognitive growth.

The Piagetian standpoint

In terms of his general theory, Piaget cannot be criticized for having neglected the role of the environment, social or otherwise, in the cognitive development of the child. He stressed that intelligence developed through the child's progressive adaptation to his environment, and in the theory of equilibration he outlined a general mechanism subserving this adaptation. But at the same time Piaget largely neglected the specific aspects of this process, and his writings offer little insight into particular cognitive sequelae of particular kinds of experience. His indifference to these issues arguably reflects his preoccupation with epistemological rather than psychological questions (Barker and Newson, 1979). In addition to this general lack of concern with environmental influences on cognition, however, there is an apparent bias towards consideration of the child's material rather than his personal environment. Piaget's experimental work over the last forty years has focused on the individual child in constructive interaction with the impersonal, physical environment. Meanwhile the socio-cultural environment of the child has been largely ignored.

The fact that Piaget preferred to focus on the dialectic between the child and his material rather than his interpersonal context can perhaps best be understood as an aspect of his reaction against a 'passive copy' model of cognitive growth. The notion of the child's mind as a bucket into which his or her elders pour knowledge was anathema to Piaget. His thesis that the child had an active, constructive role to play in the development of his own intellect could perhaps be most clearly established in situations where the possibility of social transmission of knowledge did not arise. However, as we shall argue, even a constructionist theory must at some point come to terms with the fact that other people represent a crucial part of the world to which the child has to adapt.

Only in some of his earliest writings did Piaget unambiguously argue a causal role for social interactions in cognitive development. In *The Moral Judgement of the Child* (1932) he elaborated the idea that egocentrism stands as the main obstacle to the child's progress, both in the social and in the intellectual domain. In the social domain this egocentrism was seen in the child focusing on his own viewpoint to the neglect of others. This made co-operation and effective communication difficult or impossible. In the intellectual domain, egocentrism was similarly seen in a fixation upon one aspect of a situation or a problem to the neglect of other relevant aspects. As a result, the child's reasoning was limited and distorted.

The primary developmental task for the preoperational child was therefore to achieve a *decentration* of his thinking, and Piaget maintained that social interaction held the key to this process. He took the view that the child's relationships with others of his own age group were of particular significance in this respect. He stressed the asymmetry of the adult-child relationship in terms of power and authority, and held that such asymmetry tended to reinforce rather than ameliorate the child's egocentrism. Criticism is born of discussion, Piaget wrote, and *discussion is only possible amongst equals* (1932, p. 409).

In interaction with his equals, Piaget argued, the child is exposed to differing and conflicting viewpoints, and the symmetry of the peer relationship encourages attempts to resolve the contradictions. The intellectual decentration which marks the onset of operational thinking was held to be dependent on this process of social decentration through interaction (Piaget, 1932, 1950).

This early Piagetian thesis regarding the crucial role of symmetrical peer relationships has lain latent a long time. Commentators on Piaget's work, especially those with an interest in its educational application (e.g. Elkind, 1976; Sigel, 1969) have often restated Piaget's argument on this point, but only in the last decade has the issue become a significant focus of empirical research. For this we have to thank a group of Genevan researchers led by Willem Doise. Their work, and other research stimulated by it, will be reviewed in the following section.

Child-child interaction and cognitive development

In the mid-1970s Doise and his colleagues began publication of a long series of experimental studies on the effects of peer interaction. These studies shared a basic format involving individual pre-testing of children on a particular task, followed by one or more sessions during which two or three children had experience of working on the task together, followed by individual post-tests.

The early studies (e.g. Doise *et al.*, 1975) established that the performance of children during the interaction session was typically at a higher level than that observed when children were given solitary practice on the task. Moreover, this superiority was greater than could be accounted for simply in terms of the less able children in each group imitating the performance of their more able partners. Not only was group performance superior to individual performance, but children who had had experience of peer interaction performed better on the individual post-tests than control subjects who had worked on the task alone.

The tasks employed in these studies have been few in number, being drawn mostly from Piagetian studies of concrete-operational thinking. Correspondingly, subjects have typically ranged from about 5 to 9 years of age. The tasks have included a spatial transformation problem requiring the child to 'decentre' from his own point of view, various versions of conservation of length and conservation of liquid quantity tasks, and a co-operative game involving manipulation of pulleys to keep a pencil on a pre-set path.

Particular emphasis has been placed on the conservation tasks. By presenting evidence of the use of novel justifications by children at post-test, and of generalization of acquired conservation responses to tasks other than those used in the interaction sessions (e.g. Perret-Clermont, 1980), Doise and his colleagues have been able to make the case that more is involved here than simple imitation: 'The learning acquired in social interaction arises from fundamental cognitive restructuring, and goes beyond imitative adoption of situation-specific and "superficial" behaviour patterns' (Mugny *et al.*, 1981, p. 322).

While social interaction between peers has been shown to be

capable of facilitating individual progress on all of the tasks used by Doise's group, such facilitation has been found to be conditional upon a number of factors. The relationship between task difficulty and the individual's initial level of ability turns out to be important in most cases. Only when the child already has some partial grasp of the principles involved in the correct solution of the task is interaction with a peer likely to be beneficial to him. The composition of the pairs of children involved in the interaction sessions is also important. Some degree of asymmetry needs to be present in order to ensure progress. However, this is not construed in terms of one partner providing a model for the other but (in line with Piaget's early suggestions) in terms of each child being presented with a conflict between his own response and that of the other. It does not matter if both partners are equally wrong, as long as they are wrong in different ways: 'The subject finds himself confronted with cognitive models which, although they do not offer him the correct response, suggest to him some relevant dimensions for a progressive elaboration of a cognitive mechanism new to him' (Mugny *et al.*, 1981, p. 326).

Thus the Piagetian concept of conflict between individual centrations is used to account for progress. According to this view, two children who adopted exactly the *same* incorrect approach to a problem should not benefit from interaction with one another. Mugny and Doise (1978) demonstrated this with a spatial transformation task. But in a subsequent study (cited by Mugny *et al.*, 1981) they were able to show that conflict and subsequent individual progress could be induced even in pairings of this kind. They achieved this by the simple device of putting children in different spatial relationships to the task materials, so that although they were making the same mistakes, different errors resulted.

Thus conflict is envisaged as the key to progress, whether it arises from differences in subjects' approaches to the same task or from deliberately created differences in their perspectives on the task. But what if conflict were to be engendered by, say, having a single individual occupy successively different positions in relation to a spatial task? Doise and colleagues, defending their position that inter-personal conflict is a vital element in cognitive growth, argue that such *intra*-individual conflict represents an altogether less potent stimulus to intellectual development.

Mugny and Doise (1978) have provided some evidence for the

superiority of inter- over intra-individual conflict but in a recent British study Emler and Valiant (1982) have failed to replicate this finding. While they found an advantage of social over individual practice on a spatial relations task, they also found that conflict induced at the intra-individual level could be just as facilitative of subsequent progress as conflict at the inter-individual level. Mugny and Doise's (1978) study had in fact obtained this same result in groups at certain socioeconomic levels, and Emler and Valiant suggest that socioeconomic and cultural differences may explain their discrepant findings.

Other studies have found evidence suggestive of cultural differences in the impact of inter-individual conflict on subsequent individual performance. For example, Mackie (1980) found that the relative benefits of intra- and inter-individual conflict varied as between different ethnic groups in New Zealand. Such findings obviously threaten to limit the generality of the case for peer interaction as a vital factor in cognitive development. However, we have already established that the advantage of inter-individual conflict over individual practice on the task is conditional upon the participants having a certain level of initial ability which enables them to take a systematic approach to the task from the outset. Thus where disparate findings arise from studies with different ethnic or socioeconomic groups it may be that we are dealing with differences in initial level of ability or of approach to the task rather than with cultural differences in responsivity to inter-individual conflict. This is one of the issues which is currently exercising the Genevan group (Mugny *et al.*, 1981).

A substantial and consistent advantage of peer interaction over individual practice has been found in a series of British studies by Glachan (Glachan and Light, 1982), using a complex seriation game known as 'The Tower of Hanoi'. The game involves the child (or pairs of children together) attempting to transfer a seriated stack of tiles from one to another of three pegs in as few moves as possible. Rules stipulate that only one tile may be moved at a time and that a larger one may never be placed on top of a smaller one. In most cases subjects were around 8 years of age. Individual pre- and post-tests were separated by intervention sessions of various kinds. These included individual practice, a didactic condition in which children in pairs were repeatedly led through the optimal solution by the experimenter, and an interaction condition in which children in pairs worked together to find their own solutions. This third condition was found to be by far the most effective provided that the children involved already evidenced some kind of strategy in their approach to the task, and provided also that steps were taken to prevent either partner from wholly dominating the interaction. With these provisos, the interaction condition proved to be highly effective in facilitating progress by both partners towards more efficient solution strategies at individual post-test.

Subsequent studies with a number puzzle based on the popular code-breaking game 'Mastermind' have produced similar results. Moreover using this task, which generates a high level of verbal interactions, it has been possible to make a start on the search for systematic correlations between aspects of the social interaction and the extent of progress manifested by individuals at post-test (Glachan, 1982). To achieve a clearer understanding of the relationship between quality of interaction and outcome we stand in need of a generalizable but sensitive coding scheme for such interactions. A number of attempts to provide such a scheme are under way. Miller (1981), for example, has examined ways of characterizing argumentation between peers both in relation to a moral dilemma and to a logical (balanced beam) task, and has established certain common characteristics of arguments in these two very different contexts. Vandenplas-Holpner (1982) has begun to use fine grained observational and analytical techniques to study both verbal and non-verbal interactions in triads of children working together on concrete operations tasks. Such projects are time-consuming and difficult, but should soon begin to pay dividends. In particular, they may illuminate some of the problematic issues raised in the section which follows.

Conflict or co-construction?

Little distinction has been drawn thus far between what might be called problem solving tasks on the one hand and judgement tasks on the other. For example, both of the tasks used by Glachan shared the feature that from the outset all of the children knew what they were trying to achieve, even if they had very different ideas about how to achieve it. In such problem solving situations there is room for dispute about the means, but not about the end. By contrast, in many of Piaget's classic concrete operations tasks, such as those involving conservation judgements, it is difficult to make a means-ends separation and it is clear that children may not share the same criteria for the satisfactoriness of their answers. While the 'conflict of centrations' hypothesis was developed principally in relation to tasks of the latter type, it may in fact prove to be more appropriate to the former. Some recent studies by Russell (1981, 1982a) have highlighted this issue.

Unlike Doise and colleagues, Russell has found little or no evidence of an advantage of peer interaction over working alone on conservation and other operational judgement tasks. Where experience of working in pairs did lead to gains Russell argued that these were due simply to the incorrect child's compliance with the correct answer given by his partner. Little evidence of conflict was observed. In relation to tasks of this kind Russell rejects the Piagetian hypothesis that progress results from the co-ordination of individual centrations. He suggests that the young child's judgement may diverge from that of the older child or adult not simply because he fails to take account of all relevant features of the situation but rather because he lacks an appropriate 'propositional attitude' towards the questions he is asked (Russell, 1982b). Put simply, the questioner intends the question objectively, but the child apprehends it subjectively, in terms of appearances.

Where children fail on such a task because they are approaching it subjectively there is no reason to expect that conflict will result from pairing them together, even if they disagree. Conflict will only occur, and be productive, when children already possess an 'objective attitude' towards the task in hand. Thus Russell, like Hamlyn (1982), argues that the critical developmental achievement in this domain is the acquisition by the child of an appropriate epistemic attitude, and, more particularly, of a notion of correctness versus incorrectness which is consistent with that of the adult culture: 'The main developmental task is the progressive socialization of the child's judgements, their tuning in with those of the adult by means of the appropriate public criteria' (Russell, 1982b, p. 78).

In a subsequent paper, Russell (1982c) finds some room for compromise between his position and Doise's. In the studies described earlier, Doise and colleagues reported both conflict and subsequent individual gains when preoperational children worked together on operational judgement tasks. Russell acknowledges these findings but suggests that such conflict only occurs when the children involved already have some grasp of the 'objective attitude'. Given that they have achieved this, why do they not succeed on the tasks individually? Essentially Russell's answer to this is that there is a transitional period at about 6 or 7 years during which children still tend to give subjective/perceptual answers, but abandon this preference when faced with a direct conflict of judgements. He presents some small studies which seem to show that only in situations of direct conflict can young children appreciate the distinction between assessing situations objectively and assessing them subjectively.

So conflict is important, on this view, but not for the reasons that Piaget and Doise have supposed. Rather the conflict serves to shift the issue from the subjective to the objective and thus allows the child to bring to bear understanding which he already possesses in some form. The crucial function of social interaction, from this standpoint, is to establish or clarify for the participants the nature of the questions that they are being asked. Thus the construction of 'shared meanings' comes to hold centre stage, the child's task being to find some entry into the shared meanings of the adult culture. This finds an echo in the recent work of Perret-Clermont: 'The different partners of the experimental or didactic situations are susceptible to attribute different meanings to these situations: the study of these "misunderstandings" is an intrinsic part of our study. Rather than considering them as artefacts, we will examine by what art shared social meanings are constructed' (Perret-Clermont *et al.*, in press). From this perspective, of course, the child's interactions with adults are of even greater interest than his interactions with his peers. It was suggested earlier that Piaget's original emphasis on peer rather than adult-child interaction reflected his rejection of direct social transmission as a mechanism for the growth of the child's understanding. Recent interest in adult-child interaction arises not from any wish to reassert direct social transmission as a mechanism, but rather from a desire to elucidate some of the ways in which meanings can be co-constructed and negotiated in social situations. In the following section we shall review some recent work in this field, focusing on the interaction between the research psychologist and his subject in the context of cognitive testing and training guides.

Adult-child interaction in testing and training

As Perret-Clermont and Schubauer-Leoni (1981) have pointed out, many of the same processes which are at work in the peer interaction situations they have studied are also evident in cognitive testing situations. While we have not traditionally considered the Piagetian type of cognitive test as a *social* interaction between the psychologist and the child, it nevertheless has this aspect. The research literature now contains a number of demonstrations of the impact of non-logical factors on young children's responses to concrete operations tasks. In many cases these can best be understood in terms of the effects of these factors on the children's interpretations of the experimenter's meanings and intentions. Thus, for example, McGarrigle and Donaldson (1975) showed that young children were more likely to give correct judgements in a conservation task when the materials were transformed 'accidentally' by a naughty teddy bear rather than 'deliberately' by the experimenter. Light *et al.* (1979) showed a similar facilitation of correct conservation judgements when the transformation (in this case pouring into another beaker) was effected in response to an apparently incidental difficulty (a crack in the first beaker). Similar results have been obtained in relation to other tasks, and a review of this growing literature has been provided by Neilson and Dockrell (1982). It would seem that the 'pre-operational' children involved in these studies respond to what they think the experimenter *means* when he asks them questions, rather than to the questions themselves. Their interpretation of his meaning is highly sensitive to the linguistic and extra-linguistic context of his questions. This view, for which Donaldson (1978) offers powerful advocacy, implies a rather different conception of the child's use of language from that envisaged by Piaget.

Piaget's rejection of any fundamental role for language in the genesis of concrete-operational thought seems to have been premised on a view of language as consisting largely of a collection of conventional signifier-signified relationships. Any given child will have some but not all of these within his repertoire. Provided that the relevant lexical items were within the child's spontaneous vocabulary, Piaget tended to regard any peculiarities of the child's response to questions or instructions as peculiarities of reasoning. Language was treated as unproblematic, allowing the constructor of cognitive tests a direct access to the child's underlying logical competence. By contrast, the recent studies of cognitive testing mentioned above emphasize the context dependence of the child's understanding of words and utterances. They highlight the possibility that aberrant responses may reflect systematic misinterpretation of the adult's meaning rather than any deficiencies in children's logical capabilities.

For empirical support of his position regarding language and operational thought, Piaget placed considerable reliance upon the studies of Sinclair de Zwart (1967, Inhelder *et al.*, 1974). It is therefore interesting to see that subsequent replication and extension of these studies has provided the basis for rather different conclusions. For example, in one study Sinclair selected twenty-three children at 'preoperational' and 'intermediate' levels of seriation. She trained them for three sessions in the appropriate use of the relevant verbal descriptions, especially the description of the middle term in a three-term series. She then re-tested the children to assess progress in seriation, and found that only three of them had progressed through a substantial number of sub-stages to reach a fully operational level. This was held to demonstrate the lack of a one to one relationship between the child's ability to handle the task-relevant vocabulary on the one hand and his or her operational ability on the other.

However, it is notable that the large majority of Sinclair's subjects did in fact make some progress as a result of training, and this was also found when Heber (1977) replicated this study with a more exacting seriation task and with the addition of a no-training control group. The progress made by children from pre- to post-test was not dissimilar to that reported by Sinclair de Zwart, but was significantly greater than that found in the control group. Heber (1981) went on to compare the relative efficacy of three types of training within this paradigm. An 'action' condition involved the child ordering elements in series without relevant discussion or related descriptions. A 'didactic' condition involved the child learning the appropriate descriptions of relations while he or she watched the experimenter order the elements serially. A 'dialogue' condition involved the child being asked to describe and explain the size relations of the elements he was placing: 'Discussion between the observer and child centred round the relationships which define correct placements. Decisions and actions were taken by the child himself and he was led to explore the nature of the relationships concerned and to formulate them' (Heber, 1981, p. 191).

The 'action' and 'didactic' conditions resulted in negligible gains compared to the control group, but the dialogue condition resulted in significantly greater progress, and this was sustained at a second post-test two weeks after the intervention sessions. These results suggest that while language training in a narrow sense may be relatively ineffective in stimulating the development of thought, the incorporation of speech and action within a dialogue between experimenter and child may be highly effective. Thus here again the focus has shifted from language as a formal symbol system towards language as discourse (Heber uses de Saussure's term '*la parole*').

What proved to be effective in Heber's studies was not telling the child the right answer, but guiding him towards the right considerations. This underlines the fact that adult-child interactions need not be as asymmetrical and 'one-way' as Piaget seems to have envisaged. It may be just in so far as they do not answer to this characterization that they can act as powerful stimuli to the child's cognitive development. We shall pursue this line of thought in the following section, considering two important categories of adult-child interaction. Firstly research on the cognitive sequelae of parent-child interaction will be reviewed, and then some consideration will be given to teacher-child interaction in the school.

Parent- and teacher-child interaction

The notion that different styles of parenting may have differential consequences for the child's cognitive development is by no means a new one. Indeed, the question of such a relationship was one of the first to be raised when psychologists began to examine the link between socioeconomic status and educational success in the 1960s. However, it has proved a fairly intractable problem.

Bernstein's (1965) attempt to characterize the important variables in terms of distinctive linguistic forms or codes was influential, but has not found much empirical support (e.g. Robinson, 1978). His associated analysis of different styles of family relationship (Bernstein, 1970) has nonetheless proved useful. He distinguished between positional and personal forms of relationship. In a position-oriented family, Bernstein suggested, speech typically makes implicit or explicit reference to status requirements and the child acquires a relatively communal and undifferentiated role. In a person-oriented family, by contrast, the individual motives and intentions of family members are typically made explicit in their speech, and the child acquires a more differentiated identity.

This distinction has been used as the basis of a system for coding parental techniques of social control and discipline (Cook-Gumperz, 1973). Evidence for a relationship between this aspect of parent-child interaction and the child's developing abilities has been provided by a number of studies. For example, Bearison and Cassell (1975) established that children from predominantly person-oriented families showed greater evidence of appropriately modifying their speech when dealing with a blindfolded listener than did children from predominantly position-oriented families. Some of my own research (Light, 1979) has shown a systematic relationship between person-oriented social control by the mother and successful performance by the child on a range of perspective-taking tasks. Whether similar relationships could be demonstrated with other indices of operational thinking is unclear.

However, this kind of correlational research is fraught with ambiguities. In both the studies mentioned, for example, interviews with the mothers constituted the primary source of data on family interaction patterns. Apart from the fact that here, as is so often the case, parent-child interaction reduces to *mother*-child interaction, the validity of the interview data is questionable. The finding of clear correlations between such data and the test performance of the children tells one that 'something is going on', but does not permit any confident identification of critical elements or features of parental behaviour.

A number of attempts have been made to examine the characteristics and consequences of parent-child interaction more directly. One strand of this research has employed the referential communication paradigm introduced by Krauss and Glucksberg (1969) in which two parties sit separated by a screen. One (the speaker) has to convey to the other (the listener) sufficient discriminative information about a particular referent (usually a picture) to allow the latter to pick that referent from amongst a set of possibilities available to him.

Dickson *et al.* (1979) asked mothers to describe one of a set of pictures to their own 4-year-old children. Mother and child then changed role. Referential communication accuracy for the pair was defined in terms of the accuracy of the listeners' choices. This measure was found to be predictive of the child's IQ and other cognitive test scores one and two years later. More impressively, this relationship remained significant even when measures of mother's

IQ, socioeconomic status and the child's ability at four were partialled out. These results suggest that the effectiveness of communication between mother and child may represent an important element in what the authors term the 'cognitive socialization' of the child.

A related, though more specific, observation has been made by Robinson and Robinson (1981). They compared the individual scores of 6-year-olds on a referential communication score similar to that described above with records (see Wells, 1981) of mother-child interactions obtained naturalistically in the children's homes over several preceding years. Those children who were relatively advanced in terms of their communication skills came from families where the mother would frequently tell her child explicitly when she was unclear as to exactly what the child was trying to say. The argument for a causal connection between this kind of 'metacognitive guidance' by the mother and the child's subsequent ability is made more convincing by an experimental training study which Robinson and Robinson describe in the same paper. Children were paired with an adult listener who provided one of several kinds of feedback whenever the child's descriptions were ambiguous. Feedback which made explicit why the listener could not make a confident choice on the basis of the child's description resulted in a reduction of ambiguity in subsequent descriptions. A further study (Robinson and Robinson, 1982) consolidated this finding. This bringing together of naturalistic research on parent-child interaction and laboratory training studies seems to represent one of the best available research strategies in this area.

Another strand of research on the role of mother-child interaction in the 'cognitive socialization' of children has involved mothers being asked to act as teachers in relation to their children. For example, Hess and Shipman (1965, 1972) and Brophy (1970) studied the ways in which mothers from different socioeconomic groups taught their own 4-year-olds to complete tasks such as block sorting along two dimensions. Ethnic differences have been studied in a similar fashion (e.g. Steward and Steward, 1973). In these early studies the connection between the mother's teaching on the one hand and the child's cognitive level on the other was largely inferred from their common association with socioeconomic or ethnic status. Estimates of the child's ability on the task utilized were sometimes made on the basis of his or her response in the teaching situation, but where this is done mother and child measures are inevitably interdependent.

To avoid inter-dependency between mother measures and child measures a more recent study in this tradition (Hartmann and Haavind, 1981) has adopted the following design. The experimenter taught each child (in this case they were 6-year-olds) how to play a novel competitive game. Child measures, glossed as 'educability', were derived from this situation. The mother was then taught the game, and subsequently she taught it to another child of the same age. Measures of maternal teaching strategy were obtained from this situation. A control study showed that, at least in terms of the measures used, the mother's teaching strategy was independent of whether she was teaching her own child or another of the same age.

What the authors termed decentred maternal teaching involved the mother explaining things, discerning alternatives, pointing to future consequences, and in general taking the child's role and taking account of what he needed to know in order to play correctly. In a multivariate analysis these variables were found to be significantly and substantially associated with the child 'educability' measures. These findings are broadly consistent with those of the earlier studies mentioned above, but put them on a considerably firmer footing.

A more specific analysis of maternal teaching strategies has been offered by Wood and Middleton (1975). Four-year-olds attempted to assemble a construction toy and their mothers were encouraged to help them in such a way that the children would eventually be able to do it on their own. By distinguishing different levels of specificity of intervention and instruction the authors were able to show that good subsequent performance by the child was associated not with any one level or type of instruction but with flexibility and responsiveness on the mother's part. Children of mothers who reacted contingently, systematically adjusting the specificity of their assistance in the light of the child's response to earlier interventions, were most successful later.

To clarify the causal relationships involved, Wood, Wood and Middleton (1978) conducted a further study using the same task but this time with a trained instructor in place of the mothers. Children were taught according to one of four strategies derived from the observations of mothers' behaviours made in the previous study. One was the contingent approach, outlined above, and the others were idealized versions of the teaching methods used by mothers whose children had succeeded less well. The contingently taught group fared significantly better than the other three, as predicted. It is perhaps worth noting that one of the alternative strategies was an exclusively verbal one: the child was told each step of the procedure, with no physical intervention from the instructor. Children in this condition did succeed in completing the task during the instruction phase but subsequently proved incapable of handling the task alone. The ineffectiveness of this kind of didactic approach seems to be one of the most consistent findings in this whole field of research.

Wood and Middleton concluded that effective instruction is: 'a dynamic interactive process, somewhat akin to problem solving' (1975, p. 181). Though the form of this 'interactive process' may be different with children of different ages and in different contexts, this description should embrace not only what goes on in the home but also what goes on in the school. The gulf between the traditional concerns and methods of developmental psychologists and those of educationalists remains wide, but the research we have reviewed in this chapter highlights the need to bridge it. Indeed, bridging activities are in progress, and we shall conclude this review with a brief consideration of some of these.

European researchers interested in the dynamics of peer group interaction have recently begun to move towards the use of tasks which have some 'ecological validity' in relation to education, especially in mathematics (e.g. Balacheff and Imag-Grenoble, 1982; Perret-Clermont *et al.*, in press; Schubauer-Leoni and Perret-Clermont, 1982). One clear theme of this research is that learning is often a matter of establishing shared understandings: 'We are interested in learning as a *signifying* activity' (Perret-Clermont *et al.*, in press). This emphasis on signification is shared by some researchers from a rather different tradition, also interested in mathematics learning in the classroom.

Walkerdine and Corran (1978; Walkerdine, 1982) have undertaken a detailed analysis of transcripts of the interchanges between teachers and children in the classroom. As an example, they describe the exchanges between a teacher and a group of children learning 'place value' (tens and units). They draw out the various strategies used by the teacher to get the children to see two digit numerals not as a unified value but as a union of two values. These strategies involve speech, action with concrete materials, and gesture, all integrated within dialogue. Their outcome is that the teacher and her pupils come to share certain understandings.

It is possible to describe what the child learns through such experiences in terms of signifier-signified relationships. However, it is not at all clear that in such cases the signified has priority over the signifier. In Piaget's account, signifiers are 'grafted on' (Walkerdine, 1982) to the child's knowledge, and serve as representations of it. Mathematical signifiers serve only to *represent* schemata whose origin lies elsewhere. Walkerdine and Corran's analysis suggests rather that both signifier and signified are co-constructed in the course of the teacher-pupil dialogues. While such an analysis is speculative, and its empirical foundation slight, it offers a clear reflection of an emergent theme in contemporary research.

Concluding remarks

This chapter has covered a good deal of ground, but of course much that would be relevant to its theme has been omitted. In part because of our starting point in Piaget's theory of the genesis of operational thinking, we have considered only a limited phase of development. Almost all the research reviewed has been conducted with children between the ages of 4 and 9 years. A more serious limitation, perhaps, is that throughout the chapter, 'social' has been treated as synonymous with 'inter-individual'. We have touched at times on the cultural context of interactions, especially in so far as cultural knowledge is embodied in the language used by the interactants. However, little consideration has been given to the wider cultural and ideological framework within which these interactions occur, and no attempt has been made to consider the significance of such traditional social psychological variables as social status, class or race.

Within these limitations, a considerable number of recent research projects bearing on the effects of social interactions on the child's cognitive development have been reviewed. Most encouragingly, the various strands of this research have begun to weave a pattern. Independent research projects dealing with quite different types of social interactions have come up with consistent or compatible findings. As a result, we know a good deal more than we did a decade ago about the kinds of factors which govern the cognitive outcomes of social interchanges, whether in the laboratory, the home, or the school.

This research taken as a whole highlights the inadequacy of the treatment of social interaction within Piaget's theory of cognitive development. Some of the research reviewed is nevertheless consonant with Piagetian theory, merely underlining the significance of one or another kind of social interaction for the decentration of the child's individual cognitions. Other studies suggest rather different roles for social interaction, such as establishing agreement on criteria for the truth or falsity of judgements, or agreement in respect of the signification of complex concepts. Such interpretations represent more or less substantial departures from Piaget's theory. Finally some researchers are clearly disposed toward a more radical rejection of the individualism of Piaget's theory, structuring their research around the hypothesis that all reasoning emerges from and through social processes of discourse.

So the picture is one of convergence of findings at the empirical level but divergence of views at the theoretical level. No one theory is available to integrate research in this area, but at least we are no longer stuck with the choice between a simple-minded social determinism on the one hand and a blinkered individualism on the other. A richer, if more complex, conception of the ontogenesis of thought seems to be emerging. There can be little doubt that we shall see rapid development in our understanding of these issues in the next few years, which makes it a particularly exciting field of research to be involved in.

References

Balacheff, N. and Imag-Grenoble, L. (1982) Acquisition de la notion de preuve en mathematique: elements pour une approche experimentale. Paper presented at conference on New Perspectives in the Experimental Study of the Social Development of Intelligence, Geneva.

Barker, W. and Newson, J. (1979) The development of social cognition: definition and location. In S. Modgil and C. Modgil (eds) *Toward a Theory of Psychological Development*. Windsor: NFER.

Bearison, D. and Cassell, T. (1975) Cognitive decentration and social codes: communicative effectiveness in young children from differing family contexts. *Developmental Psychology* **11**: 29–36.

Bernstein, B. (1965) A socio-linguistic approach to social learning. In J. Gould (ed.) *Social Science Survey*. Harmondsworth: Penguin Books.

Bernstein, B. (1970) A socio-linguistic approach to socialization with some reference to educability. In J. Gumperz and D. Hymes (eds) *Directions in Socio-linguistics*. New York: Holt, Rinehart & Winston.

Brophy, J. (1970) Mothers as teachers of their own preschool children: the influence of SES and task structure on teaching specificity. *Child Development* **41**: 79–94.

Cook-Gumperz, J. (1973) *Social Control and Socialization*. London: Routledge & Kegan Paul.

Dickson, W., Hess, R., Miyake, N. and Azuma, H. (1979) Referential communication accuracy between mother and child as a predictor of cognitive development in the United States and Japan. *Child Development* **50**: 53–9.

Doise, W., Mugny, C. and Perret-Clermont, A. N. (1975) Social interaction and the development of cognitive operations. *European Journal of Social Psychology* **5**: 367–83.

Donaldson, M. (1978) *Children's Minds*. London: Fontana.

Elkind, D. (1976) *Child Development and Education: A Piagetian Perspective*. New York: Oxford University Press.

Emler, N. and Valiant, G. (1982) Social interaction and cognitive conflict in the development of spatial co-ordination skills. *British Journal of Psychology* **73**, in press.

Glachan, M. (1982) *Peer Interaction: Its Role in Cognitive Development*. Ph.D. thesis, University of Southampton.

Glachan, M. and Light, P. H. (1982) Peer interaction and learning. In G. E. Butterworth and P. H. Light (eds) *Social Cognition: Studies of the Development of Understanding*. Brighton: The Harvester Press, and Chicago: University of Chicago Press.

Hamlyn, D. (1982) What exactly is social about the origins of understanding. In G. E. Butterworth and P. H. Light (eds) *Social Cognition: Studies of the Development of Understanding*. Brighton: The Harvester Press, and Chicago: University of Chicago Press.

Hartmann, E. and Haavind, H. (1981) Mothers as teachers and their children as learners: study of the influence of social interaction upon cognitive development. In W. P. Robinson (ed.) *Communication in Development*. London: Academic Press.

Heber, M. (1977) The influence of language training on seriation in 5- to 6-year-old children initially at different levels of descriptive competence. *British Journal of Psychology* **68**: 85–95.

Heber, M. (1981) Instruction versus conversation as opportunities for learning. In W. P. Robinson (ed.) *Communication in Development*. London: Academic Press.

Hess, R. and Shipman, V. (1965) Early experience and the socialization of cognitive modes in children. *Child Development* **36**: 869–86.

Hess, R. and Shipman, V. (1972) Parents as teachers: how lower-class and middle-class parents teach. In C. Lavatelli and F. Stendler (eds) *Readings in Child Behaviour and Development* (3rd edn). New York: Harcourt, Brace, Jovanovich.

Inhelder, B., Sinclair, H. and Bovet, M. (1974) *Learning and the Development of Cognition*. London: Routledge & Kegan Paul.

Krauss, R. and Glucksberg, S. (1969) The development of communication competence as a function of age. *Child Development* **40**: 255–66.

Light, P. H. (1979) *The Development of Social Sensitivity*. Cambridge: Cambridge University Press.

Light, P. H., Buckingham, N. and Robbins, A. (1979) The conservation task as an interactional setting. *British Journal of Educational Psychology* **49**: 304–10.

McGarrigle, J. and Donaldson, M. (1975) Conservation accidents. *Cognition* **3**: 341–50.

Mackie, D. (1980) A cross-cultural study of intra- and inter-individual conflicts of centrations. *European Journal of Social Psychology* **10**: 313–18.

Miller, M. (1981) Cognition and moral argumentation: five developmental levels. Paper presented at conference on Social Interaction and Sociocognitive Development, Max Planck Institut, Starnberg, W. Germany.

Mugny, G. and Doise, W. (1978) Socio-cognitive conflict and structuration of individual and collective performances. *European Journal of Social Psychology*, **8**: 181–92.

Mugny, G., Perret-Clermont, A. N. and Doise, W. (1981) Interpersonal coordinations and sociological differences in the construction of the intellect. In G. N. Stevenson and G. B. Davis (eds) *Applied Social Psychology*, vol. I. Chichester: John Wiley.

Neilson, I. and Dockrell, J. (1982) Cognitive tasks as interactional settings. In G. E. Butterworth and P. H. Light (eds) *Social Cognition: Studies of the Development of Understanding*. Brighton: The Harvester Press, and Chicago: University of Chicago Press.

Perret-Clermont, A. N. (1980) *Social Interaction and Cognitive Development in Children*. London: Academic Press.

Perret-Clermont, A. N., Brun, J., Saada, E. and Schubauer-Leoni, M. L. (1982) Learning: a social actualization and reconstruction of knowledge. In H. Tajfel (ed.) *The Social Dimension*. London: Academic Press, in press.

Perret-Clermont, A. N. and Schubauer-Leoni, M. L. (1981) Conflict and co-operation as opportunities for learning. In W. P. Robinson (ed.) *Communication in Development*. London: Academic Press.

Piaget, J. (1932) *The Moral Judgement of the Child*. London: Routledge & Kegan Paul.

Piaget, J. (1950) *The Psychology of Intelligence*. London: Routledge & Kegan Paul.

Robinson, E. J. and Robinson, W. P. (1981) Ways of reacting to communication failure in relation to the development of the child's understanding about verbal communication. *European Journal of Social Psychology* **11**: 189–208.

Robinson, E. J. and Robinson, W. P. (1982) The advancement of children's verbal referential communication skills: the role of metacognitive guidance. *International Journal of Behavioural Development* **5** (3): 329–55.

Robinson, W. P. (1978) *Language Management in Education*. Sydney: George Allen & Unwin.

Russell, J. (1981) Why 'socio-cognitive conflict' may be impossible: the status of egocentric errors in the dyadic performance of a spatial task. *Educational Psychology* **1**: 159–69.

Russell, J. (1982a) Dyadic interaction in a logical reasoning problem requiring inclusion ability. *Child Development*, in press.

Russell, J. (1982b) Propositional attitudes. In M. Beveridge (ed.) *Children Thinking Through Language*. London: Edward Arnold.

Russell, J. (1982c) What studies of dyadic interaction may tell us about the young child's concept of truth. Paper presented at conference on New Perspectives in the Experimental Study of the Social Development of Intelligence, Geneva.

Schubauer-Leoni, M. L. and Perret-Clermont, A. N. (1982) Interactions sociales dans l'apprentissage de connaissances mathematiques chez l'enfant. Paper presented at conference on New Perspectives in the Experimental Study of the Social Development of Intelligence, Geneva.

Sigel, I. (1969) The Piagetian system and the world of education. In D. Elkind and J. Flavell (eds) *Studies in Cognitive Development*. New York: Oxford University Press.

Sinclair de Zwart, H. (1967) *Acquisition de Language et Développement de la Pensée*. Paris: Dunod.

Steward, M. and Steward, D. (1973) The observation of Anglo-, Mexican- and Chinese-American mothers teaching their young sons. *Child Development* **44**: 329–37.

Vandenplas-Holpner, C. (1982) Social interactions and cognitive development: towards a micro-analytical interaction approach in semi-structured situations. Paper presented at conference on New Perspectives in the Experimental Study of the Social Development of Intelligence, Geneva.

Walkerdine, V. (1982) From context to text: a psychosemiotic approach to abstract thought. In M. Beveridge (ed.) *Children Thinking Through Language*. London: Edward Arnold.

Walkerdine, V. and Corran, G. (1978) Cognitive development: a mathematical experience? Paper presented at conference of the British Psychological Society, Developmental Section, Southampton.

Wells, C. G. (1981) *Learning Through Interaction*. Cambridge: Cambridge University Press.

Wood, D. and Middleton, D. (1975) A study of assisted problem solving. *British Journal of Psychology* **66**: 181–91.

Wood, D., Wood, H. and Middleton, D. (1978) An experimental evaluation of four face-to-face teaching strategies. *International Journal of Behavioural Development* **1**: 131–47.

4 Assessment of cognitive development

Ingrid Lunt

Introduction

In recent years there has been a move away from intelligence testing as the major means of assessing cognitive development. Early enthusiasm for comparison and classification by means of the IQ score has given way to attempts at description and diagnosis, while preoccupations with statistical, norm-referenced measurements are being replaced by more descriptive, often criterion-referenced accounts of what a particular individual can and cannot do in a range of cognitive areas. Psychological measurement is generally indirect and characteristics have to be inferred from selected behavioural observations usually presented as scores on a particular test or task. When an individual's performance or score is compared with the average, or norm, for a defined group (e.g. his age group), the measure is norm-referenced. On the other hand, when an individual's score indicates the kinds of items or information he has successfully mastered (from a specified criterion or set of educational objectives), the measure is criterion-referenced. Since the purpose of assessing children's cognitive development is usually to clarify and solve a (learning or developmental) problem, recent assessment techniques focus more directly on the attainments which are causing concern and often include some suggestions for remediation. Any cognitive assessment involves a sampling of a range of cognitive behaviours from which to infer, first, developmental level; second, areas of strength and weakness; third, individual strategies and nature of learning and development. There is an increasingly widely held view amongst those involved in the assessment of cognitive development that this sample needs to be closely related to a finely worked hierarchy of developmental steps in the different areas: this is made possible by the increased use of criterion-referenced measurements rather than norm-referenced IQ tests (Simon, 1953; Gillham, 1974 and 1978; Maloney and Ward, 1976).

The use of intelligence tests assumes that it is possible to infer level of ability from a child's performance on a number of tasks selected on the basis that older children could succeed at them more easily than younger children (rather than according to a developmental theory). Cognitive ability is equated with the construct intelligence, and the designation of a number or IQ score suggests a unitary monolithic ability (rather like Spearman's (1927) 'g') with the IQ as the quantitative index of how much 'g' an individual possesses. In addition to overall IQ, it is possible to look at a profile of subtest scores in order to gain a picture of an individual's comparative scores on different subtests (so Thurstone's (1938) primary mental abilities: number, word fluency, verbal meaning, memory, reasoning, space, perceptual speed). But, like IQ, this data offers limited description or explanation. As the purpose of assessment is diagnosis with a view to remediation, statistical scores showing peer-related comparisons are not the most useful. The move within educational psychology is therefore away from norm-based tests of cognitive constructs such as intelligence towards more direct descriptions and measures of children's cognitive abilities.

In this chapter I am going to consider some alternative approaches to cognitive assessment, based broadly on developmental theories, and to raise some of the issues involved in accurately describing a child's cognitive functioning. The first issue, stages of development, has been much debated in developmental psychology. It is relevant to a consideration of assessment since the assumption of qualitatively different but interrelated stages of cognitive development might call for qualitative rather than quantitative distinctions at different levels. The second issue, the competence-performance distinction, emphasized by Chomsky (1968) and made again in intelligence testing as aptitude-performance or ability-achievement, is important in any consideration of what to observe in the limited sample of the child's cognitive repertoire. The third issue to be examined will be the nature of cognitive development and assumptions made by developmental and psychometric theories. The majority of intelligence tests were constructed without a thorough theoretical rationale; 'conceptually the tests were constructed with a multiple-factor view of intelligence, but they did not sample all of the hypothesized factors and what they did sample was done in a haphazard, non-systematic way. The main derivation of these tests, the IQ, while contrary to the notion of multiple factors, is most aligned with Spearman's monolithic "g"' (Maloney and Ward, 1976). Finally, I shall look at some suggestions for assessing cognitive development based on a broadly developmental approach.

Stages of development

The task of assessment implies placement along a continuum or on a series of steps or stages arranged in logical (developmental) sequence. It is generally recognized that 'whether growth is quantitative and continuous or qualitative and discontinuous is partly a function of the rate at which it is taking place. When the rate of change is slow, development tends to occur within the framework of qualitative consistancy. . . . But when the rate of change is more rapid, qualitative differentiation also tends to occur' (Ausubel and Sullivan, 1970). Cognitive development appears to follow this pattern, with new abilities gradually taking over from earlier forms. Recognition that the continuity/discontinuity issue in development (whether development is a process of gradual, quantitative and continuous change or a process of uneven, discontinuous and qualitatively different steps) constituted a false dichotomy and that development can be both continuous and discontinuous at different times and in different abilities has enabled developmental psychologists to concentrate on the developmental process itself.

Although theories based on developmental stages might be thought to imply discontinuity, and have been criticized for doing this, in reality stage theory implies nothing more than the orderly sequence of identifiable steps or stages in development which are qualitatively distinct from preceding and succeeding stages. Stage theory need not imply abrupt or sudden breaks or spurts in development, and the transition from one stage to another is usually achieved gradually and with considerable overlap while one constellation of abilities assumes prominence over a previous one.

Piaget's (1950) exposition of stage theory implies that each stage is characterized by the complexity and organization of its schemes and defined by a structured whole. So Piaget's first stage (sensori-motor stage) is characterized by practical schemas, the following stage (preoperational stage) is characterized by symbolic schemas, and the final stage (concrete-operational stage) is characterized by symbolic schemas which are organized into a coherent network to form a logical system. Each stage depends on the one before it; development from one to the next involves realignment and integration of previous skills with new ones and a reorganization of the whole network of competencies in the organism (Uzgiris and Hunt, 1975), and is seen in terms of transformations of competencies (see also Flavell, 1972). The sequence of stages is invariant (implied in the previous statement) and the abilities of one stage combine and evolve to constitute the abilities of the next stage. In this way, there is a continuous thread or 'link' in the development of the child progressively creating order out of his experiences in the world, yet the manifestations of this development (stages) may be seen as qualitatively distinct.

Implicit too, in Piaget's theory, is the idea of 'readiness': the idea that different maturational stages enable individuals to cope with differing cognitive demands. School readiness implies levels of development in different areas which are said to facilitate a child's progress from the stimulation provided by school. Thus 'by virtue of his distinctive degree of cognitive sophistication at every age level, the child has a characteristic way of approaching learning material . . . the pedagogic problem in readiness is to manipulate the learning situation in such a way that one takes account, and optimal advantage, of existing cognitive capacities and modes of assimilating ideas and information, as for example, the learner's objectivity/subjectivity, his level of generality or particularity, and the abstractness and precision of his conceptualizations' (Ausubel and Sullivan, 1970). As we shall see later, this is also an issue in relation to assessment.

For Piaget, each stage is characterized by a particular mode of thinking or viewing the world which may be appropriately nurtured, and progress assessed by particular problems and tasks. Such a theory suggests the need to identify substages, subskills and hierarchies of competencies and to assess each of these almost as a separate whole before progressing to the next stage. When the child has mastered the competencies of one stage (the 'criterion' of the criterion-referenced measurement) he is ready to move to the next (different) stage of competencies.

In his own studies Piaget was as interested in the wrong answers provided by children as the correct ones, since both revealed the nature of the children's thinking. Stage theories provide a scaffolding within which to build a systematic assessment scale of tasks illustrating a child's competencies at each level; the interrelatedness of levels shows how it is possible to investigate a child's thinking by presenting slightly different but related tasks. Piaget combines the interdependence of stages with an explanation of continuity/discontinuity in cognitive development; he suggests that phases of continuity alternate with discontinuity and are defined in terms of relative dependence or independence of new behaviour with respect to earlier behaviour. 'Indeed, it seems as if during the formation of a structure of reasoning (characteristic of Stage A) each new procedure depends on those the child has just acquired. Once achieved, this structure serves as a starting point for new acquisitions (characteristic of Stage B), (Inhelder, 1962). In order to assess the cognitive development of a child, sensitively structured tasks are required which trace the essential continuity and which are responsive to a child's readiness to tackle new kinds of problem and to progress to more abstract ways of organizing information.

Piaget provides the most detailed exposition of a stage theory and his description of stages, particularly the detailed substages of the sensori-motor stage, offer the background for a scale which might follow the development of particular cognitive abilities as the child progressively creates order out of his increasingly complex experiences in the world. Although several attempts have been made to construct scales using Piagetian stages as a theoretical underpinning (for example, by Vinh-Bang), no generally useful scale of assessment has been developed, mainly because of the practical difficulties (and some theoretical problems) of using this approach.

Piaget did not concern himself with individual differences (a basic point of reference from intelligence testers) but aimed to discover universal abilities or structures underlying a particular stage; and he described his children in terms of that stage. For example, all children go through four major steps in the acquisition of 'conservation', at first concentrating on only one property of the task, gradually hesitating, and finally attending to the successive transformations and 'discovering' conservation. The order is invariant, though the exact age is unimportant.

Piaget's broad, but detailed, stage theory has been criticized as we shall see later (Bryant, 1974; Donaldson 1978; Brainerd, Chapter 2; Meadows, Chapter 1). One of the main difficulties of his theory is the empirical validation needed if these stages are to be used as the basis of assessment scales. Children's performance on Piagetian tasks is affected by context, mode of presentation of the task and the nature of the materials used. Although the significance of Piagetian questioning and enquiry is lost if it becomes constrained by standardized questions (and more normative scores), the significance of Piagetian stages has also been increasingly questioned by the finding that children succeed on Piagetian tasks at even younger ages than he proposed of the tasks if the tasks are presented in an appropriate way (Bryant, 1974; Donaldson, 1978). It has been shown that young children are capable of much more than implied by Piaget's theory. Bower argues that 'development is a cyclic process with competencies developing and then disappearing to reappear anew at a later age; development is not a continuous linear process but rather a series of waves, with whole segments of development reoccurring repetitively' (Bower, 1974). He has shown this by the way in which particular abilities, for example in the development of the object concept and in the development of conservation, appear and then disappear in the young child's behavioural repertoire. This regression may be seen in terms of continuous reorganization within normal development. In Piaget's terms, simpler versions of the same ability are integrated with other abilities and then evolve into more sophisticated competencies. However, it is important to distinguish between normal variations in competency (which may be seen as reorganizations) and abnormal regression or fixation where an individual reverts to an earlier cognitive level, often for emotional reasons.

A detailed knowledge of stages of development and their interrelationships may constitute a valuable background to assessment where what is needed is a detailed and accurate description of a child's present level of functioning. However, attempts to develop such assessment scales are fraught with the difficulties inherent in the identification and specification of subskills necessary to a particular cognitive process. Piagetian tasks involve a set of somewhat abstract subskills (albeit within a theoretically logical framework). The problem in assessment is to know the appropriate subskills and their development and thence to identify their presence or absence in a particular child in order to facilitate progress or remediation.

Factors affecting performance

A common criticism of assessment procedures is that the test situation may affect an individual's performance, usually for the worse; for example, factors such as anxiety or social class or race may adversely affect a child's performance on cognitive tasks. Furthermore (Meadows, this volume), recent work concerning children's performance on Piagetian-type tasks suggests that the manner in which the task is presented affects performance and that young children are capable of much more than was implied by Piaget's theory. Bryant (1974) has shown that it is possible to manipulate some of the conditions of Piaget's reasoning tasks and affect the child's ability to solve the problem. If the task is presented in a manner relevant to the child's logic and he is helped to remember relevant information, he is more likely to succeed. Similarly, Donaldson (1978) has shown that changing the language, the task material and the way in which the problem is presented dramatically affects the child's performance and ability to solve the problem.

These and other studies suggest that, at least in certain tasks, children fail Piaget's tasks because they do not realize that they need to apply particular skills which they already possess. These findings emphasize the ways in which children's performance may be affected by a range of important and different variables. Although Piaget's methods allowed him the freedom to explore in detail the development of children's thinking, the competence-performance distinction failed to evolve as an issue, partly because of the methodological weaknesses implied above. Because children's development is complex, task performance (including the nature and presentation of the task) is an important variable.

The assessment of cognitive development involves inferring competence from behaviour on a particular task. Such inferences are more justifiable when the task refers directly to a particular subskill. Since different abilities and subskills develop at different rates even within one individual, accurate assessment involves devising several scales each with a sequence of finely graded stages from which to infer the nature and stage of cognitive operation.

The nature of cognitive development

It is generally accepted that development involves both quantitative and qualitative changes in various abilities and that although a broad concept of stages is a useful framework, assessment requires more detailed knowledge of hierarchies of subskills. For the purposes of assessment it is useful to assume age (stage)-level changes in major areas of cognitive function, such as language, problem-solving, perception, concept formation, symbolization. There is also a general shift through infancy and childhood from concrete to abstract, and from egocentricity to other-centredness. It has been demonstrated that as children grow older, they demonstrate an increasing ability to understand and use abstract symbols and classificatory schemata (Inhelder and Piaget, 1958), they are more able to understand abstract relationships without using concrete images (Inhelder and Piaget, 1958); they can infer properties of objects from class membership rather than from direct experience (Wohlwill, 1960); they gradually use abstract symbols rather than concrete imagery to represent concepts (Bruner, 1964); and their thought becomes increasingly abstract. This clearly has implications for the tasks used to assess development.

Psychologists agree that development is a gradual (and complex) process rather than an all-or-none acquisition of knowledge. New abilities develop gradually, alternating with previous abilities, then taking over and replacing earlier abilities. Hamlyn (1971) discusses conservation of volume:

> We have no right to suppose that there are bits of understanding – the understanding of what water is, the understanding of what volume is and the understanding of what mass is – so that we can compare and contrast the relations that hold between them in a linear way. The child's understanding of what water is will be quite different on the occasions when he does not know or appreciate that water poured from one vessel into another of a different kind remains the same water, when he appreciates this but does not appreciate the constancy of volume and when he appreciates all of these things. Hence, there is danger in speaking of a concept of water as if a child might have this by itself without other connected concepts of the kind which I have been considering. To have a concept is not an all-or-none affair; there are degrees of understanding and degrees in the complexity of what is understood. Conceptual development is as much as anything an initiation into a web of understanding which may be more or less involved at any given time.

As shown earlier, the nature of cognitive processes and the kind of thinking vary according to the stage of development; assessment procedures need to reflect stage-related, qualitative changes in thinking (Flavell, 1963; Smedslund, 1964). Different kinds of task and activity will be appropriately observed at different ages in order to make a full and accurate assessment of present functioning. Later we will consider some attempts to devise developmentally based assessments. One of the main differences between these (criterion-referenced) assessments and psychometric (norm-referenced) measures is that psychometric tests (for example, intelligence tests) only convey how a child's performance compares to a notional average child of the same age, whereas developmental assessments attempt to describe an individual's present level of functioning in terms of the presence or absence of specific subskills.

Intelligence and intelligence tests

Intelligence is the abstract and hypothetical measurement construct which has been used to measure general level of cognitive functioning. Psychometric theories assumed intelligence to be an 'innate mental ability', 'a capacity', and 'stable quality and so predictive of future performance' (Gillham, 1981). Although there is considerable theoretical background to the psychometric theory of intelligence (Spearman's (1927) general 'g' and specific 's' intelligence; Thurstone's (1931) 'multiple factor theory of ability'; Guilford's (1967) 'structure of intellect' factorial model, to name but a few theoretical propositions) intelligence tests have not usually been derived from a particular theory of intellectual development, but have rather sampled aspects of cognitive behaviour which have been found to differentiate between the average performance of groups of children of different ages. In a practical sense intelligence has become 'what intelligence tests measure' and is synonymous with IQ. IQ is a statistical formulation which places a child below average, average or above average for his age, as measured by his performance on a sample of subtests, and has some predictive validity when the criterion is academic performance. Intelligence tests sample an individual's present cognitive repertoire (the Wechsler Intelligence Scale samples skills in general knowledge, vocabulary, arithmetic, comprehension, memory, reasoning, non-verbal puzzles and reasoning, symbolization, all 'academic' skills which have been found to differentiate between school children of different ages), and give a measure of a child's performance on particular subtests. The way in which Binet, and later Wechsler, selected items to be included in the Binet and Wechsler intelligence tests did not reflect a theoretical viewpoint, but rather the fact that these items differentiated between groups of children, and being related to school-related activities, were predictive of later school success. The items selected for early intelligence tests were a rather arbitrary sample of the cognitive repertoire which had been found to be of practical use. The continual search to measure abstracts such as 'g' or 'intelligence' depended on clumsy and concrete measuring instruments.

More recent attempts to construct an intelligence test (British Ability Scales, 1978) have suffered also from the fact that 'the norm-referenced test is only as good as its constructs or content'. The BAS (British Ability Scales) test consists of subscales within six Thurstonian-type factors: speed, reasoning, spatial imagery, short-term memory, retrieval and application of knowledge, perceptual matching. Although some items are designed to give qualitative information about levels of cognitive development along the lines of Piagetian theories, the BAS uses abstract and hypothetical factors to give a measure of 'potential' and still offers no explanation as to a child's success or failure on particular items. In the same way as earlier intelligence tests give scores of achievement on different sub-tests (as do reading and arithmetic tests) so also the BAS shows how far a child succeeds or fails on a particular task (for example, matching letter-like forms, or recalling digits). This offers no further explanation than that obvious from the task itself.

Referring to infant intelligence tests, Stott and Ball (1965) note that:

> the present tests are designed on the theory of a constant general intelligence rather than a developmental sequence of qualitatively different levels of functioning, (and) fail to register adequately the developmental change taking place. It would seem, as a result, that a promising approach to the construction of mental tests for early childhood might be along the lines established by the work of Piaget.

To an extent, the statement holds true for all intelligence tests, which aim to explain success or failure in terms of abstract and hypothetical factors. Standardized tests attempt to infer competence from performance on a small sample of cognitive tasks, largely ignoring the rich qualitative variety and uneven course of development, and providing little 'information on the processes and strategies of problem-solving' (Mittler, 1973). For these and other reasons, psychologists are shifting the focus away from norm-based assessment towards more criterion-referenced testing or an 'experimental approach' as opposed to a 'standardized one' (Mittler, 1973). Still relatively recent, these developments manifest themselves in the form of observation procedures, rating scales and developmental checklists.

Assessment of cognitive development

One of the main purposes of assessment is diagnosis with a view to remediation (assessment is also used to predict future success). IQ tests are usually of limited diagnostic use and do little to explain why a child succeeds or fails at a particular task. The norm-referenced intelligence test compares individuals with others of the same age, but gives little information as to how the individual thinks, approaches the task, why or how he has problems, what he might need to make progress.

Although classification along Piagetian stages provides little further explanatory information than classification by intelligence test, Piagetian methods of observation and investigation suggest methods of assessment which might be of more explanatory and therefore remedial value. There have been some attempts to construct forms of assessment based on Piagetian theory, usually consisting of an open-ended series of questions (such as, 'Which is bigger?', 'Why?') whose answers give a more complete description and explanation of the child's thinking. In the same way that Piaget considered wrong answers to be as informative as correct ones, the Piagetian method (as opposed to standardized questions) enables further questions to be pursued along lines of interest. 'Piagetian methods of investigation – adaptive to and interpretive of the dynamics of the stituation – would be of value if the child's point of breakdown in the hierarchical sequence of development and instructions could be first determined' (Gillham, 1974). Advantages of this kind of assessment are: first, that it is more than an empirical sampling of items at different age levels, since the selection of tasks and questions derives from Piaget's theory, each item being selected to show the presence or absence of a certain stage of cognitive functioning; second, the Piagetian method is sensitive to the dynamics and complexities of the assessment situation; third, what is important is the quality of answer, not a pass or fail score. However, the difficulties in constructing scales using this approach are shown by the fact that they have been of limited practical use.

Flavell (1963) quotes some attempts to construct tests based on Piagetian theory. Vinh-Bang and Inhelder created a standardized developmental scale based on about thirty Piaget tasks drawn from various content areas (number, quantity, space, geometry, movement, velocity, time, chance and others). Attempting the same kind of task, Pinard constructed a theoretically based scale of mental work (5 on time, movement and velocity; 4 on quantity and number; 6 on space; 5 on causality and chance; 3 on the child's beliefs about the world; 4 on logical deduction and the logic of relations).

A more ambitious ordinal scale of infant assessment has been devised by Uzgiris and Hunt (1975) and will be discussed here to illustrate some of the ways in which Piagetian theory has formed the background of assessment. They start from broadly Piagetian assumptions concerning the hierarchical and epigenetic nature of development, the mutual interaction and influence between infant and environment, and the importance of this interaction for assessment and a focus on sequence rather than stages in development. Uzgiris and Hunt (1975) aim

> to develop a tool of assessment grounded in the theory that development is an epigenetic process of evolving new, more complex, hierarchical levels of organization in intellect and motivation . . . a tool wherein the actions of infants would serve to indicate directly their level of cognitive organization, a tool which in use can extend our understanding of psychological development . . . a tool which would facilitate the study of the influence of various kinds of circumstances on development, a tool which would ultimately help guide the efforts of those attempting to devise circumstances to foster the development of very young children.

These principles suggest a basis for assessment through the whole range of development.

The scales of Uzgiris and Hunt will be considered here in some detail as a case study example of the way in which Piagetian stages have been used as the model for assessment scales. Uzgiris and Hunt began by selecting the various actions of infants described by Piaget as indicative of new levels of cognitive organization or structure. From these they selected, adapted and used those situations which could be reproduced in the home and observed by a tester. Critical actions were defined as those which indicated that an infant had reached a particular level of functioning. Assuming differential rates of development in different aspects of cognitive functioning they devised six separate scales:

Development

(1) Visual pursuit and the permanence of objects
(2) Means for obtaining desired environmental events
(3) Imitation; vocal and gestural
(4) Operational causality
(5) Object relations in space
(6) Schemas for relating to objects

The assessment takes place in the home with the tester attempting to create familiarity, interest and maximum motivation by also involving the caretaker. An example of instructions might be: 'Attempt to create a spectacle which the infant finds interesting by using your hands and face. Actions such as drumming on a surface with the fingers, snapping the fingers, or making facial grimaces often are successful. Stop abruptly and observe the infant's behaviour . . .' Assessment takes the form of observing the child in a familiar setting with conditions organized so as to obtain the best performance possible. Although the Uzgiris and Hunt scales are not widely used by practising psychologists, they illustrate some important factors in assessment. One of these is the importance of making observations in a familiar (natural) environment.

Observational methods have increasingly played an important role in all forms of assessment, whether of an infant at home or pre-school (Sylva *et al.*, 1980), of a child using observational procedures in the classroom or of an individual engaged in a particular task. 'The skilful psychologist . . . recognizes that it may take several visits to secure an adequate assessment, that observation of the child's behaviour and the quality and nature of his free play may be as valuable as a formal result in some circumstances' (Mittler, 1970). There is an increasing awareness of the limitations of the 'single performance' on an intelligence test and a recognition that such tests should only be the first step in an assessment process which then needs to explore the quality of the child's thinking and problem-solving, asking such questions as 'How does he solve the problem?' rather than 'How much can he do?', and considering how 'children's problem-solving behaviour [can be] investigated and explored rather than passed or failed' (Gillham, 1974). A consideration of qualitative changes in children's thinking as they grow older has led psychologists to select a range of items and tasks from different sources in order to observe and explore a child's level of thinking, motivation and approach to the problem. These tasks are used not so much as measures but as clues in the process of understanding how a child makes sense of his world and the problems he is confronted with. Examples of such an approach are observation procedures such as the ILEA Classroom Observation Procedure, rating scales such as the IRS (Infant Rating Scales, Lindsay, 1981) and other criterion-referenced approaches used with older children. Bricker and Bricker (1973) suggest 'a move from standardized assessment of "intelligence" to a learning approach involving the teaching of behavioural competencies relating to actual environment settings' with a set of hierarchies of subskills along which an individual can be helped and progress assessed.

In line with the increasing trend towards criterion-referenced assessments, involving the use of a sample of criterion behaviour which provides information about a particular cognitive process which is of use diagnostically and remedially, Gillham (1978) has summarized the necessary stages for assessment.

(1) Accurate identification of those children whose level of attainment constitutes a handicap
(2) An expanded (i.e. curriculum-referenced) assessment to determine precisely what a child can and cannot do; i.e. what a child needs to be taught and what he already knows
(3) An investigation of how the child views or understands the learning tasks and of how instruction has been organized – not to identify 'causes' but to ascertain where the difficulties lie and what can be changed to improve learning performance
(4) Bearing in mind the objectives defined in the curriculum – referenced assessment, the more-or-less detailed specification of remedial procedures
(5) Determining criteria and methods for evaluating progress.

A criterion-referenced assessment specifies criteria in terms of a hierarchy of subskills relevant to a particular cognitive skill and may also refer to age or stage levels. In fact the concept of age-norms does not preclude other forms of reference such as classification in terms of qualitative changes since these are usually age-related. More important it does not preclude the use of criteria-referenced forms of assessment. In fact they are mutually inclusive because the order and hierarchy of attainment objectives in an educational curriculum or programme reflects an age-progression, the psychological progression of learning development. (Gillham, 1978)

Conclusions

Awareness of the limitations of traditional assessment tools (intelligence tests) has led to a consideration of the whole issue of assessment. Developmental psychologists have contributed to the foundations laid by Piaget in his exploration of children's thinking, and many of his methods have proved useful in the development of assessment procedures. Amongst these are the concept of broad developmental stages, the open-ended clinical exploration, the investigation of 'process' rather than product, the detailed description and exploration of a child's cognitive functioning and the crucial importance of observation in assessment. The assessment of a child's ability to deal with the situation before him and to make sense of his immediate environment is a dynamic process of interaction in which the child plays an active and influential part. Assessment is rarely an isolated event, but is usually part of an ongoing process of diagnosis and remediation in which the child may influence the course of events as much as the assessor. The diagnosis implies a clear and accurate description of the child's present functioning in several different areas including his responses to different experimental tasks and learning situations.

One of the main problems in the assessment of cognitive development both for the researcher and the practitioner is 'to steer a course between the Scylla of flexibility and the Charybdis of objectivity' (Mittler, 1970). What is still needed is to combine the flexibility and sensitivity of the developmental approach with the objectivity implicit in the psychometric approach while still avoiding the pitfalls to which both are susceptible.

References

Ausubel, D. P. and Sullivan, E. V. (1970) *Theory and Problem of Child Development*. (2nd edn). New York: Grune & Stratton.

Bowen, T. G. R. (1974) Repetition in human behaviour. *Merrill Palmer Quarterly* **30** (4): 303–18.
Bricker, W. A. and Bricker, D. (1973) Behaviour modification programmes. In P. Mittler (ed.) *Assessment for Learning in the Mentally Handicapped*. Edinburgh and London: Churchill Livingstone.
Bruner, J. S. (1960) *The Process of Education*. Cambridge, Mass.: Harvard University Press.
Bruner, J. S. (1964) The course of cognitive growth. *Amer. Psychol.* **19**: 1–15.
Bryant, P. E. (1974) *Perception and Understanding in Young Children*. London: Methuen.
Chomsky, N. (1968) *Language and Mind*. New York: Harcourt, Brace & Jovanovich.
Donaldson, M. (1978) *Children's Minds*. London: Fontana.
Flavell, J. H. (1963) *The Developmental Psychology of Jean Piaget*. Princeton, NJ: Van Nostrand.
Flavell, J. H. (1972) An analysis of cognitive developmental sequence. *Genetic Psychology Monographs* **86**: 279–350.
Gillham, W. E. C. (1974) The British intelligence scale; à la recherche du temps perdu. *Bulletin of the British Psychological Society* **27**: 307–12.
Gillham, W. E. C. (1978) The failure of psychometrics. In B. Gillham (ed.) *Reconstructing Educational Psychology*. London: Croom Helm.
Gillham, W. E. C. (1981) Intelligence tests and educational practice. In C. I. Howard and W. E. C. Gillham (eds) *The Structure of Psychology*. London: George Allen & Unwin.
Guilford, J. P. (1967) *The Nature of Human Intelligence*. New York: McGraw-Hill.
Hamlyn, D. W. (1971) Epistemology and cognitive development. In T. Mischel (ed.) *Cognitive Development and Epistemology*. New York: Academic Press.
Inhelder, B. (1953) Criteria of the stages of mental development. In J. M. Tanner and B. Inhelder (eds) *Discussions on Child Development: A Consideration of the Biological, Psychological and Cultural Approaches to the Understanding of Human Development and Behaviour*. WHO Study Group, vol. 1. New York: International Universities Press.
Inhelder, B. (1963) Some aspects of Piaget's genetic approach to cognition. In W. Kessen and C. Kutilman (eds) Thought in the young child. Monograph. *Soc. Res. Child Develop.* **27**: 19–40.
Inhelder, B. and Piaget, J. (1958) *The Growth of Logical Thinking from Childhood to Adolescence*. London: Routledge & Kegan Paul.
Inner London Education Authority (1975) *Classroom Observation Procedure*. London: ILEA.
Lindsay, G. (1981) *Infant Rating Scale*. London: Hodder & Stoughton.
Maloney, M. P. and Ward, M. P. (1976) *Psychological Assessment: A Conceptual Approach*. Oxford: Oxford University Press.
Mittler, P. (1970) Assessment of handicapped children. In P. Mittler (ed.) *The Psychological Assessment of Mental and Physical Handicaps*. London: Methuen.
Mittler, P. (1973) Purposes and principles of assessment. In P. Mittler (ed.)

Assessment for Learning in the Mentally Handicapped. Edinburgh and London: Churchill Livingstone.

Piaget, J. (1950) *The Psychology of Intelligence*. London: Routledge & Kegan Paul.

Simon, B. (1953) *Intelligence Testing and the Comprehensive School*. London: Lawrence & Wishart.

Smedslund, J. (1964) Concrete reasoning: a study of intellectual development. Monograph. *Soc. Res. Child Develop.* **29** (93): 1–39.

Spearman, C. (1927) *The Abilities of Man: Their Nature and Measurement*. New York: Macmillan.

Stott, L. H. and Ball, R. S. (1965) Infant and preschool mental tests: review and evaluation. Monograph. *Soc. Res. Child Develop.* **30**: 101.

Sylva, K., Roy, C. and Painter, M. (1980) *Childwatching at Playgroup and Nursery School*. London: Grant McIntyre.

Thurstone, L. L. (1938) Primary mental abilities. *Psychometric Monographs*, no. 1. Chicago: University of Chicago Press.

Uzgiris, I. C. and Hunt, J. McV. (1975) *Assessment in Infancy: Ordinal Scales of Psychological Development*. Urbana, Ill.: University of Illinois Press.

Wohlwill, J. F. (1960) Developmental studies of perception. *Psychol. Bull.* **57**: 249–88.

5 Metacognitive development

Elizabeth Robinson

Introduction

One of the most interesting characteristics of people is that they not only behave, but can watch themselves behaving and believe they can exert a certain amount of control over how they behave. People are not mere victims of their immediate abilities and dispositions, but active agents who can be aware that things are or are not going as intended, who can deliberately optimize their performance, and who can learn from having become aware of their mistakes.

In everyday life we explain behaviour by making reference to knowledge of capabilities ('I couldn't do that exam question because I remembered nothing about metamemory') or knowledge of whether desired goals are being achieved and how to improve the likelihood of achieving them ('I keep forgetting to check that reference; I'll write a note to myself'). Yet there has been a long period when psychologists have attempted to understand how people remember, solve problems, or communicate information to others, without taking into account people's ability to monitor and control their own activity. Perhaps this has been due to the influence of behaviourists' reaction against introspection, along with a failure to distinguish people's ability or inability to be aware of their thinking process from their knowledge or ignorance about what they know. People can know that they know without having been conscious of mental processes leading to that knowledge.

In some research, people's awareness of and ability to control their own cognitive activity has been seen as a disadvantage (how to prevent subjects from knowing that we are interested in how much they are learning, in case that knowledge changes their strategies for learning), or as an asset (the subjects can tell us how they solved the problem and hence reveal their thinking processes to us), or even as a way of distinguishing between people (how accurately can subjects predict their skill at performing a particular task). In contrast, in the work on metacognition to be discussed in this chapter people's knowledge about their own cognitive activities has been the focus of interest, even if the reason for being interested in it has been in order to understand better the cognitive activities themselves.

In the most recent literature, the excitement of working from this perspective seems to have worn off, and there have been expressions of disappointment at the number of 'demonstration studies', which merely show what children of different ages know about how to remember, which tasks are easy or hard, how to communicate a particular meaning unambiguously, and so on. In this chapter I hope to avoid inducing disappointment in the reader; I shall not present a comprehensive review of the literature, but will instead focus on some of the interesting problems still to be solved. For example, is awareness of inadequacy in one's current way of thinking responsible for advances? On the other hand, is awareness of one's thinking activity a relatively late development which allows that activity to become more planful and regulated? Does one become aware of how one is thinking when problems arise, or when one is coping easily with spare cognitive capacity to watch what one is doing?

I shall follow the distinction made by Flavell (1981) between metacognitive experiences and metacognitive knowledge: the former are conscious experiences such as a feeling that you do or do not understand, whereas the latter is 'accumulated world knowledge that has to do with people as cognitive agents, and with their cognitive tasks, goals, actions and experiences' (p. 40). For example, when they are reading this chapter, some people might turn over the pages, and having reached the end, realize that they have been thinking about something else and have taken in nothing about the content of the chapter. This realization is an example of a metacognitive experience. Other readers might come to this realization after two or three pages, and then begin to monitor their reading activity more closely, perhaps by testing themselves after each paragraph or by making written summaries. Knowing which strategies increase the chances of concentration remaining focused on the task in hand is an example of metacognitive knowledge. However, the actual use of these strategies ('knowing how') will not be considered to be an example of metacognitive knowledge ('knowing that') and in this respect I am taking a narrower definition than has been used by some others (e.g. Brown, 1978; Flavell, 1981; Lefevbre-Pinard, 1981). Relationships between using strategies and knowing that one is using them are discussed in a later section.

Knowing that you don't know

Simply being aware that one does not know what to do, does not understand, or that one's behaviour has not produced the intended outcome, may be important for bringing about change in the strategy one is using. Under what circumstances do children become aware of problems of this kind, and what might be the developmental significance of their becoming aware? These are the questions to be discussed in this section.

Conflict between children

One theory in which conflict is seen as an impetus to cognitive development is that of Piaget. The conflict may be between a child's expectation of the outcome of a certain action, and the actual outcome, or it may be between alternative contradictory interpretations of a situation. It is not clear in Piaget's account (Piaget, 1957, 1970) that *awareness* of the conflict is necessary, nor that if awareness occurs, if has any developmental significance (it could be a mere by-product), although in Piaget's work on children's awareness of their own activities (which is discussed in the section on 'knowing that and knowing how'), he makes the point that awareness of the intended outcome and of whether or not that is achieved, develops very early. There is one aspect of Piagetian theory in which it seems clear that awareness is held to play a significant role in development: that is the account of how children are forced to take into account other points of view through contacts with peers (Piaget, 1928, 1932). There was no experimental work relevant to that view when Piaget wrote about the importance of peer interaction, but more recently Doise and his colleagues have carried out a large number of experiments in which they have begun to clarify the conditions under which inter-child interaction will produce cognitive progress (Doise and Mugny, 1981). Similar procedures have also been carried out by Emler and Valiant (1982), Glachan and Light (1982) and by Russell (1981, 1982a and b).

In experiments such as these, children are pre-tested individually on some Piagetian task such as conservation of length or perspective taking, and are classified as not exhibiting the concept in question, or as intermediate, or as exhibiting mastery of the concept. Each child is then paired with another at the same level, a lower level or a higher level, and pairs interact verbally to reach agreement in a task in which members of a pair are likely initially to give contradictory judgements. For example, in a conservation of length task, children might be asked to reach agreement about the relative length of two sticks. The task would be constructed and the children positioned so that one child within a pair of non-conservers would be likely to judge one stick to be the longer, and the second child to judge the other to be longer. Finally, children are given an individual post-test.

In some but not all of the experiments following a design of that kind, some children who in the pre-test showed no sign of understanding the concept being tested, had advanced by the post-test. This seems particularly likely to happen to children who had been paired with an intermediate, but can, it appears, even occur when both members of the pair showed no initial understanding. When such advances occur, they have been interpreted as being a consequence of the conflict experienced during the interaction with a partner. In a review of their series of experiments, Mugny, Perret-Clermont and Doise conclude 'The subject is emotionally activated when he is involved in interpersonal conflict. He becomes aware of the existence of different centrations, and must come to view his own centration individually' (1981, p. 326). That is, in this work on inter-individual conflict, children's *awareness* of a problem is considered to be in part responsible for their advancing to a higher level of understanding.

Two possible general difficulties can be raised about an approach such as this one. One applies to any conflict theory of development (whether or not awareness is involved) and has been widely remarked upon: the mere realization that one's current way of dealing with a task does not work is not sufficient for one's coming to deal with that task in a more appropriate way. Clearly something else must enter into an explanation of how children eventually come to the more advanced solution. Bryant (1982) has proposed an alternative to a conflict model of development, that children learn when strategies agree rather than when they conflict. If two strategies produce the same answer, the child can assume both are appropriate. This hypothesis suffers from an equivalent difficulty: like the conflict model it does not specify how the correct strategy enters the child's repertoire in the first place. Unless one is prepared to argue that all strategies are available to children from birth, the suggested alternative has no clear advantage over a conflict theory.

A second difficulty with a theory that children can advance cognitively as a result of inter-individual conflict is that the theory must specify when children become aware that their partner's judgement is contradictory to their own. Russell (1981, 1982a, 1982b) has produced evidence that it is only non-conservers who are already on the verge of concrete-operational thinking who perceive the other's judgement as contradictory to their own, and that these children already have a receptive grasp of conservation. He argues that non-conservers who are not marginal, in contrast, are unaware of a contradiction because they do not appreciate that their judgements are objectively true or false. Rather, their judgements are more like opinions: 'You think it's more, I think it's less' is treated in a similar way to 'You like that one, I like this one'. Russell's evidence for this view comes in part from analyses of interactions between peers in experiments similar to those of Doise and his colleagues. The member of a non-conserving pair who had his or her judgement accepted by the other, tended to be the one who was more dominant in a different task in which the children operated jointly an 'Etch-a-Sketch' toy. However that was not true when non-conservers were paired with conservers: then, when the conserving judgement was adopted this was irrespective of dominance, presumably because the conserver knew and the non-conserver recognized that it was true. On the rare occasions when pairs of non-conservers produced conserving judgements, these were given spontaneously rather than following argument. Russell concludes on the basis of this and other evidence that these children could equally well have come to the conserving judgement without interacting with their partner. That is, there are no grounds for supposing that it was awareness of a contradiction between own and other's judgement that was crucial for advancement to a higher level of understanding.

With further work in this area it should become clearer under what conditions children can learn as a result of arguing with equals. The important point here is that exposing children to what from the adult point of view would be an inadequacy in their way of thinking, may not be sufficient for children to become aware of that inadequacy. Even if children do become aware, that awareness may or may not have developmental significance. And even if it is of developmental significance, it remains to explain why children come to think in a more advanced way rather than just remaining puzzled.

Similar issues arise in work on verbal communication in children, and here we shall see that children who become aware of a problem may solve it pragmatically without necessarily having explicit knowledge of why that solution is appropriate.

Knowing that you don't understand a verbal message

When adults become aware that they have not understand what a speaker means, they can bring into play various ways of dealing with their non-comprehension, and they may consider the possibility that further information is necessary to guarantee that they make the correct interpretation. That is, it seems that among adults, awareness of a difficulty with interpreting a message may lead the listener to use strategies appropriate for dealing with the difficulty. Studies of children's verbal referential communication skills show age-related differences in speaking and listening behaviour. In a typical study of children's communication skills, a child and his or her partner (who might be the experimenter or another child) sit separated by an opaque screen. They have matching sets of materials, often drawings, and one of them, the speaker, describes one item in the set so that the other, the listener, can pick up the matching item from his or her set. The experimenter may be interested in the quality of the child speaker's messages, or in the child's judgements of their quality, or in the child listener's preparedness to interpret ambiguous messages, or in the child's judgements about why the listener chose correctly or incorrectly.

There is a body of evidence which shows that young children tend to act upon ambiguous messages or instructions rather than seek further information (Cosgrove and Patterson, 1977; Ironsmith and Whitehurst, 1978) and also that they judge ambiguous messages to be adequate (Flavell, Speer, Green and August, 1981; Patterson and Kister, 1981; Robinson and Robinson, 1976a and b, 1977). These data have been interpreted as suggesting that young children understand neither that verbal messages can be ambiguous, nor that ambiguity can cause communication failure. If this is so, we have the problem of explaining how they come to achieve understanding about the requirements of effective communication and the causes of communication failure, and it could be that their awareness or lack of awareness of difficulty with interpreting ambiguous messages will figure in such an explanation.

Children who judge ambiguous messages to be adequate, may nevertheless have shown verbal or non-verbal signs of uncertainty when they were attempting to interpret those messages (Bearison and Levey, 1977; Patterson, Cosgrove and O'Brien, 1980). For example, they may show facial expressions of puzzlement, they may hesitate, or they may say something like 'There are two of those!' It has been suggested (Flavell *et al.*, 1981) that these children may not be aware that they are puzzled, or they may be aware but not realize the significance of their uncertainty. Yet some children clearly are aware of a problem even though they do not judge the message to be ambiguous: these same authors found that some children, after having made their interpretation of an ambiguous message, denied or doubted that it was correct but nevertheless asserted that the speaker had 'done a good job of telling'.

This phenomenon has been confirmed in other studies (Beal and Flavell, 1982; Robinson and Robinson, in press, b), and in the Robinson and Robinson study it was found that children who were unsure about the correctness of one interpretation of an ambiguous message, did not necessarily realize that they could not tell which of two possible interpretations was the right one. They knew that they had a problem, but did not know that the source of the problem was the message. It seems clear then that awareness of difficulty with interpreting an ambiguous message is not sufficient for children to understand that messages can be ambiguous. There is even some weak evidence to suggest that such awareness may not be necessary for coming to understand about ambiguity: in the Robinson and Robinson study, a number of children were identified who correctly judged messages to be ambiguous once they knew that their interpretation had been wrong, but who had been confident in the correctness of their interpretation at the outset. It may be that an account of the development of understanding about ambiguity will be in terms of information given to children following communicative success or failure, rather than in terms of dawning awareness of uncertainties within children (e.g. Robinson, 1981a and b). Perhaps it is only when children have been informed directly or indirectly by others that there can be ambiguity in a message that they come to interpret their uncertainty as a sign of possible ambiguity in particular cases.

Whether or not children's awareness of uncertainty helps them to achieve explicit knowledge of the causes of communicative success or failure, it could be responsible for their coming to use appropriate strategies to deal with uncertainty. One such strategy is question-asking, and, as mentioned above, there is evidence that in experimental situations at least, younger children are less likely than older ones to ask disambiguating questions. It is also the case that children who ask fewer necessary disambiguating questions are less likely to identify ambiguous messages as such (Robinson and Robinson, in press, a). However, such children readily learned to ask disambiguating questions when they were encouraged to do so over a number of training sessions, even though they continued to judge ambiguous messages to be adequate. In that study, children practised listening and speaking in small groups, and the experimenter encouraged listeners to ask questions when they did not know precisely which of a set of objects or events the speaker meant. Children readily learned to do that, even if in their post-test performance they did not identify ambiguous messages as such. It is conceivable that children first learn to ask questions as a way of dealing with uncertainty, without at that time realizing that they were uncertain *because* the original message contained insufficient information. These children may ask questions merely as one possible way of solving a practical problem of how to interpret a verbal message; they may assume that with sufficient effort on their part they could equally well work out the correct interpretation without additional information. That is, children may learn to use an appropriate strategy for dealing with a problem of which they are aware, without necessarily knowing why that strategy is appropriate. We might, however, expect their use of that strategy to be less efficient than that of children who know why the strategy works; this will be discussed further in the section on 'Knowing that and knowing how'.

In the work on verbal communication discussed so far, the focus has been on children who *are* aware of a problem when they attempt to interpret an ambiguous message. A slightly different approach is illustrated by the work of Markman (1977, 1979, 1981) on children's skill at monitoring their level of comprehension. Markman argues that young children fail to notice when they do not understand, and makes suggestions as to why this is. In one experiment, Markman (1977) presented first, second and third graders with incomplete verbal instructions about how to perform a magic trick and a game. Children were given a sequence of probes to find out whether they spotted the ambiguities and omissions from the instructions. The youngest children were less likely than the older ones to question the adequacy of the instructions until they actually attempted to perform the tasks or saw them demonstrated. Grade three (8 years old) children, in contrast, more frequently identified omissions in the instructions after only the verbal presentation. Markman suggested that the youngest children did not notice the problems because they failed to execute the instructions mentally. 'In contrast, when the [youngest] children attempt to perform the instructions they literally confront the problems, and then become aware of their failure to understand' (p. 989).

There is, however, in Markman's procedure a certain confusion between knowing *that* you don't know, and knowing *why* you don't know. It is clear from the work mentioned above that children can be aware that their interpretation may be wrong without necessarily knowing that it may be wrong because the message was ambiguous: children may say both 'I'm not sure that I'm right' and 'You did tell me enough to get it right'. Of the probes given to the children in Markman's study, the early ones seem to focus on whether the child located the instructions as the source of the difficulty, e.g. 'Did I tell you everything you need to know to play the game?' whereas the latter ones focus upon whether the child was confident that his or her interpretation was correct, e.g. 'Do you think you can play?' It was during this later stage in the probing that children were invited to try to play the game. It may be then, that at this stage in the probing children's attention was directed from 'Did I tell you enough?' to 'Do you know what to do?' and that the younger children could answer the second question but not the first.

This point is mentioned to illustrate how crucial it is to analyse precisely which features of a child's metacognitive knowledge are being assessed by a particular procedure. Further illustrations appear in the discussion of methodology in the next section.

Knowing what to do

By far the greatest body of work on metacognition consists of investigations of what children of different ages know about how to tackle various cognitive problems, particularly problems of remembering, and what they know about how easy or difficult such problems are likely to be. Reviews of this work appear in Brown, 1978; Brown and de Loache, 1978; Cavanaugh and Perlmutter, 1982; Flavell, 1977; Flavell and Wellman, 1977. Not surprisingly, older children are found to know more than younger ones.

Three possible ways of structuring this work will be suggested: by filling in the cells of a taxonomy of metacognitive knowledge, by relating studies to descriptive accounts of age-related differences in metacognitive knowledge, and on the basis of the methodology used. The third way will be developed in most detail.

Kinds of metacognitive knowledge

One way of ordering this body of work is to fill in the cells of a taxonomy such as the one provided by Flavell (1981) which is an elaboration of the taxonomy of metamemory devised by Flavell and Wellman (1977). Flavell points out that we can know about task variables (knowing which of two tasks is likely to be easier, for example), about person variables (knowing that you are better at one kind of task than another, or that two people or categories of people differ in their skill at certain tasks), about strategies (how to tackle a particular task) and about 'sensitivity' (knowing what is appropriate at any particular time). If the published literature is fitted into a taxonomy such as this one, we can begin to identify which kinds of metacognitive knowledge are exhibited by children of different ages, and we have a fairly clear description of what we have to explain in an account of metacognitive development.

Age-related differences

A second way of ordering the work is to use it to assess the value of descriptive accounts of differences between younger and older children. One such account has been suggested by Brown and de Loache (1978). They use the dimension of novice-expert to describe the differences between young children and adults. They point out that novices at any task not only lack the skills needed to perform it efficiently but are also deficient in 'self-conscious participation and intelligent self-regulation of their actions' (p. 13). 'Thus, an explanation of why young children have such generalized metacognitive deficits . . . is that most of our experimental tasks are both new and difficult for them' (p. 13). They speculate that we might find the following pattern of behaviour both developmentally and within any task in which an individual progresses from being a novice to being an expert. At first, there would be little or no intelligent self-regulation. Then, as the role and sub-processes become familiar, there would be a period of deliberate self-regulation. Finally, as the necessary components become overlearned, they would become relatively automatic: the individual is then described as an expert. Brown and de Loache acknowledge that one difference between child novices and adult novices is that the latter, unlike the former, will have available general metacognitive skills which can be applied to a wide range of problems. It is perhaps this characteristic of adult novices which prompted Flavell (1978) to speculate that novices would indulge in a lot of, rather than a little, metacognitive activity. Brown and de Loache's account is elaborated by Markman (1981) to describe differences between younger and older children in their skill at comprehension monitoring. A similar, but more detailed, three-stage description of understanding of verbal communication has been put forward by W. P. Robinson (1982).

The value of describing age-related differences in terms of the novice-expert dimension would be strengthened by evidence that such differences can be reversed when it is the adult who is the novice and the child who is the expert. Comparisons by Chi (1978) between good child chess players and poor adult ones, could have provided such evidence but in fact no significant differences were found between them in their accuracy at predicting their memory for positions on a chess board. There are at least two possible reasons why this lack of evidence is not critical for Brown and de Loache's account: first, players of chess do not, I understand, practise predicting their memory for chess positions. There may be other forms of metacognitive knowledge which are more likely to be familiar to expert than to novice chess players. Second, predicting what one can or cannot remember may be one of the general metacognitive skills which adults can apply to novel situations.

The question of age-related and task-related differences in the amount of conscious processing is an important and interesting one, and it is a pity we have so little evidence.

It may be more fruitful to try to identify more precisely in what respects children are novices at the tasks we present them with in the laboratory, rather than to try to make adults behave like children and children like adults. To describe a person as ignorant does not tell us anything about what that person has yet to learn or how it could be learned. In any case, Brown and de Loache seem to be suggesting that children are not merely ignorant of content, but also deficient in skills or strategies for processing that content. To describe both deficiencies with the single term 'novice' is unlikely to be illuminating.

A further problem with the 'making adults look like children' approach may be that adults tend to apply their general metacognitive skills to any novel task, whereas children may lack those general skills. Yet if that proves to be a problem it would suggest that this difference between adult and child novices in their use of such skills must be taken into account in any description of age-related differences. That is, if it is necessary to take steps to prevent adult novices from using general metacognitive skills, that alone would suggest that the description in terms of a novice-expert dimension is too simplistic.

There has been very little experimental work on the development of general metacognitive knowledge which can be applied to a wide range of problems. One study (Yussen and Bird, 1979) has been carried out to examine children's knowledge about tasks involving remembering, communicating and attending to a visual array. The aim was to find out whether children knew that in all three kinds of task, the task was harder if it involved more items, if it was carried out in the presence of noise, and if less time was allowed. Even 4-year-olds apparently recognized the effects of noise and length of list, but the effects of time allowed were better known by 6-year-olds. The pattern of judgements was similar across the three kinds of task, suggesting that the children had already acquired some general metacognitive knowledge about factors which make tasks easy or hard. However, we do not know whether such young children would have general knowledge about how to tackle a novel problem.

Shatz (1978) provides a more detailed description of age-related differences, and in some ways her account can be seen as a specification of what it might mean to be a 'novice' or an 'expert'. Shatz's description is in terms of information-processing capacity: conscious monitoring occurs only when capacity is not fully taken up with actually carrying out the task in hand: 'Metacognitive ability depends on an objectivization of process resulting from the release of consciousness from the major chores of selecting and controlling processing operations' (p. 25). Since adults have more well learned routines than children, they are more likely to have the spare capacity necessary for indulging in metacognitive activity. (Presumably there could then be positive feedback in that having indulged in metacognitive activity successfully, efficiency at the task in hand could be improved, hence leaving more capacity for more metacognitive activity.) As in the Brown and de Loache account, children could in principle indulge in it under suitable conditions. Again, support for Shatz's view would come from evidence that variations in familiarity of task are related to variations in metacognitive activity and some such evidence is provided. Shatz predicted that children would be more likely to give appropriate reasons for their behaviour, as well as behave appropriately, when the operations required to produce that behaviour were well-learned. In a task in which 4- and 5-year-olds were asked to select toys suitable for younger or same-age children, both 4- and 5-year-olds chose appropriately for a 2-year-old when the number of toys from which they could choose was small, but as the number of potential choices was increased, the performance of the 4-year-olds declined more than that of the 5-year-olds, presumably because the younger children were less able to deal with the larger set of items. That is, the task was apparently easier for 5-year-olds than 4-year-olds. As expected, the older children were also more likely to give appropriate reasons for their choices. These data, then, are interpreted as consistent with the view that metacognitive activity (giving appropriate reasons for choices in this case) is more likely to occur when the task itself imposes less strain on the individual's cognitive capacity.

Although Shatz's account could, as mentioned above, be seen as a specification of what is meant by a 'novice' or an 'expert', there is still no attempt to identify what experience is necessary for people to become capable of indulging in metacognitive activity. Furthermore, it focuses only on *when* metacognitive activity can occur, and not on what the content of that activity can be. For example, the account is not relevant to our understanding of how children come to know what is the best way of tackling a memory task, or how they come to know that they must gain further information to guarantee a correct interpretation of a verbal message. In any case, even if one is capable of introspecting more accurately on one's thinking activity *on command* when the task is easy rather than difficult, that may not be relevant to real life: it may still be when problems arise with difficult tasks that one *spontaneously* becomes aware of one's activity.

Finding out what people know

Two general methodological issues are relevant to work on metacognition. First, how are we to interpret failures to find signs of metacognitive activity? In work on Piagetian tasks, enormous efforts have gone into showing that when procedures are changed in certain ways, it is possible to reduce the age at which children exhibit mastery of the concepts in question. A similar movement could begin in work on metacognition, but it may be more profitable to focus on how children of different ages interpret the world, than to conceive of younger children as deficient or not deficient relative to older children and adults. For example, the approach taken by Jackson and Jacobs (1982) is more useful than that taken by Robinson and Robinson (1967a and b, 1977) in the latters' description of young children's failure to recognize that verbal messages can be ambiguous. Jackson and Jacobs tried to find out what strategies these children use when they are confronted with an ambiguous message and identified two such strategies. Whereas older children and adults may refuse to interpret an ambiguous message without further information, younger children try to make a sensible interpretation on the basis of current or prior information.

The second issue, which is related to the first, is that of reliance on verbal methods. There is an assumption that people can have metacognitive knowledge without being able to express it verbally, and that verbal methods may therefore provide an underestimate of what people 'really' know. On the other hand, verbal accounts may sometimes provide an overestimate of what people can put into practice: we can know that we should do something without necessarily being able to do it.

In what follows, the first issue will be discussed within the context of the second, and both will be examined within a more general attempt to illustrate the close relationships between conceptual and methodological issues. There have been two useful recent discussions of the value of verbal reports of mental processes, although neither focused directly on metacognition. Nisbett and Wilson (1977) and Ericsson and Simon (1980) aimed to specify when verbal reports are and are not useful. Nisbett and Wilson tend to emphasize examples in which people did not give an accurate account of their own mental processes. For example, in one experiment (Nisbett and Schachter, 1966), half the subjects were given a placebo pill and were told that it would have certain physiological effects such as heart palpitations and hand tremor, which were in fact like those associated with electric shocks. The control group were given no placebo. Experimental and control subjects were then given electric shocks, and it was found that people who had received the placebo were prepared to accept higher levels of shock than the controls. Yet when they were told that they had withstood unusually high levels, experimental group subjects did not report that it was because they had attributed the symptoms to the placebo. Even when this hypothesis was made explicit to them, they did not accept it as applicable to themselves. However, as Ericsson and Simon point out, the design was a between-subjects one, and so it is not surprising that individual subjects could not interpret their own behaviour in the same way as the experimenters did. In other experiments, Nisbett and Wilson show that individuals are no more accurate than outside observers at commenting on their mental processes.

In contrast, Ericsson and Simon (1980) present experiments in which individuals were able to comment usefully on how they tackled certain tasks, and they develop a model to predict when verbal reports will and will not provide accurate data about mental processes. For example, they show that when the input to be commented upon is in short-term memory, and the input is easily coded or re-coded into verbal form, then people can describe how they are tackling a problem without the commenting process changing the way they do so. In one experiment (Karpf, 1973) half the subjects were asked to report how they were performing a discrimination task, and half were not. On each trial, subjects were shown a pair of letters, which differed on a single dimension such as size, colour or texture, and the subjects were to identify this difference. There was no difference between groups in accuracy of performance, although those who reported were slower, as would be expected if they had to re-code from verbal to visual mode. Ericsson and Simon made the useful point that if we are to use verbal reports as data, we need some kind of theory, however rudimentary, of how those verbal reports are made. Once we have such a theory, then not only can we use verbal reports to find out about mental processes, but we can also interpret differences between tasks in terms of ease or accuracy of making such reports.

The value of these two papers is that instead of just expressing a worry about the value of using verbal reports, as a number of authors have been content to do, they have examined the evidence and attempted to draw some conclusions about when it is appropriate to use them.

Some of the work on metacognition will now be summarized to illustrate different degrees of reliance on verbal report.

Asking people how they remember, communicate or solve problems is surely the most obvious way of finding out what they know about their own cognitive processes, and this approach has been used most boldly by Piaget in *Success and Understanding* (1978). In an earlier volume, *The Grasp of Consciousness*, are reported studies in which children performed actions which they could either do already (e.g. crawling) or which they could readily learn (e.g. ejecting a stone from a sling). They were asked how they performed the actions, and if necessary they performed them again with the instruction to watch how they did so. This work does not really come within the boundary of 'metacognition' since the activities performed were not cognitive ones. However, that work was followed by the studies presented in *Success and Understanding*, in which children tried to perform more difficult tasks, and in which there was the opportunity to think about what was involved, to verbalize theories in response to questioning, and to learn to act more effectively as a result of the verbalization. For example, children were asked to use a set of more and more complex levers to lift a sugar lump or a matchbox. As children tried out the levers they were questioned about what was happening and what would happen. It is not clear how much children's explicit understanding of tasks was influenced by the questioning, nor have we any idea whether children would have been aware of or even held hypotheses without such questioning. From the Piagetian point of view this may not matter (Piaget states that the series of lever problems were treated as a training programme), but if one is interested in the interaction between cognition and metacognition in a self-directed situation, perhaps a less intrusive use of 'how did you do it?' would be judged more appropriate.

An example of such use is provided by Waters' (1982) study of metamemory among adolescents. Before they were given a memory task people were warned that they were going to be asked how they did it. The task involved learning word pairs, and at the end they were told that four commonly used strategies were reading each word pair carefully, rehearsing, combining the words in an image, and combining the words in a verbal phrase. They were asked to indicate which of these strategies they had used for each word pair. That people could report accurately on the strategy they used is suggested by the results: the more they reported using the more effective visual or verbal elaboration strategies, the greater their recall scores.

A variation of 'How did you do it?' is to ask 'How would you do it better next time?' This has been used to find out what children know about the requirements of effective verbal communication and the causes of communication failure (Robinson and Robinson, 1978). When children had given the experimenter an ambiguous description of which one of a set of drawings they had chosen, and the experimenter had made the wrong interpretation, the children were asked 'How could we make sure we got it right next time?' Children whose other judgements and behaviour indicated that they realized ambiguous messages could cause communication failure said 'I'll have to tell you more about it' or mentioned the message in some other way. In contrast, children whose other judgements and behaviour had given no indication of understanding about ambiguity, said 'You'll have to think harder' or 'We'll get it right'. That is, as in the Waters study, children's verbal judgements were consistent with expectations formed on the basis of other data.

One further example is provided by the study mentioned earlier, Yussen and Bird (1979). Children were shown pairs of pictures. Within each pair, one picture showed what was from the adult point of view an easier problem than the other. For example, one pair showed a girl trying to remember three items, and a girl trying to remember ten items. Children were asked 'Which girl has the harder job, or do you think they will both find the job about the same?' Children were also asked to give a reason for their judgement, but these data were analysed separately since the authors 'were not willing to assume that silence or incoherent explanations can be equated with inferior understanding' (p. 307). However, it appears that the pattern of findings was not changed when the criterion for a correct judgement included the giving of an appropriate explanation; the scores were lower, although it is not stated whether the difference was significant. Presumably there could not have been correct explanations of incorrect judgements; and presumably children who did not understand could have given correct judgements (without explanations) by chance. It would then have been surprising if the explanation criterion had *not* produced lower scores. Hence Yussen and Bird's data could have been taken (but were not) to suggest that there was little need to worry about children understanding without being able to verbalize that understanding.

It appears then that at least in some circumstances children can give accurate verbal accounts of how they did perform a task or how they should perform a task. Yet in the published literature, the worry remains that children can have metacognitive knowledge without being able to express it verbally. For example Brown (1978) cites the case of a 7-year-old who physically sorted items to be remembered into categories, but who said both before and after the task that he just looked at the items. However, this apparent discrepancy between what the child's verbal and non-verbal behaviour revealed about his metamemory can be resolved by making the distinction between knowing how to use strategies, and knowing that one is using them. As mentioned in the introduction, Brown and others appear to include both within a single category of 'metacognition', and if one does this it may well appear that verbal methods of assessment provide an underestimate of metacognitive ability. This distinction between knowing how and knowing that is discussed in more detail in the next section.

The least intrusive way of using verbal reports as indicators of metacognitive activity, is to examine naturalistic data. Clearly this would be more appropriate for establishing the presence of such activity rather than its absence, and for such a purpose it has been used in studies of metalinguistics more than it has in work on metacognition. For example, Clark (1978) quotes an example from Limber (1973): a girl aged 2:10 said 'When I was a little girl I could go "geek-geek" like that. But now I can go "This is a chair".' This and other examples were used to illustrate Clark's point that children begin to reflect on certain properties of language at an early age. Unfortunately there do not seem to be any analyses of bodies of naturalistic data (as opposed to isolated examples), nor analyses of what input children receive from adults which might encourage them to indulge in metacognitive activity.

In any case, with spontaneous utterances, problems of interpretation or categorization can arise. For example, in an analysis of children's indicators of failures to understand occurring in naturalistic data (Robinson and Robinson, 1981), examples ranged from 'Uh?' through to 'What do you mean?' or 'I don't know what you mean'. The latter seems to be a clear example of awareness of non-understanding, but what about the others? They could merely be children's ways of solving the problem of not knowing what to do in response to another person's utterance: that children can solve communication problems effectively without necessarily understanding why the solution is appropriate has already been pointed out in connection with question asking. Furthermore, if we include verbal comments, what about looks of puzzlement or even silence? Without accompanying experimental work of the kind mentioned earlier, we have little basis for deciding how to interpret naturalistic data.

An example of the value of combining laboratory with more naturalistic studies comes from the work of Silbereisen and Claar (1982), who have shown that a conflict model of cognitive development which has been found in laboratory studies to be predictive of development, may not be applicable to children's everyday lives. In a number of laboratory studies, it has been found that children advance most in their mastery of certain concepts when they are presented with an 'optimal mismatch' with their current level of thinking (e.g. Kuhn, 1972) (that is, when they are presented with a level of thinking a little more advanced than their current stage, but not so discrepant that the new input cannot be incorporated into their present style of thought). Silbereisen and Claar pre-tested 5-year-olds on a verbal communication task in which the child described one of a set of pictures so that the experimenter could identify it in his matching set. Children in the experimental group were then watched by a parent as they played another communication game, and parents could help if they wanted to. Children in the control group played the same game without their parents being present. Finally, all the children were post-tested. The difference between pre- and post-test scores was no greater for experimental than for control children: the parents had apparently not succeeded in teaching their children how to communicate more effectively. Analyses of the parent-child interactions showed that parents did not employ strategies which could be described as conflict-induction: 'neither stimulating question techniques, nor contradictions to the children's activities occurred in any considerable frequency' (p. 13). Rather, there were vague directives such as 'You have to tell it the right way'. Subsequent interviews with the parents suggested that they were unaware that their children's difficulties with the task could have been due to an 'insufficient level of socio-cognitive development' (p. 14). Hence in this work it is lack of metacognitive knowledge among the parents which is used to account for their behaviour towards their children.

Similarly, Robinson and Robinson (1981) have shown in experimental studies that telling children explicitly when and why their verbal communications were not understood, helped them to understand that messages can be ambiguous and that ambiguity can cause communication failure. This finding was confirmed by naturalistic data, but these data also revealed how rarely such explicit information was given to young children at home or at school. It seemed therefore inappropriate to try to account for the development of explicit knowledge about communication solely in this way. Children may benefit from the occasions when the social environment does, by chance rather than by design, provide 'optimal mismatch' or explicit information about communication, but it may well be that an account of development cannot rely on their occurrence.

If any conclusion can be drawn from this discussion of methods used to find out what people know, it is that we are likely to build up the best picture by using a variety of methods. Rather than assume that verbal reports will underestimate what children really know, researchers can compare data obtained by different procedures, taking care to analyse precisely what is being assessed by each. Certainly we can never be sure that children are incapable of doing things we have not seen them do, but on the other hand there is no value in imputing understanding unnecessarily.

Knowing that and knowing how

One of the main reasons for being interested in metacognition is that it is assumed, in the adult at least, to influence cognitive behaviour. It is surprising, therefore, that there have been relatively few investigations of relationships between what people know about how to tackle particular problems on the one hand, and how they actually do tackle those problems on the other. In the literature there seems to be more speculation about the difficulty of identifying such relationships, than there have been attempts to establish empirically what relationships are found and to account for them.

Expectations about relationships between knowing that and knowing how will differ according to the task being considered. For some tasks (e.g. some of those in Piaget's *Grasp of Consciousness* such as crawling), it is to be expected that success will precede understanding. Indeed, Piaget (in Bringvier, 1980) reports that the task of describing how they crawled was given to some of the distinguished guests who had been invited to comment on the work on consciousness. The physicists and psychologists gave accurate descriptions, but the logicians and mathematicians gave inaccurate but logically simple accounts.

At the other extreme would be tasks success at which could be guaranteed only if activity was directed by knowledge of how to proceed. For example, one could not expect to be successful at teaching a child how to play chess if one was not aware of the requirements of effective verbal referential communication and the causes of communication failure.

There are two complementary ways in which relationships between knowing and doing have been examined. On the one hand, the researcher can focus on what happens when a person of a particular age tackles some cognitive task: what does that person know about how to proceed and about how things are proceeding, and how does that knowledge relate to their actual performance. People of different ages may differ not only in their knowledge of what to do, but also in the extent to which they use their metacognitive knowledge and experiences when they are actually performing tasks. That is, children may not only be more ignorant than adults, but also weaker at using what knowledge they have to optimize their performance at any particular time.

On the other hand, the researcher can take a developmental perspective. What children know about their cognitive activity at one point in time may influence their performance at a later point; what they observe about their performance at one point in time may lead to the development of knowledge about how to proceed at a later point in time.

In what follows, both approaches will be discussed. It will become clear that in both cases, one problem is being ignored: that of specifying a mechanism by which metacognition and cognition can influence each other. Flavell (1981) avoids the problem by drawing boxes with arrows between, as do Marshall and Morton (1978) in their discussion of language awareness. It will be assumed here that if concordances are found empirically, then it may prove valuable to interpret them causally, while accepting that the point made by Markman in connection with comprehension monitoring applies more generally to relationships between cognition and metacognition: 'much information about one's comprehension is a by-product of active attempts to understand and not just of attempts to monitor' (1981, p. 75). In everyday life it often makes sense to think of people as acting in certain ways *because* they know certain things; it may prove equally sensible to do so in psychology.

Cross-sectional approaches

In work on verbal communication, children's explicit knowledge about ambiguity in verbal messages has been shown to be closely related to their level of performance in verbal communication tasks. In a series of experiments (Robinson and Robinson, 1982 a and b; in press) children instructed the experimenter or another child how to build a model out of Lego or a picture out of felt pieces. Whether the listener played a passive role or asked questions when in doubt about what to do, strong positive relationships were found between children's judgements about quality of instructions and responsibility for communication failure on the one hand, and quality of their instructions on the other: children with more accurate explicit knowledge about communication gave more informative instructions about the pieces to be placed and where to place them.

However, in work on relationships between memory and metamemory, low correlations have often been found. These studies have been summarized by Cavanaugh and Perlmutter (1982) who also discuss when one might expect to find high and low correlations. This discussion draws largely on the work of Flavell (1981) who points out that people may be most likely to use their knowledge of the best memory strategy for a particular task when they are motivated to perform well and when there are not too many constraints on time and effort. We would expect there to be occasions when people fail to behave in what they know to be the most effective way, because it is easier or quicker to tackle the problem in a less effective way.

One further reason why we might find 'knowing without doing' is suggested by Ringel and Springer (1980), who point out that if people are to use the most effective strategy for a particular task, they must be capable of monitoring strategy effectiveness. That is, metacognitive experience of success may be necessary for metacognitive knowledge to be put into practice subsequently. Ringel and Springer were attempting to account for previous research findings that children can be trained to use particular strategies for improving their memory performance, but often fail to use those strategies spontaneously in a post-test. These authors carried out an experiment in which 7-, 9- and 11-year-olds were shown and told how to sort pictures into semantic categories in preparation for a recall test. Some of the children were told in addition that they had remembered more because they used that strategy: 'I guess using that idea of placing pictures together that go together really helps us remember more'. Among the first graders (6 years old), there was little transfer of use of the sorting strategy whether or not children were given this further information. However, third graders (8 years old) who were given this information showed greater transfer than those who were not. Fifth graders (10 years old) apparently had no need to be told that the sorting strategy was effective: they continued to use it whether or not they were given the information.

There are also likely to be circumstances when people use effective strategies without being able to formulate them explicitly: 'knowing how without knowing that'. This is illustrated by work on children's analysis of the important parts of prose passages. Brown and Smiley (1977) found that third graders, unlike fifth graders, could not identify the most important sections of a prose passage, even though their recall of the main ideas was better than their recall of the peripheral ones, suggesting that they had processed the structure implicitly but failed to do so explicitly.

A further example of 'doing without knowing' is provided by the work on question-asking, where it was also suggested that we might find differences in the efficiency of use of effective strategies according to whether or not the person has explicit knowledge about those strategies. For example, in a series of investigations of children's skill at reformulating their messages in response to their listener's non-understanding, it was found that most 5- and 6-year-olds said something new about what they meant when the listener said 'I'm not sure what you mean. Can you help me?' Whether or not their judgements in other tasks revealed explicit understanding about message ambiguity, these children could apply the strategy

'Say something more when the listener does not respond correctly to the original message'. However, those whose other judgements revealed explicit understanding about ambiguity were much more likely than the others to give new information which was informative rather than redundant. Those who apparently did not yet have explicit knowledge of *why* the listener needed more information, did not apply the strategy effectively. An alternative way of describing these results would be to say that the two groups of children were in fact applying different strategies: 'Say something more' in contrast to 'Say something which reduces the number of potential referents from which the listener has to choose'. It may be the case that other apparent examples of 'knowing how without knowing that' can also be described in that way. That is, when children come to have explicit knowledge of how to handle a task their strategies for tackling it may themselves change. If so, this would be an argument for taking a developmental approach to relationships between knowing that and knowing how.

Developmental approaches

The work on verbal communication which was summarized at the beginning of the previous section on cross-sectional approaches, has been followed up with a more developmental approach (Robinson and Robinson, in press, c). The aim of this study was to compare the effects of two forms of intervention on children's performance in and explicit understanding of communication tasks. Of particular interest were any changes in relationships between knowing and doing which might have been found following the intervention: would we find children whose communicative performance advanced without any associated improvements in explicit knowledge about the requirements of effective communication and the causes of communication failure? On the other hand, would we find children who came to know more about communication without being able to perform any better? During the intervention, 4- and 5-year-olds practised listening and speaking in small groups. The groups were homogeneous with respect to initial level of explicit knowledge about communication. Half the groups were practice groups: the children played games in which they took turns at listening and speaking, and on the experimenter's turns she modelled appropriate listener and speaker behaviour. The other half of the groups were guidance groups: the children had the same practice at listening and speaking, but in addition they were told when and why listeners understood or failed to understand what the speaker meant. In previous experimental work this explicit information had been found to be an effective way of advancing children's explicit knowledge about communication, and the experimental results had been confirmed by analyses of naturalistic data. After six weekly half-hour sessions, the children were given immediate and delayed post-tests.

Children in the guidance groups improved more than those in the practice groups in both level of performance in communication tasks, and in degree of explicit knowledge about message ambiguity and its role in causing communication failure. However, practice as well as guidance groups improved significantly in both respects, with no regression in the delayed post-test. The relationships between explicit knowledge and level of performance remained unchanged: whichever form of intervention the child received, there were no signs of advances in performance only or of advances in explicit knowledge only. The exception was the asking of questions which, as mentioned earlier, improved without there necessarily being associated improvements in explicit knowledge of why questioning in the face of ambiguity is appropriate.

These results suggest that in development advances in knowing and doing can occur together; how such joint emergence might happen is discussed in the next section.

A very much more thorough examination and interpretation of developmental changes in relationships between knowing that and knowing how has been made by Piaget (1978, and summarized by Sinclair, 1978). As mentioned earlier, in one chapter of *Success and Understanding*, Piaget describes children's attempts to use more and more complex levers to lift a lump of sugar or a matchbox. As children tried out the levers, they were questioned about what had happened and what would happen next. As usual, children's responses were classified into a number of supposedly age-related levels. At the lowest level there was inaccurate observation of the action of one of the simplest levers, a horizontal bar with a central pivot: children said that their finger (at one end of the bar) had gone down when the sugar (at the other end) had also gone down. However, children at more advanced levels could describe accurately what was happening with the simple pivot and learned by trial and error how to use some of the more complex levers. According to Piaget, children first become aware of the intended outcome of their actions, and of discrepancies between that and actual outcome. Subsequently, children become increasingly aware of the actions themselves, and also of the ways their actions react with the physical world. At this stage, actions can be the result of prior hypotheses, and themselves lead to subsequent hypotheses: there is an alternation of conceptualizations and actions.

If this work were to be followed up from outside the Genevan framework it would be important to establish what happens when children are allowed to formulate explicit hypotheses spontaneously rather than under questioning from the experimenter, and also to begin to identify what input from children's physical or social environment is relevant to changes in the relationship between knowing and doing.

This kind of approach has been taken in work on children's awareness of language: workers in this area have used naturalistic data, as mentioned earlier, and have also begun to examine what environmental events might be relevant to the development of awareness and how that awareness might interact with language use. This work may provide useful models for investigations of metacognitive development. Particular attention has been paid to the awareness of language which is associated with learning to read and write. For example, Ehri (1979) points out that lexical awareness may interact with the process of learning to read, existing both as a consequence of what has occurred and as a cause of further progress. Hjelmquist (1981) further suggests that children's awareness of the nature of written language leads them to have a distorted picture of what spoken language is like, and this in turn leads, for example, to errors of memory for conversation.

Learning to read and write have themselves been seen to have more general cognitive consequences (Donaldson, 1978, 1982; Olson, 1977, 1981, Chapter 6): '[logical] development [in a literate culture] consists of learning to confine interpretations to the meaning explicitly represented in the text and to draw inferences exclusively from that formal but restricted interpretation' (Olson, 1977, p. 274). Skill at doing this is held to be a consequence of schooling, and in particular of learning to read. The influence of schooling is discussed again in the next section.

Coming to know

Just as it is assumed that in adults, metacognition functions as an error-detecting and error-correcting device (Brown, 1978; Flavell, 1981; Marshall and Morton, 1978) it is also assumed that the occurrence of errors provides the incentive for metacognitive development. The suggestion is that when an expected outcome is not achieved, children become aware of a problem and then have the opportunity to reflect upon their behaviour or thought processes. Complications arising from putting forward such a view are discussed in the section above on 'Knowing that you don't know'. As part of an explanation of cognitive development, it is necessary to specify the conditions under which children do become aware of problems. The specification might be in terms of events in the external environment and/or in terms of prerequisites within the child.

In this section, the focus will be on events in children's environments which may be linked with metacognitive development.

Both those interested in metamemory and metalinguistics have noticed a close correspondence between advances in these skills and attendance at school. This has led them to wonder whether schooling could be a cause of advancement. In the previous section relationships were mentioned between learning to read and write on the one hand, and language awareness on the other. In the case of metamemory, Brown (1978) suggests that it is only in school that people are expected to remember material without the use of external aids and with no particular goal in mind. She argues that before going to school, and in unschooled communities, there is no need to use mnemonic strategies since external aids to memory may be used. Some cross-cultural studies suggest that such strategies are less used in unschooled than in schooled communities (e.g. Cole, Gay, Glick and Sharp, 1971). In cross-cultural work it is hard to separate effects of schooling from effects of an urban environment. Wagner (1978) successfully did that in his investigation of schooled and unschooled, urban and rural Moroccans. Metamemory (in the sense of verbal accounts of how they remembered items) was not tested, but the strategies used for remembering were inferred from patterns of recall scores, and effects of both urban environment and schooling were detected. Cross-cultural work will not be discussed further here since it has been concerned with strategies used rather than with explicit knowledge of these strategies.

Having identified the existence of schooling as a possible cause of the development of mnemonic strategies, we still need to find out precisely what happens in school to help children learn them. In some cases they may be taught explicitly, but in others it may well be that children, given the task of memorizing material, work out suitable strategies for themselves. Events in the home may be relevant even when tasks themselves are imposed by the school. For example, Beveridge and Dunn (1980) have begun to identify parental ways of interacting with preschool children which are related to reflective thinking. They suggest that there is a 'package' of behaviours in which some mothers indulge and which are particularly effective for promoting reflective thinking. Discussions between mother and child about motives, feelings and intentions are considered to be important. Similar work relating mothers' behaviour styles to communication skills has been reported by Light (1979). Naturalistic studies such as these may usefully be followed up by experimental ones so that developmental relationships can be worked out in detail. Just because mothers who do one thing also tend to do another, and the occurrence of both is related to reflective thinking, does not necessarily mean that both maternal behaviours are causally related to the development of that thinking. This kind of question is likely to be answered most accurately in experimental work.

In work on verbal communication there have also been speculations about the importance of schooling, and it is still not clear precisely what it might be about schooling that is important. It has been found that telling children explicitly when they have or have not been understood, is an effective way of advancing their explicit knowledge about message ambiguity (Robinson and Robinson, 1981). We assumed initially that it was the information itself which was in some way responsible for the advances. However, we failed to notice that when a speaker is told 'I don't know what you mean', the subsequent interaction between listener and speaker is defined in certain ways: it is the speaker rather than the listener who must take responsibility for solving the problem of non-comprehension, and it is implied that the speaker has a particular meaning in mind. In contrast, when a listener says 'Is it the big one?' the listener has taken responsibility for divining an acceptable interpretation of the original message, and the speaker is free to accept a suggestion made by the listener even if it is not what was originally intended. That is, whether or not the speaker is given explicit information that the listener has failed to understand can have consequences for the speaker's subsequent behaviour. It could be that behaviour which is important for advancement, and not the information about non-comprehension.

This possibility was suggested by the results of the intervention study summarized above in which it was found that children in the practice groups (who received no explicit information about listeners' comprehension or non-comprehension but who were expected to behave *as if* they understood the requirements of effective communication) advanced significantly in their explicit knowledge about communication. A further experiment was designed to try to separate out effects of being told explicitly about listener's non-comprehension, and being encouraged to behave in a way consistent with understanding about message ambiguity.

The results supported the idea that being encouraged to behave in certain ways could be sufficient to advance explicit knowledge. Children underwent one of three forms of intervention. One group was given explicit information 'I don't know what you mean because . . . ' *after* their message had been interpreted, so that their behaviour as speakers was not influenced on that particular trial: these children made no advances in explicit knowledge about message ambiguity. A second group was encouraged to behave as if speakers should take responsibility for conveying a particular meaning unambiguously, but without being given explicit information about listener's comprehension or non-comprehension: this group did advance. However most advances occurred in the third group, which was told 'I don't know what you mean because . . . ' *before* their message was interpreted, so that their behaviour on that trial was influenced. These children received both explicit information (which alone seemed to be ineffective) and they were encouraged to behave as if they knew the requirements of effective communication (Robinson and Robinson, 1982a and b).

The suggestion is, then, that children can advance in their metacognitive knowledge as a result of being expected to behave in a way consistent with that knowledge. In a way, this suggestion is consistent with a view that as they get older children's thinking becomes less influenced by context and more 'disembedded' (Donaldson, 1978). For example, with a task such as a conservation problem in which children are expected to make judgements, they may initially be led to make the correct judgement by social or other environmental cues, and as a consequence of having produced that judgement, somehow come to understand why that judgement is correct.

This implies a receptive grasp of the concept in question (Russell, 1982a and b) in that the child, having produced the correct response, recognizes why it is correct.

In the case of coming to know about verbal communication, as in the case of metamemory and metalinguistics, events in school may be important for advances to occur. It is in explicitly educational settings, as contrasted with settings which are social in function, that it becomes crucial to convey particular meanings unambiguously, and to achieve full understanding in the listener. Hence it may be in explicitly educational settings that children are expected to behave in a way consistent with these aims. The validity of this speculation remains to be tested.

Conclusion

Clearly we are not yet experts on metacognitive development, but neither are we complete novices. In the published literature there is evidence of awareness that problems are perhaps not being approached in the best way, and there is speculation about what might be better ways. There is a useful body of information about what children of different ages know about how they carry out or should carry out each of a variety of tasks, and there are valuable general descriptive accounts of age-related differences in such knowledge. However, as yet there is very little information about variables relevant to advances in metacognitive knowledge and no precise specification of necessary or sufficient factors. Neither is there any clear account of when or how children's metacognitive knowledge influences their cognitive activity in everyday life.

A number of possible views about aspects of metacognitive development have been formulated, and we can now begin to ask more specific questions the answers to which should increase our knowledge. For example, possibilities have been made explicit about the circumstances under which children of different ages become aware of or become capable of reflecting upon their own cognitive activities. Probably no one of these possibilities is correct or incorrect. Now we can begin to find out under what conditions younger children are more likely than older ones to know what they are doing and why, under what conditions difficult and problematic tasks lead to this knowledge and under what conditions easy and familiar ones do so. Similarly, we can now formulate contrasting views about the role of awareness in cognitive development: is awareness a necessary impetus to cognitive development from the earliest ages, or a relatively late development allowing deliberate planning and regulation of cognitive activity? Again, we should probably not expect to accept or reject either view, but try to identify conditions under which each might be applicable.

Many of the problems of how best to conceive of metacognition have already been discussed by philosophers, and perhaps the best way of clarifying our ideas in order to ask the right questions will be to pay attention to those discussions. An example of how fruitful such an approach can be is provided by Russell's (1978) volume (particularly pages 249–57) and his subsequent experimental work (e.g. 1982b and c).

It is to be hoped that readers will not accept the view mentioned at the beginning that the recent work by psychologists has been disappointingly unproductive, but instead recognize that as a result of the efforts made in the 1970s and early 1980s we are in a position to formulate the right questions, use the right techniques and procedures to answer them, and in the next few years make real progress in our understanding of metacognitive development.

Note

I would like to thank W. P. Robinson and James Russell who both made very helpful comments on earlier versions of this chapter.

References

Beal, C. R. and Flavell, J. H. (1982) The effect of increasing the salience of message ambiguities on kindergarteners' evaluations of communicative success and message adequacy. *Developmental Psychology* **18**: 43–8.

Bearison, D. J. and Levey, L. M. (1977) Children's comprehension of referential communication: decoding ambiguous messages. *Child Development* **48**: 716–20.

Beveridge, M. and Dunn, J. (1980) Communication and the development of reflective thinking. Paper presented at the Annual Conference of the Developmental Section of the British Psychological Society, University of Edinburgh.

Bringvier, J. (1980) *Conversations with Jean Piaget*. Chicago: University of Chicago Press.

Brown, A. L. (1978) Knowing when, where and how to remember: a problem of metacognition. In R. Glaser (ed.) *Advances in Instructional Psychology*. New York: Halsted Press.

Brown, A. L. and de Loache, J. S. (1978) Skills, plans and self-regulation. In R. S. Siegler (ed.) *Children's Thinking. What Develops?* Hillsdale, NJ: Lawrence Erlbaum Associates.

Brown, A. L. and Smiley, S. S. (1977) Rating the importance of structural units of prose passages: a problem of metacognitive development. *Child Development* **48**: 1–8.

Bryant, P. (1982) The role of conflict and of agreement between intellectual strategies in children's ideas about measurement. *British Journal of Psychology* **73**: 243–51.

Cavanaugh, J. C. and Perlmutter, M. (1982) Metamemory: a critical evaluation. *Child Development* **53**: 11–28.

Chi, M. T. (1978) Knowledge, structure and memory development. In R. S. Siegler (ed.) *Children's Thinking. What Develops?* Hillsdale, NJ: Lawrence Erlbaum Associates.

Clark, E. (1978) Awareness of language: some evidence from what children say and do. In A. Sinclair, R. J. Jarvella and W. J. M. Levett (eds) *The Child's Conception of Language*. Berlin: Springer.

Cole, M., Gay, J., Glick, J. and Sharp, D. (1971) *The Cultural Context of Learning and Thinking*. New York: Basic Books.

Cosgrove, J. M. and Patterson, C. J. (1977) Plans and the development of listener skills. *Developmental Psychology* **13**: 557–64.

Doise, W. and Mugny, G. (1981) *Le Développement Social de l'Intelligence*. Paris: Intereditions.

Donaldson, M. (1978) *Children's Minds*. London: Fontana.

Donaldson, M. (1982) Conservation: what is the question? *British Journal of Psychology* **73**: 199–207.

Ehri, L. C. (1979) Linguistic insight: threshold of reading acquisition. In T. G. Waller and G. E. MacKinnon (eds) *Reading Research Advances in Theory and Practice*, vol. 1. London: Academic Press.

Emler, N. and Valiant, G. L. (1982) Social interaction and cognitive conflict in the development of spatial coordination skills. *British Journal of Psychology* **73**: 295–303.

Ericsson, K. A. and Simon, H. A. (1980) Verbal reports as data. *Psychological Review* **87**: 215–51.

Flavell, J. H. (1977) Paper given at NATO Advanced Study Institute on Structural Process Theories of Complex Social Behaviour, Banff, Canada.

Flavell, J. H. (1978) Comments on Brown and de Loache's paper in R. S. Siegler (ed.) *Children's Thinking. What Develops?* Hillsdale, NJ: Lawrence Erlbaum Associates.

Flavell, J. H. (1981) Cognitive monitoring. In W. P. Dickson (ed.) *Children's Oral Communication Skills*. New York: Academic Press.

Flavell, J. H., Speer, J. R., Green, F. L. and August, D. L. (1981) The development of comprehension monitoring and knowledge about communication. *Monographs of the Society for Research in Child Development*, serial no. 192.

Flavell, J. H. and Wellman, H. M. (1977) Metamemory. In R. U. Kail and J. W. Hagen (eds) *Perspectives on the Development of Memory and Cognition.* Hillsdale, NJ: Lawrence Erlbaum Associates.

Glachan, M. and Light, P. (1982) Peer interaction and learning: can two wrongs make a right? Paper given at conference on New Perspectives in the Experimental Study of the Social Development of Intelligence, Geneva.

Hjelmquist, E. (1981) A note on adults' conception of language and communication. *Osnabrücker Beiträge zur Sprachtheorie* **20**: 62–74.

Ironsmith, M. and Whitehurst, G. J. (1978) The development of listener abilities in communication: how children deal with ambiguous information. *Child Development* **49**: 348–52.

Jackson, S. and Jacobs, S. (1982) Ambiguity and implicature in children's discourse comprehension. *Journal of Child Language* **9**: 209–16.

Karpf, D. A. (1980) Thinking aloud in human discrimination learning. Referred to in K. A. Ericsson and H. A. Simon, Verbal reports as data. *Psychological Review* **87**: 215–51.

Kuhn, D. (1972) Mechanisms of change in the development of cognitive structures. *Child Development* **43**: 833–44.

Lefevbre-Pinard, M. (1981) Understanding and auto-control of cognitive functions: implications for the relationship between cognition and behaviour. Paper given at Sixth Biennial Meetings of the International Society for the Study of Behavioral Development, Toronto.

Light, P. (1979) *The Development of Social Sensitivity.* Cambridge: Cambridge University Press.

Limber, J. (1973) The genesis of complex sentences. In T. E. Moore (ed.) *Cognitive Development and the Acquisition of Language.* New York: Academic Press.

Markman, E. M. (1977) Realizing that you don't understand: a preliminary investigation. *Child Development* **48**: 986–92.

Markman, E. M. (1979) Realizing that you don't understand: elementary school children's awareness of inconsistencies. *Child Development* **50**: 643–55.

Markman, E. M. (1981) Comprehension monitoring. In W. P. Dickson (ed.) *Children's Oral Communication Skills.* New York: Academic Press.

Marshall, J. C. and Morton, J. (1978) On the mechanics of Emma. In A. Sinclair, R. J. Jarvella and W. J. M. Levett (eds) *The Child's Conception of Language.* Berlin: Springer.

Mugny, G., Perret-Clermont, A. and Doise, W. (1981) Interpersonal coordinations and sociological differences in the construction of the intellect. In G. K. Stephenson (ed.) *Progress in Applied Social Psychology*, vol. 1. London: Wiley.

Nisbett, R. E. and Schachter, S. (1966) Cognitive manipulation of pain. *Journal of Experimental Social Psychology* **2**: 227–36.

Nisbett, R. E. and Wilson, T. D. (1977) Telling more than we can know:

verbal reports on mental processes. *Psychological Review* **84**: 231–59.

Olson, D. R. (1977) From utterance to text: the bias of language in speech and writing. *Harvard Educational Review* **47**: 257–81.

Olson, D. R. (1980) Some social aspects of meaning in oral and written language. In D. R. Olson (ed.) *The Social Foundations of Language and Thought*. New York: Norton.

Patterson, C. J., Cosgrove, J. M. and O'Brien, R. G. (1980) Non-verbal indicants of comprehension and noncomprehension in children. *Developmental Psychology* **16**: 38–48.

Patterson, C. J. and Kister, M. C. (1981) The development of listener skills for referential communication. In W. P. Dickson (ed.) *Children's Oral Communication Skills*. New York: Academic Press.

Piaget, J. (1928) *Judgement and Reasoning in the Child*. New York: Harcourt Press.

Piaget, J. (1932) *The Moral Judgement of the Child*. London: Routledge & Kegan Paul.

Piaget, J. (1957) Logique et equilibre dans les compartements du sujet. In *Etudes d'Epistemologie Génétique*, vol. 2. Paris: Presses Universitaires de France.

Piaget, J. (1970) Piaget's theory. In P. H. Mussen (ed.) *Carmichael's Manual of Child Psychology* (3rd edn). New York: Wiley.

Piaget, J. (1978) *Success and Understanding*. London: Routledge & Kegan Paul.

Ringel, B. A. and Springer, C. J. (1980) On knowing how well one is remembering: the persistence of strategy use during transfer. *Journal of Experimental Child Psychology* **29**: 322–33.

Robinson, E. J. (1981a) The child's understanding of inadequate messages and communication failure: a problem of ignorance or egocentrism? In W. P. Dickson (ed.) *Children's Oral Communication Skills*. New York: Academic Press.

Robinson, E. J. (1981b) Conversational tactics and the advancement of the child's understanding about referential communication. In W. P. Robinson (ed.) *Communication in Development*. London: Academic Press.

Robinson, E. J. and Robinson, W. P. (1976a) Developmental changes in the child's explanation of communication failure. *Australian Journal of Psychology* **28**: 155–65.

Robinson, E. J. and Robinson, W. P. (1976b) The young child's understanding of communication. *Developmental Psychology* **12**: 328–33.

Robinson, E. J. and Robinson, W. P. (1977) Development in the understanding of the causes of success and failure in verbal communication. *Cognition* **5**: 363–78.

Robinson, E. J. and Robinson, W. P. (1978) Development of understanding about communication: message inadequacy and its role in causing communication failure. *Genetic Psychological Monographs* **98**: 233–79.

Robinson, E. J. and Robinson, W. P. (1980) Egocentrism in verbal referential communication. In M. V. Cox (ed.) *Are Young Children Egocentric?* London: Batsford.

Robinson, E. J. and Robinson, W. P. (1981) Ways of reacting to communication failure in relation to the development of the child's understanding about verbal communication. *European Journal of Social Psychology* **11**: 189–208.

Robinson, E. J. and Robinson, W. P. (1982a) Understanding about verbal communication: causes and consequences. Paper given at conference on New Perspectives in the Experimental Study of the Social Development of Intelligence, Geneva.

Robinson, E. J. and Robinson, W. P. (1982b) The advancement of children's verbal referential communication skills: the role of metacognitive guidance. *International Journal of Behavioural Development* **5**: 329–55.

Robinson, E. J. and Robinson, W. P. (in press, a) Coming to understand that referential communication can be ambiguous. In W. Doise and M. Palmonari (eds) *Social Interaction in Individual Development*. Cambridge: Cambridge University Press.

Robinson, E. J. and Robinson, W. P. (in press, b) Children's uncertainty about the interpretation of ambiguous messages. *Journal of Experimental Child Psychology*.

Robinson, E. J. and Robinson, W. P. (in press, c) Communication and metacommunication: quality of children's instructions in relation to judgements about the adequacy of instructions and the locus of responsibility for communication failure. *Journal of Experimental Child Psychology*.

Robinson, W. P. (1982) The child's development of understanding about ambiguity in referential speech. *International Journal of Psycholinguistics*, in press.

Russell, J. (1978) *The Acquisition of Knowledge*. London: Macmillan.

Russell, J. (1981) Dyadic interaction in a logical reasoning problem requiring inclusion ability. *Child Development* **52**: 1322–5.

Russell, J. (1982a) Cognitive conflict, transmission and justification: conservation attainment through dyadic interaction. *Journal of Genetic Psychology* **140**: 283–97.

Russell, J. (1982b) Propositional attitudes. In M. Beveridge (ed.) *Children Thinking Through Language*. London: Edward Arnold.

Russell, J. (1982c) The child's appreciation of the necessary truth and necessary falseness of propositions. *British Journal of Psychology* **73**: 253–66.

Shatz, M. (1978) The relationship between cognitive processes and the development of communication skills. In B. Kearey (ed.) *Nebraska Symposium on Motivation*. Lincoln: University of Nebraska Press.

Silbereisen, R. K. and Claar, A. (1982) Stimulation of social cognition in parent-child interaction: do parents make use of appropriate interaction strategies? Paper given at conference on New Perspectives in the Experimental Study of the Social Development of Intelligence, Geneva.

Sinclair, H. (1978) Conceptualization and awareness in Piaget's theory and its relevance to the child's conception of language. In A. Sinclair, R. J. Jarvella and W. J. M. Levett (eds) *The Child's Conception of Language*. Berlin: Springer.

Wagner, D. A. (1978) Memories of Morocco: the influence of age, schooling and environment on memory. *Cognitive Psychology* **10**: 1–28.

Waters, H. S. (1982) Memory development in adolescence: relationships between metamemory, strategy use, and performance. *Journal of Experimental Child Psychology* **33**: 183–95.

Yussen, S. R. and Bird, J. E. (1979) The development of metacognitive awareness in memory, communication and attention. *Journal of Experimental Child Psychology* **28**: 300–13.

6 Literacy and cognitive development: a conceptual transformation in the early school years

David R. Olson and Nancy G. Torrance

In this paper we shall consider some of the ways in which literacy may interact with cognitive development. Since the influential writings of Piaget and Vygotsky it has been generally agreed that an important intellectual transformation occurs during the early school years. For Piaget, this transformation is characterized as the development of operational thought which underlies such achievements as reversibility, class inclusion and transitivity. An important part of this development is the child's growing ability not only to represent objects and events but also voluntarily to reassign 'descriptions' or representations to the same object or event in a number of ways or from a number of perspectives. Thus the child comes to call a particular household pet *Rover*, a *dog*, a *pet*, an *animal* and the like without contradiction. Further, the child recognizes that there are more animals than dogs, that dogs may be both bigger than cats and smaller than wolves and so on.

Other theorists note that these descriptions and redescriptions depend upon the availability of a language for redescription and that language seems to depend upon the lexical resources of the culture in which the child finds himself or herself. For that reason theorists such as Vygotsky attribute an important causal influence in cognitive development to the structure of the culture, particularly the structure and uses of language. For Vygotsky, then, this intellectual transformation in the early school years is characterized by the development of a systematic, 'schooled' form of thought which at first parallels and eventually transforms the spontaneous and commonsensical concepts of the child.

The argument which we shall advance in this paper is, in a sense, between Piaget and Vygotsky. It adopts from Piaget (1960) the notion that the child must construct his or her own cognitions; they cannot simply be transmitted, taught, or internalized from the culture. It adopts from Vygotsky (1962) the notion that what the child constructs is not simply 'homemade' or spontaneous but rather reflects very closely the cultural patterns of the adult society, especially those patterns reflected in the forms of talk and thought of that culture. And finally it goes somewhat beyond both by arguing that it is not merely the language of the culture that is important but also the medium of expression and communication used in that culture – writing, printing, picture making, television or computing – and the metalanguage constructed around these media. The medium of interest herein is print, and the skills of concern are those of literacy – children's competence with reading and writing.

The relationship between a medium of expression such as writing or printing, competence with that medium of expression, and cognitive development is quite complex. First, one may argue that the mere fact that a child grows up in a literate environment may influence his or her cognitive processes. But here the problem is one of specifying just how that culture could have an impact on the child. We have already mentioned that theories relating culture to cognition, such as that of Vygotsky, rely upon relatively simple and unsatisfactory models of learning and development, such as internalization or socialization. Such models are of course appropriate for some purposes; they fail only in that they assume a rather passive learner and ignore the process by means of which a child comes to resemble an adult. In a word they lack the constructive aspects of Piaget's theory.

Secondly, one may argue that it is the actual process of learning to read and write that has an impact on the cognitive processes. Literacy in this sense, is a form of competence derived from skill in reading and writing. Literacy skills then have their effects on cognition through altering the ways in which people get access to information – through reading; how they store information – in notes rather than through oral mnemonics; how they retrieve information – through reading rather than through asking; how they decide what is true – by consulting an encyclopedia, and so on. Literacy skills undoubtedly serve a large number of intellectual and social functions of the sort described. But it is not clear that such uses of reading and writing have any important effects upon the structure and functions of the mind. One could speak of literacy skills – reading and writing – but not of a 'literate mind'.

Thirdly, one may argue that the basic processes of learning to read and write do not have any particular effects upon the cognitive processes, but that the acquisition of these skills makes accessible the world of literature. On this view it is access to and participation in the world of literature, science and philosophy which is important in the formation of a literate or educated mind. A literate person in this sense, thinks differently only in that he or she brings to bear not only personal experience or the social experience of the community but also the historical, comparative, disciplined perspectives provided by a literary tradition.

In fact the OED offers both of these senses of *literate* – able to read and write, and having some acquaintance with literature. And both of these uses of literacy have cognitive consequences which are sufficiently well known and agreed upon to warrant the teaching of both literacy skills and literature to children.

But our concern is somewhat more general. Does children's participation in a literate culture, whether through their forms of talk and thought or through their learning to read and write or through their more literary activities, have an effect upon their cognitive processes? Does it permit a distinctive form of mental operations? And if it does, how does that effect come about?

The recent writings of a number of psychologists and anthropologists including Scribner and Cole (1981), Heath (1982), Schieffelin and Cochrane-Smith (in press) and others, reveal another difficulty in untangling the nature and consequences of literacy, namely the varying uses of literacy in different societies. These differences make it impossible to state in a general way the consequences of literacy; consequences depend upon the type of literacy and the uses to which it is put in a particular social world. Hence when we look for the cognitive consequences of literacy, we are not making universal statements about a medium and a form of cognition but rather about one presumably important intellectual use to which literacy is put in a particular social world.

Given these complexities in the concept of literacy and the complexity in the uses to which reading and writing can be put, what can we say about the relation between literacy and the cognitive development of children? Our hypothesis is that an important conceptual transformation occurs during the early school years for children in a literate bureaucratic society such as ours which is related, either directly or indirectly, to literacy. This conceptual transformation depends upon the development of a new orientation to language, specifically, an attention to and a competence with the structure of language *per se* as opposed to an attention to competence with the contents, intentions or messages expressed by the language. As we shall argue, it has to do with learning to differentiate form from content, what is *said* from what is *meant*.

Another way of expressing this hypothesis is to say that the cognitive consequences of literacy spring from the knowledge that language exists as an artefact, that it has a structure, that it is composed of syntactic units such as sounds, words and sentences, and that it has a semantic structure or meaning, and finally, that all of these aspects of structure may be referred to by a metalanguage. In a word, it is the belief that language can be treated opaquely, as a structure in its own right.

Now, if the awareness of linguistic form is the means whereby literacy has its cognitive effects, it is possible that the awareness of this form does not arise exclusively through learning to read and write or any other actual literate activity. Rather, the metalanguage, expressing particular structures of the language and thereby rendering them opaque, can be acquired through other devices such as the oral language practices of literate adults or for that matter through any other lexical or intonational devices for making language explicit. Thus Schieffelin and Cochrane-Smith (in press) have shown that among the Kaluli there appears to be considerable attention to the language, not merely its meanings, even if the people are non-literate. Further, the hypothesis allows the possibility that people may be somewhat literate without having worked up any degree of competence in treating language as an object in its own right. Hence, we cannot expect to find a simple causality between reading and writing and the orientation to language that we have described as literate. Pattison (1982) has recently made the same point, namely, that what is decisive is the attitude to language, not the simple skill of reading and writing.

Nonetheless, there is an important relation between the orientation to language as an object and the nature of literacy. Derrida

(1978) puts it this way: 'Inscription alone . . . has the power to arouse speech from its slumber as sign. By enregistering speech, inscription has as its essential objective . . . the emancipation of meaning' (p.12). That is, writing permits the language user to notice that speech is not merely a means for expressing the speaker's meanings and intentions. The user comes to note that language has a structure and a meaning in its own right. Differentiating language as sign from language as structure is tied to writing in that writing preserves form, or surface structure, 'the very words', which can therefore be subjected to analysis, study and interpretation, none of which are particularly encouraged by oral language (Olson, 1977). Writing makes the language, otherwise ephemeral, into a visual artefact: Its physical structure invites naming and analysis. However, the mere physical presence does not cause the language to be treated as an object. That comes, as we suggested above, from the invention of concepts and symbols for referring to that visible artefact, namely, the invention of a metalanguage. And once coded in the metalanguage, the concepts may be taught and learned quite independently of learning to read and write. In fact, however, as Francis (1975) and others have shown, for most children the process of learning to read and write is the occasion for learning the metalanguage.

The notion that what is important is treating the language as an object may be somewhat misleading since this can be accomplished in a number of ways. A rough gloss such as 'metalinguistic awareness' while somewhat similar to the notion advanced herein is, in our view, somewhat mischievous. It assumes that awareness is a general or conscious psychological process, like using a mirror to reflect a pattern. No such notion is advanced here. Our argument is simply that treating the language as an object means literally that; it involves 'nominating' language, using nouns and verbs to refer, not to the world, but to language. Hence the word *language*, used and understood conventionally, in a sense creates an object, the language, which is nominated, or referred to by the word *language*. Of course, many aspects of language may be so nominated or designated by language and each such designation makes up part of the metalanguage.

No natural language, presumably, exists without at least some metalanguage. Thus *say* is a part of the metalanguage which is, apparently, universal. But note that it is a rather elementary metalanguage. More elaborated metalanguage is called for in the attempts to refer more specifically to parts of language, through such words as *word, sound, paragraph* or whatever, or for referring to types of talk, through such metalinguistic terms as *pray, curse, whisper, ask, promise* and so on. Hence, there is nothing abstract about our concept of treating language as an object; we are simply referring to a person's knowledge and use of the metalanguage. Everyone has some such knowledge; but literate persons, by our hypothesis, possess an elaborate, and perhaps distinctive metalanguage by means of which they treat various structures and functions of language as objects. Our question then becomes one of finding the structure, acquisition, and cognitive implications of that metalanguage.

Let us summarize to this point. The cognitive transformation which, by hypothesis, is related to literacy, may be a consequence of the child's learning to treat language as an object. But treating language as an object, as we have seen, is simply the consequence of learning and using a metalanguage for referring to linguistic forms. All speakers have some such metalanguage even if it merely discriminates talk from song, or prayers from curses. The metalanguage of concern here is that for referring to more detailed levels of structure, particularly that for referring to parts of the linguistic code – words, sentences, and the like – and that for referring to the meanings, intentions, and beliefs expressed by the code – assertions, questions, promises, and the like. In the remainder of this paper, we shall consider evidence that this metalanguage is aquired about the time that the child learns to read and write, that this acquisition is related either directly or indirectly to literacy, and that its acquisition has the kinds of cognitive uses we have described as a cognitive revolution.

From intended meanings to sentence meanings

An important part of conceptual development during the school years, we have suggested, is a consequence of the progressive realization of the relations between the forms and meanings in the language and the meanings that people entertain and express through language, that is the difference between what sentences mean and what people mean by them. How then do children handle this problem of meaning and how does it change with development? Our suggestion is that there is a shift from attention to the beliefs and intentions of persons towards the meanings and structures of sentences; a shift from intended meanings to sentence meanings. This shift, as we shall see, is marked by a significant change in the metalanguage. The metalinguistic verb *say* comes to be differentiated into the verbs *say* and *mean*. But let us firstly clarify this distinction.

Grice (1957) was among the first to develop an intentionalist theory of meaning and we shall adopt his distinction between sentence meaning and speaker's meaning here. Sentence meaning refers to the literal or conventional meaning of what was in fact said, including the linguistic form or semantic structure, the very words employed and their syntactic relations. The precise structure of an expression, of 'sentence meaning', is a vexed issue which has been attacked by several writers including Searle (1979), Bierwisch (1979) and Hildyard and Olson (1982). But its precise structure is not the major concern here. Rather, we are concerned with children's and adults' beliefs and assumptions about semantic structure, that is about linguistic form and meaning, and how those beliefs as assumptions influence how they talk and think.

Speaker's meaning, in contrast to sentence meaning, refers to the underlying intentions a speaker holds (and a listener recovers) in uttering a particular sentence. Again, we are less concerned with a full theory of intentionality than we are in speakers' assumptions and beliefs about their meanings and intentions. And as we hinted, we may get a fairly accurate picture of speakers' ideas about both intentions and expressions through looking at their metalanguage for referring to intentions and expressions.

Grice (1975) has provided several examples in which what a sentence means and what a speaker means by it do not coincide. If in writing a letter of recommendation for a student, one says 'Mr X writes with a steady round hand', one is not saying that the student is not academically promising, but one means and implicates precisely that. Simpler examples of the discrepancy between what sentences mean and what speakers mean by them may be found in hyperbole, sarcasm, indirect speech acts, and the like.

Now, how do children handle this relation between what they mean and what words and sentences mean? In a sense, children already implicitly know about sentences and intentions in that they successfully use the former in the service of the latter. What he or she apparently fails to do is to differentiate the two and to pay attention to the latter. Alternatively expressed, the child uses sentence meanings to express or compute intended meanings but, as many writers have pointed out, the sentence meaning remains implicit and, hence, transparent (Polyani, 1958, p. 92; Cazden, 1975). What he or she begins to do primarily under the impact of literacy and schooling, is to become aware of, to make explicit, the sentence meaning. The child does so, we suggest, through learning the concepts expressed by the metalanguage.

Consider some of the evidence for this view. In one study (Olson and Hildyard, 1981), kindergarten (5-year-old) and grade 2 (7-year-old) children were read a story which told about two children, Kevin and Susie, who went to a movie, bought and shared some popcorn, and who then argued about the justice of the distribution, Kevin complaining to Susie, 'You have more than me!'. When subsequently asked what Kevin had *said*, more than half of the kindergarten children replied, 'Give me some!' That is, of course, what he meant but not exactly what he had said. By grade 2, the majority of the children reported verbatim what had been said, and when asked, indicated that they knew what had been meant as well.

Yet even younger children will use *say* to refer to the linguistic form as for example when young children are asked to 'say' new or complex words in the process of learning to talk. The adult says 'Say *chicken*!' and the child answers 'Chicken'. Thus for children the verb *say* does not distinguish form from meaning; it refers to both. Of course, there is a colloquial use of 'say' which means, roughly, *mean* in adult usage. But most adults note the ambiguity of such requests as: 'Can you say that chickens have fur?' They reply, 'Well, you can *say* it but it wouldn't be true.' Children apparently do not see the ambiguity.

A study by Elizabeth Robinson in Bristol and by Goelman and Olson in Toronto shows the development of this distinction in the early school years. In some of their earlier studies, Robinson and Robinson (1977a and b) had discovered that in cases of communication failure in which the responsibility could be logically traced back to the speaker and his or her inadequate message, children invariably 'blamed the listener'. To illustrate, if a child in a communication game intends to say 'blue flower' (that is what the child means), and inappropriately says just 'flower', and the listener picks a red flower in response to the command, the child blames the listener for not picking the right one. As the Robinsons point out, it seems not to occur to the child that the speaker or his message may be at fault. This tendency disappears after a year or two of schooling.

In a collaborative study, Robinson, Goelman and Olson (in press) attempted to determine if the pattern of 'blaming the listener' was the result of the inability to differentiate what the speaker means or intends from what the sentence means, a conflation of the two types of meaning. To this end, Robinson in the UK and Goelman and Olson in Canada, repeated the communication game but this time on each occasion that the child inappropriately blamed the listener, they asked the child what the speaker had said. This question was asked only when, by looking (on the sly) at the object in the speaker's hand, it was clear what the actual intended object had been. Hence, they had independent evidence both of what was *said* (and thereby what the sentence meant) and what the speaker had *meant* or intended. The hypothesis was that the listener-blamers were not aware of the difference between what the speaker meant and what the sentence meant and of the possible discrepancy between the two. If children conflate the two they should answer the question with a correct description of the intended object rather than with a correct repetition of the sentence. If they differentiate the two, they have the option of saying something of the form 'I (you) said *x*, but I (you) meant *y*'. Specifically, the authors looked at cases in which there was a discrepancy between what was said and what was meant. The results were just as predicted. To refer again to our earlier example, if the child said 'flower' while holding (intending) a *blue* flower, and the listener picked up a *red* flower, the message may have resulted in a failure of communication. If the child was then asked: 'What did you say?', the child tended to reply 'The blue flower'. That, of course, is what he meant but not what he said. Conversely, children who blamed the speaker for the inadequate message, generally the older children, admitted that they had said *flower* but meant *blue flower*. Such studies indicate that the youngest children assumed, with Popeye, that they say what they mean and they mean what they say, and it is only with some further development that they make the differentiation and use that distinction in their own thinking. Finally, it should be noted that the conceptual distinction between what the sentence means and what the child means by it is perfectly reflected in the child's knowledge of the metalanguage. If the child discriminates an inadequate message from an adequate one, he knows the metalanguage for marking that distinction, namely, what 'say' and 'mean' mean.

A recent study by Newman (1982) reports a similar finding in children's interpretation of lies. He showed first- to sixth-grade children (6–11 year olds) a Sesame Street television segment in which Ernie says to Bert: 'I'm going to divide this banana up so both of us can have some', whereupon he eats the whole banana and gives Bert the skin, saying: 'See, I took the inside part and here's the outside part for you'. The question is whether or not Ernie lied. First-grade children think that he did; by grade three children begin to notice that the sentence is both true and false. It is true by virtue of its 'sentence meaning'; it is false by virtue of its putative intended 'speaker's meaning'. In terms of the hypothesis described above, children come to notice that language may be treated either in terms of sentence meanings or speakers' meanings and, when so treated, the two may be discrepant. But both come to be noticed, in part, because the child is attempting to construct meanings for the metalinguistic terms he is hearing, specifically, 'what did you say?', 'what did you mean?' 'what did it say?', and 'what did it mean?', where 'it' can be any linguistic level ranging from a word, to a sentence to a text.

In fact, in our study of children's oral language competence, we have observed how children begin to mark this distinction in the early school years.

Teacher: What's a bicycle?

Child: Bicycle's got three wheels, I mean, two wheels.

Notice the child's use of the word 'mean'. It is the child who 'means' two wheels. Contrast this use with the following:

J: Dads are supposed to be strong but my dad's puny. Do you know what puny means?

L: Yes.

J: It means scrawny.

Here it is not the child but the word which 'means' scrawny. The metalinguistic use of the verb 'mean' to refer to an aspect of language is an important part of coming to treat language as an object. The importance of this verb and its cognates such as *understand* is indicated in another study by Robinson and Robinson (1981). The children of mothers who used such expressions as 'I don't know what you mean' and 'I hear you but I don't understand what you're saying' and the like, were the very children who succeeded in the task of blaming speakers for their inadequate messages from a relatively early age. That is, the use and understanding of the metalanguage appears to be a good indication of the tendency to treat language opaquely. Indeed, as we suggested, it is possible that all that is meant by treating language opaquely is the knowledge and use of the metalanguage.

Similar findings have been reported from somewhat different research perspectives. Donaldson (1978) reports a series of studies in which children systematically misinterpret sentences in an experimental task. Thus if children were shown an unequal number of cars and garages and asked to judge the truth of such sentences as: 'All the cars are in the garages' or 'All the garages have cars in them', children younger than 7 years tended to make incorrect judgements. They would, for example, deny that all the cars were in the garages when there were three cars, all in garages, but one empty garage in addition. Similarly they would claim that all the cars were in the garages when all the garages were full but an extra car sat beside the full garages. Donaldson concluded that the children were ignoring these variations in linguistic form and judging the statement: 'All the garages are full'. She infers that 'the child is unable to pay scrupulous attention to the language in its own right' (p. 70) particularly when the child is required to comprehend a sentence out of its normal context of comprehension. Paying attention to the language, we may add, is a matter of recognizing that what sentences mean may both be discrepant from what we as speakers mean by them and from what we as listeners expect others mean by them. The child recognizes that what sentences mean may be differentiated from what people mean, or presumably, mean by them.

Karmiloff-Smith (1979), too, in discussing language development in school-age children found that children use 'pragmatic' procedures for understanding language. That is, they draw upon context and prior knowledge in interpreting sentences, sometimes at the expense of the particular linguistic form involved. Thus, she told stories to children which were somewhat counter to usual pragmatic factors and which therefore put a heavy communicative burden upon a particular linguistic form, the singular definite article. Children were told a story involving a dog who had gone into a garden and had crushed *the* flower, from which the children were to infer that the garden contained only one flower. The majority of children under 8 years did not pick up the clue from the definite article; they claimed there must have been many flowers 'because gardens usually have many flowers, so there must have been several' (p. 321). Even more interesting, when they did begin to make the correct inference, in telling back the experimenter's story, they insisted that she had said: 'He crushed the only flower'. Children seem to assume that a modest article could not, by itself, carry such a heavy semantic burden. Karmiloff-Smith concludes that much of this development occurs from the child's constructive interaction with linguistic 'objects', on their working out the structures of language, 'treating language as a problem space' rather than simply working on the structure of the world. 'Only after 8 years does language seem to become *solely* the important instrument for representing and communicating thought' (p. 323). This view is similar to that discussed here. We would add only that, in our view, treating the language as a problem space is crucially dependent upon learning and using the metalanguage.

The most ambitious study of the cognitive consequences of literacy has been carried out by Scribner and Cole (1981). In a 7-year study, they examined the nature, uses and cognitive consequences of literacy in the indigenous Vai script, a syllable-based script invented some hundred years ago and used primarily for letter writing by about 25 per cent of the adult men in the society. For comparative purposes they also studied the effects of formal schooling in which English is the language of instruction, and Arabic literacy that is used primarily for liturgical and religious practices. While non-schooled literacies had some important cognitive effects, such as enhancing literates' abilities to describe the structure and rules of a game, and many other more contextually specific skills that are not of concern here, by far the most general of the measured cognitive skills were related to schooling rather than to indigenous literacy. Students were able to offer more adequate explanations of their logical inferences in syllogistic types of tasks, of their classification strategies and of their knowledge about language – the relative arbitrariness of the relation between objects and names, their knowledge of 'word' – than were those who were literate in the Vai script but had not been to school. Literate Vai who had not been to school were not discriminable from those who were not literate in the Vai script. Scribner and Cole conclude that: 'under literacy circumstances in Vai country, knowledge of reading and writing does not have the same intellectual consequences as schooling' (p. 254). And further that: 'school effects are not brought about through the ability to read and write *per se*' (p. 255).

On the one hand, these findings support the argument about the attention to language that develops during the school years, the ability for example to draw and justify formal inferences, to know what a word is or what a word means and the like, but, on the other hand, they contradict the argument that this development is directly related to the ability to read and write. Scribner and Cole suggest that schooling has the intellectual effects it does in part because the types of questions used to measure these intellectual effects reflect rather directly the types of questions teachers ask in school: 'Why do you say that?' 'How do you know?', 'How can you tell?', and so on. In fact, this may be the link we require for our argument, namely, that the route through which literacy normally (in our society) has its effect on cognition is through leading children and adults to treat language as an object. The means for treating the language as an object is through the metalanguage. But if it is the metalanguage that is critical, it leaves open the route through which the learner may acquire the metalanguage, whether through talk with literate parents, who may treat the language as an object (Olson, in preparation), or through teachers who use that form of talk (Mehan, 1979, cited by Scribner and Cole, 1981), through literacy events, such as bedtime story reading (Heath, 1982), or through learning to read and write (Francis, 1975). At best, we may say that the metalanguage is related either directly or indirectly to literacy. Reading and writing is neither a necessary nor a sufficient condition for learning the metalanguage. However, the metalanguage, as we shall argue presently, may be based on writing.

From the metalanguage to a mode of thought

To this point we have summarized some of the evidence that children in the early school years, in our society at least, begin to treat language as an object, presumably by means of the mastery of the metalanguage. We have now to show that the mastery of this metalanguage can have important intellectual uses. Obviously, children who know what a word is can understand such questions as 'What does the word *x* mean?' better than if they do not know the metalinguistic noun 'word'. Similarly for the word 'mean'. But does it have any more general use? The structure of the metalanguage is vast, including the set of speech act verbs (say, ask, promise, order) and the corresponding set of mental state verbs (believe, want, intend), as well as taxonomic structural nouns (letters, words, sentences) and the nouns representing specialized genres of both written texts and oral discourse (essays, letters, songs, prayers, chants and so on). Our concern here is with the restricted set having to do with *say* and *mean* and their application to persons and to linguistic structures. What then can we say about the possible cognitive uses of this small set of metalinguistic devices?

In part we have already answered this question. In discussing our work and that of Donaldson, Karmiloff-Smith, and Scribner and Cole, we pointed out that children and adults who could discriminate what the sentence said from what they would ordinarily have assumed that the speaker meant by it, could solve the problems posed for them, while those who failed to make the differentiation could not. Hence it seems clear that there is a range of intellectual tasks, tasks which we in a literate society take as descriptive of 'intelligence', which cannot be handled easily by subjects who do not make that distinction. To provide a simple illustration, in an experiment by Hildyard and Olson (1982), preschool and school-aged children were given inferential tasks involving complex verbs. Children were told, for example: 'John forced Mary to eat the worm', or 'John forced Mary to eat the ice-cream'. The verb *forced* is interesting because it implies both that she did not want to, hence she had to be forced, and that she actually did the eating. Preschool children's responses to both of these questions were overridden by children's expectancies. To the first they reply: 'Oh no, she didn't eat the worm. Nobody eats worms'. To the second they reply: 'Oh yes, she wanted to eat the ice-cream. Everybody likes ice-cream'. As in the studies cited above, when the language conflicts with the expectancies in the situation, it is the language which gives way. With a few years of schooling, that pattern changes. We say that the child starts to treat sentences *literally*, and to see that what the sentence says and means may be discrepant from what the speaker means (and in the secondary sense, says) by it.

Piaget's concrete-operational tasks may be looked at in the same way. When Piaget shows the child a collection consisting of two ducks and three rabbits and then asks the child: 'Are there more rabbits or more animals?', the child fails to 'pay scrupulous attention to the language'. So he responds 'More rabbits'. When asked why, he replies: 'Because there are only two ducks'. The child has ignored the meaning in the language and replaced it by the meaning he supposes, incorrectly in this case, that the adult has in mind. Again, he does not differentiate what the sentence means from what he supposes a speaker means by it.

But perhaps our hypothesis is too general. It may be that the problem is not with the metalanguage – the difference between what the sentence means and what the speaker presumably means – but rather simply in the language. The child simply does not know what the comparative *more* means, or in the other studies discussed above, what *the* means, or what *forced* means and so on. Development, by this account, would be tied to linguistic development, not metalinguistic development. But that account fails because, in fact, the children in all the studies cited above know the critical terms and use them productively in their own speech. They fail only when the sentences contradict the more probable contextual meaning, that is, when the sentence meaning differs from the putative intended meaning. Hence, it is not the meaning of the word, the knowledge of the language, that is relevant, it is the knowledge of the metalanguage, of the difference between what is said and what is meant. This is further shown by the justifications which Karmiloff-Smith, Newman, Scribner and Cole, and Hildyard and Olson reported their subjects giving. In all of these cases the child appeals to the lexical structure of the language. The child picks the word out of the sentence and justifies his or her decision on the basis of the meaning of the word. Thus, older subjects in the Hildyard and Olson study say, 'You said that John had to *force* her' (p. 176). Piaget, of course, is concerned with the child's epistemology, the child's beliefs about the world. Yet if the characteristics of thought that we take as sophisticated depend upon a particular orientation to language, then we can reopen the question regarding the role of language, or symbols generally, in cognition (cf. Gardner, in preparation).

But even if the language and the metalanguage are important in cognition, we must not overlook the Piagetian point we introduced at the beginning of this paper. The existence of a symbol in the culture, or even the child's superficial knowledge of the word or symbol, will not, in and of itself, explain the cognitive uses of that symbol. What is critical is that the child has to invent the semantic structure or meaning for a symbol. This is a process that in many cases involves many false starts, revisions and corrections before she arrives at the culturally conventional meaning (cf. Ferreiro, in preparation). And it is only the meaning, the concept expressed by that symbol, that is responsible for the conceptual uses of symbols. Hence, it is not sufficient to note that the child hears the words that make up the metalanguage; he or she must construct the concepts that those words represent. But on the other hand, in the absence of such expressions as *say* and *mean*, the child would be unlikely to initiate the attempt to construct such contrastive concepts.

It is important to point out that the absence of a metalanguage for referring to words or sentences as opposed to intentions does not imply that the structures of thought are somehow illogical or irrational. As Donaldson pointed out in her studies of children, even children are rational; they simply reason from different grounds than those expressed by sentences. Similarly, if some of Cole and Scribner's subjects failed to draw the valid inference in a syllogism, it was not because they lacked rules of logic but because they treated the questions as factual rather than hypothetical. Rationality is presupposed in all such analysis; what is at stake is the ground of inference. Schooling and literacy, we have suggested, make that ground the meaning of sentences rather than the intended meaning of persons.

From literacy to the metalanguage

It remains only to discuss some possible relations between literacy and the metalanguage. As we have suggested, following Scribner and Cole, literacy by itself is neither a necessary nor a sufficient condition for the kinds of effects we have discussed. We suggested that this could be true if the mediating factor between literacy and the cognitive effects we have discussed was the knowledge of the metalanguage. If what is required is that one distinguish what people say and mean from what words or sentences say or mean, then that knowledge could derive from any one of a number of sources. We mentioned them earlier: from classroom talk (Mehan, 1979 cited by Scribner and Cole, 1981), from preschool literacy events (Heath, 1982), from conversations with literate adults (Robinson, 1980), and from being taught how to read and write (Francis, 1975). None of these contexts has yet been thoroughly investigated for either the children's or the parent's uses of metalinguistic nouns and verbs or their metacognitive counterparts. The evidence that exists suggests that children's knowledge of these verbs is closely related to their reading abilities. Thus, Bissex (in preparation) quotes one of her early readers as saying: '*Hate* is about the only word I can read but can't spell. I always spell it h-a-t' (p. 7). Note the rich metalanguage, *word, read, spell,* and indirectly the letters, *h, a* and *t*. Along the same line, one of the properties of children's oral language use that correlated consistently and significantly with children's progress in learning to read in our longitudinal study, was children's use of metalinguistic and metacognitive verbs (Torrance and Olson, in preparation). Again we note that it is not merely the words that are important, it is the concept or meaning that those words express. And a great deal of cognitive activity goes into the construction of those meanings. But the occasion for that constructive activity is a particular world, the world of language and literacy.

Conclusions

In this paper, we have considered some of the ways that literacy is related to cognition. Written language is not a simple cause of a conceptual change but is a result of the child's attempt to make sense of an environment made up in part of literate artefacts – books, notes, lists and so on – and in part by literate practices – story-reading, schooling, and learning to read and write. It is children's attempts to cope with this environment and these practices that produces the cognitive changes we have discussed. But what, precisely, is the child constructing? The concepts that the child constructs are, in large part, concepts marked in the metalanguage that adults use in talking about and dealing with the literate environment. It is the mastery and use of the metalanguage, and hence, of these metalinguistic concepts, that permits children to deal with both their language and their world in a new way. The basic achievement is to come to treat language not merely as an expression of the intentions of a speaker or writer, what we have called the 'speaker's meaning', but also to treat language, including words, sentences and texts, as having a meaning in their own right, a 'sentence meaning', and thereby come to live in a world 'opened up by texts' (Ricoeur, 1973).

References

Bierwisch, M. (1980) *Utterance, Meaning and Mental States*. Mimeo.

Bissex, G. L. (in preparation) The child as teacher. In F. Smith and H. Goelman (eds) *Children's Response to a Literate Environment*.

Cazden, C. B. (1975) Play with language and metalinguistic awareness: one dimension of language experience. In C. B. Winsor (ed.) *Dimension of Language Experience*. New York: Agathon Press.

Derrida, J. (1978) *Writing and Difference*, translated by Alan Bass. Chicago: University of Chicago Press.

Donaldson, M. (1978) *Children's Minds*. London: Fontana.

Ferreiro, E. (in preparation) Literacy development: a psychogenetic perspective. In D. Olson, N. Torrance and A. Hildyard (eds) *Literacy, Language and Learning: The Nature and Consequences of Reading and Writing*.

Francis, H. (1975) *Language in Childhood: Form and Function in Language Learning*. London: Paul Elek.

Gardner, H. (in preparation) *The Idea of Multiple Intelligences*.

Grice, H. P. (1957) Meaning. *Philosophical Review* **66**: 377–88.

Grice, H. P. (1975) Logic and conversation. In P. Cole and J. L. Morgan (eds) *Syntax and Semantics*, vol. 3. New York: Academic Press.

Heath, S. B. (1982) Protean shapes in literacy events: ever-shifting oral and literate traditions. In D. Tannen (ed.) *Spoken and Written Language*, vol. 9 in Advances in Discourse Processes. Norwood, NJ: Ablex Publishing Corporation.

Hildyard, A. and Olson, D. R. (1982) On the structure and meaning of prose text. In W. Otto and S. White (eds) *Reading Expository Material*. New York: Academic Press.

Karmiloff-Smith, A. (1979) Language development after five. In P. Fletcher and M. Garman (eds) *Language Acquisition*. Cambridge, Mass.: Cambridge University Press.

Newman, D. (1982) Perspective-taking versus content in understanding lies. *The Quarterly Newsletter of the Laboratory of Comparative Human Cognition* **4** (2): 26–9.

Olson, D. (1977) From utterance to text: the bias of language in speech and writing. *Harvard Educational Review*, **47**: 257–81.

Olson, D. (in preparation) See! Jumping! In F. Smith, H. Goelman and A. Oberg (eds) *Awakening to Literacy*.

Olson, D. R. and Hildyard, A. (1981) Assent and compliance in children's language. In W. P. Dickson (ed.) *Children's Oral Communication Skills*. New York: Academic Press.

Pattison, R. (1982) *On Literacy*. New York: Oxford University Press.

Piaget, J. (1960) *The Psychology of Intelligence*. Paterson, NJ: Littlefield Adams.

Polyani, M. (1958) *Personal Knowledge: Towards a Post-Critical Philosophy*. London: Routledge & Kegan Paul.

Ricoeur, P. (1973) Creativity in language: word, polysemy and metaphor. *Philosophy Today* **17**: 97–111.

Robinson, E. J., Goelman, H. and Olson, D. R. (in press) Children's understanding of the relation between expressions (what was said) and intentions (what was meant). *British Journal of Developmental Psychology*.

Robinson, E. J. and Robinson, W. P. (1977a) Children's explanations of failure and the inadequacy of the misunderstood message. *Developmental Psychology* **13**: 151–61.

Robinson, E. J. and Robinson, W. P. (1977b) The young child's explanation of communication failure: a reinterpretation of results. *Perception and Motor Skills* **44**: 363–6.

Robinson, E. J. and Robinson, W. P. (1981) Ways of reacting to communication failure in relation to the development of children's understanding about verbal communication. *European Journal of Social Psychology* **11**: 189–208.

Schieffelin, B. B. and Cochrane-Smith, M. (in preparation) Learning to read culturally. In F. Smith and H. Goelman (eds) *Children's Response to a Literate Environment*.

Scribner, S. and Cole, M. (1981) *The Psychology of Literacy*. Cambridge, Mass.: Harvard University Press.

Searle, J. R. (1979) Metaphor. In A. Ortony (ed.) *Metaphor and Thought*. Cambridge, Mass.: Cambridge University Press.

Torrance, N. G. and Olson, D. R. (in preparation) Talking and learning to read: oral and literate competencies in the early school years. In D. R. Olson, N. G. Torrance and A. Hildyard (eds), *Literacy, Language and Learning: The Nature and Consequences of Reading and Writing*.

Vygotsky, L. S. (1962) *Thoughts and Language*. Cambridge, Mass: MIT Press.

7 Experience and cognitive processing

Maggie Mills and Elaine Funnell

Much of the research of the last ten years on the cognitive processing of young children can be summed up in the maxim that children think to better effect when the information they are asked to deal with makes sense to them. It is the aim of this chapter to examine the role of experience as it relates to children's ability to make inferences and their acquisition of the concepts and translation processes involved in learning to read.

A familiar situation or one incorporating a child's frame of reference maximizes understanding. In this there is no difference between children and adults. A now famous experiment by Wason and Johnson-Laird (1973) asked university students to formulate circumstances under which a conditional rule would be true when they were asked to select examples to prove their case either from two-sided cards on which there was an arbitrary assignment of abstract symbols and letters or from an array of envelopes bearing two-stamp values, which came sealed or unsealed. While the logical structure of the two tasks was identical in that students were told 'if a card has a vowel on one side, then it has an even number on the other side', and 'if a letter is sealed then it has a five-penny stamp on it', the success rates in choosing the correct examples to illustrate the truth were not. Many more students gave the right answer when the problem was based in everyday reality. Psychologists assumed that the end goal of developing cognition was formal logic unsupported by context, what Donaldson (1978) calls 'disembedded thought'. Yet it is the habitual mode of thought only of a minority and many adults never attain formal thought at all (Ennis, 1975; Taplin and Staudenmayer, 1973; Weitz *et al.* 1974). If this had been realized we would probably not have spent years baffling generations of young children with the kind of abstract thinking tests Piaget used. Furthermore, when a transition to more formal modes of thought is achieved it is usually assumed to come about through cognitive meta-awareness and the conscious use of control processes and self-reflecting techniques in problem-solving acquired in school and more properly regarded as a post-literacy not pre-school accomplishment (see Olson, Chapter 6).

If one seriously entertains the notion that child and adult thinking processes are not that different, but what has to develop in the child through experience is first his understanding of events in the world and second his meta-awareness for the deployment of cognitive strategies, then the nature of experience which differentiates children from grown-ups and from children in different cultures, becomes crucial. When the child's personal experiences are plugged into by the happy selection of experimental tasks that fit into the child's world (Hughes, 1975; McGarrigle, 1974; Light, Buckingham and Robbins, 1979) or by the child himself initiating activity and volunteering conversation about his experiences (Slobin and Welsh, 1973; Donaldson, 1978; Cole *et al.*, 1978) then he may well be capable of deductive reasoning.

Very young children can take two separate pieces of information and combine these to draw a conclusion that is not just plausible but is the result of a valid and necessary inference. They may not provide Piagetian 'justification' for their conclusions but should we expect the knowledge of such young children to be explicit (see Robinson, Chapter 5)? We do not claim that a young child can display a full mastery of formal logic. They may not make all the necessary conclusions and only the necessary conclusions all the time but then neither do adults (Wallington, 1974). The operation of propositional logic requires the concept of logical necessity, that is, only certain relations between premises are seen to produce necessarily true conclusions. Young children are more likely to interpret circumstantial facts in an argument as being as useful in reaching a valid conclusion as logically critical ones, although they are still more likely to choose the latter in constructing their arguments (Bereiter and Hidi, 1977). Also while understanding the presuppositions in an argument and making inferences from them, children arrive at the indirect and often pragmatic implications of statements by using their own real-world knowledge about the content of a particular argument

(Omanson, Warren and Trabasso, 1978; Hidi and Hildyard, 1979).

The issue therefore becomes one of how children acquire, code and store the familiar situations and context that makes deductive reasoning possible for them. Piaget himself envisaged that children could conjure up an image from a particular state of affairs, use personal schemes of analogy or memories of earlier reasoning, and then read off conclusions from their internal representation in dealing with logical arguments (Piaget, 1928, 1959). Schank and Abelson (1977) have suggested that adults and children code experience in episodic form. If a sequence of activities occur together, that is how they will be stored in memory, often effectively in one trial. Memory is grouped contextually and the associations that connect objects and events are automatically preserved in a quite stereotyped way as scripts. Possible scripts for a child might be 'going to a party', 'hair-washing night' or 'a visit to the shops'. This last example Schank has recorded from the spontaneous conversation of a $2\frac{1}{2}$-year-old child with its parent: 'Next time when you go to the market I want you to buy straws, pay for them and put it in the package and take home. Okay?'

The suggestion that the child acquires a general list of specifications as a prototype is plausible, given that essential word meaning is often stored by prototypical reference (Bowerman, 1976). Schank argues that new scripts are learnt by organizing them around the primitive actions they enable – ingestion, physical movement of self, etc. We already know that toddlers observed at home show linguistic comprehension of nine of Schank's twelve primitive action schemes (Booth, 1978) and Piaget, bearing in mind his sensori-motor theory of early intelligence, would hardly quarrel with such a thesis.

Scripts become organized by direct or vicarious experience. They become elaborated with continuous exposure and would fade out without it. Eventually the child develops a parsimonious distribution of knowledge so that some experiences get handled by the same script and others do not. Going to tea with granny, for example, while it might contain features such as best dress, requirement to hug ageing relative, minding manners, and sweeties as a reward for intact porcelain on departure, would still carry the more general features of 'An Event': going out, cleaner clothes, travelling, something to eat, fun/boredom, etc.

We want to argue that scripts help reasoning in an important way because once a script is activated children know what to expect. A particular situation or problem the child encounters can be slotted into an already understood set of relationships. These help to make explicit or predict the connections between the things the child is experiencing and so aid understanding. A preschooler's comprehension, for instance of linguistic instruction, is governed by the canonical relationships of the objects he is instructed to manipulate (Hoogengraad, Grieve, Baldwin and Campbell, 1978). As would be expected from everyday commerce with objects, things get put *on* inverted boxes but *in* upright ones. Thus the expectation of what is meant is shaped by context, and no script means no understanding.

There is no doubt that children as young as 5 years can operate a broad range of inference types and all equally well (Warren, Nicholas and Trabasso, 1980). These include an understanding of physical and psychological causation, motivation, enabling situations and moral and social judgements depicted in text. The details of handling ever-proliferating episodic stores however, like so much else in semantics, still require prolonged study.

Nevertheless, two powerful methods of script acquisition are well known. First, through the child's imaginative play, and second, through parental support, the cognitive scaffolding that Bruner (1975) supposes adults provide in the years before formal education begins. Dunn and Wooding (1976) gave us a clue when they reported that, regardless of class differences, mothers were more likely to intervene in and extend their 2-year-old's play when it could be described as being symbolic or representational in content.

But the main evidence for our assertion that parents of preschoolers rehearse, activate and elaborate the episodic memory and scripts of their offspring, and that this is related to their reasoning ability, comes from home observations collected as part of the South London Under-Fives Project. Findings are reported from three hours of natural observation made on each of sixty mother/child pairs when the child was between 2–3 years of age (Mills and Puckering, 1982). Children with expressive language delay were excluded from the analysis. Families were all working class (Registrar General's non-manual 3, 4 and 5 categories) and not particularly disadvantaged. Mother and index child spent at least half of every day together.

When we were satisfied that each pair was mutually involved in joint activities or chat at a level that made possible reciprocal contributions from them both, we recorded all such contributions provided that each contribution introduced or expanded the ongoing activity or chat between them at some conceptual level. We also specified that maternal contributions had to be relevant to the child's ongoing behaviour and appropriate to his level of cognitive development (hence we call this measure a link). We stipulated that the mother had to plug into some aspect of the child's world before we were interested in her contribution. This contextual constraint we argue should dramatically facilitate the 2-year-old child's understanding by tapping his knowledge-base at the right level and thus enable him to activate scripts almost as easily as when he volunteers spontaneous contributions of his own.

Some mothers mentally situate the child within his own family and social context and take pains to make his current experiences relevant to him. Others do not. All mothers tend to respond when the child, looking at a book or picture, says 'That's a cow' by saying, 'Yes it says moo' or 'Yes there are two of them, do you see the other one?' or 'Yes it is lying down, perhaps it doesn't feel well.' But only some mothers would be likely to say, 'Yes, do you remember that weekend when Daddy took us on a picnic and the cow ate your hat?'. Or 'It's the same colour as the cow who fell in the canal – you used to love that story when you were little.'

What we have found is that only those mothers who make these definite personalized attempts to match their contribution to the child's experience have children who make 'Donaldson-type' inferences spontaneously at some time during the conversation when we are present taking data. These maternal contributions we have called world links. This relationship is only found between maternal world links and child deductive reasoning, it is not found for the ordinary links which all mothers of 2-year-olds make. The number of ordinary links made does not relate to children's inferential ability, but it is possible that categorizing ordinary links in more detail by type of information proffered might relate to child reasoning. This has not yet been looked at. Interestingly mothers who make world links spend the most time in imaginative and pretend play with their children.

Tizard *et al.* (1982) found that very few working-class mothers facilitated their child's intellectual inquiry as evidenced by responding to 'why' questions when they were observed at home with their 3–4-year-old children. And when these mothers asked questions which required the child to give a label, description, explanation or recall of events, children gave adequately explicit and focused replies to less than half the total number of maternal inquiries made. Here conversational interplay between the two did not seem to influence the child's intellectual status (Stanford Binet) or efficient cognitive meshing. Was it perhaps unproductive for child cognition simply because, as Tizard observes, the things that enthuse and interest a child and on which he will spontaneously comment are not discussed with him? (This is particularly true of nursery schools (Wood *et al.*, 1980)).

In specifying a contextually appropriate constraint on maternal contributions our study may be reporting on children whose interest has already been aroused through maternal selection of material likely to activate and elaborate scripts. In our study less than 10 per cent of all links, and even fewer world links, received no adequate response from the children. Nevertheless, our correlational evidence is at best suggestive. What is required is to establish the existence or absence of certain scripts in a sample of young children and then get them to comment on situations which might require these scripts to be used in order to solve some problem involving the making of inferences.

Not all the examples of deductive thinking however that came from our sample of 2–3-year-olds could be said to come from specific scripts. About half developed out of social discourse and argumentation in which the child seemed to identify the mother's plan and intentions. If children can identify the goal or goals of a set of actions these direct the course of inferences from actions, defining the relationships between them. They also specify the constraints on, and choices open to, actions.

That young children have sophisticated social scenarios, is evidenced by their undoubted ability to manipulate their social environment, using pragmatic considerations. Dore (1976) in bugging 3-year-olds' conversation in nursery school, describes how a couple of small boys who wished to exclude a third from their play did so by remarking – when the victim positioned himself alongside them – 'We don't sit on tables in this school'.

Again, during our observations, a mother was struggling to occupy her child with a difficult jigsaw puzzle and watch the TV racing at the same time. As her 2½-year-old clumsily dislodged a piece the mother had just successfully placed, the mother commented, 'I'm only going to do this once you know', to which the child, quick as a flash, replied 'I don't have to do it at all'. This conscious deployment of social skill and pragmatic presuppositions suggests an underlying knowledge-base built up from experience which we might call social scripts or scenarios. We argue that they facilitate deductive thinking in just the same way as Schank's specific scripts and that they are learned and used very early in life.

Thus, as mother and child ($2\frac{1}{2}$ years) made Lego houses together, the conversation went as follows:

M: Whatever happened to all the Lego we had?
K: I lost it.
M: Yes, I thought it might have been you.
K: No, it was Ann [sister] who did it.
M: I should Koko. (Derisory tone, not believing child)
K: I couldn't have lost it, cause it's here. See. (Child goes to pockets of dressing gown on bed and gets out quantities of Lego.)
K: And that red one's [dressing gown] not mine, is it?

1st premise: Lego is lost – someone, possibly index child, did it.
2nd premise: Sister is responsible – Lego found in her garment.
Conclusion: Index child not responsible and anyway Lego not lost, so no problem.
Pragmatic consideration: Mother cross Lego is lost and mistakenly blames child.

Social scaffolding does not always have to be provided by an adult for deductive thinking to occur. Consider the following example. A child, almost 3 years old, had been trying physically to prevent her 2-year-old sibling from jumping on and off the sofa with her. Finally she said:

People with shoes on can't jump.
I haven't got them on, so I can jump
but you can't you've got shoes.
So there.

This child even put the first premise by enumerating explicitly the general rule to be considered. One imagines she might have assumed the pragmatic force of her utterance to be supported by a common social scenario that children are not often allowed to stand on the furniture in shoes.

Clementson-Mohr (1982) makes a strong case that we should study the processes of the mind by integrating social and practical intelligence by supposing that their ontogeny is not separately derived. He discusses the nature of imitation but his claim that this is a social event 'and will undergo successful developmental investigation only within the context of naturalistic and semi-naturalistic observation of meaningful social interaction' could equally well be applied to children's thinking.

In a replication of McGarrigle's naughty teddy conservation task with 4–6-year-olds, Dockrell *et al.* (1980) reconcile the facilitative effect of teddy with Rose and Blank's (1974) pragmatic viewpoint that the experimenter's second question must require a different answer since he couldn't be stupid enough to repeat himself. They suggest that teddy in distracting the experimenter sets up a social scenario such that the child can understand teddy's role. 'It seems to us', they say, 'that behavioural interpretation of setting is not a variable that functions autonomously like reading or counting but rather pervades all communicative interactions and reflects the status of other aspects of the communicator's knowledge.' What could do this so well as a social scenario?

We should not assume that the activation and use of social scripts is in any sense secondary or less important than those which encapsulate past and present experience of a conceptual or historic kind. Tizard *et al.* (1982) notice that cognitive demands frequently have a pragmatic function – particularly so at home when children are often asked to justify their actions. For example, when a child is asked: 'Why are you jumping on the sofa?' The answer: 'You said I could if I took my shoes off' certainly fulfils a 'cognitive' function, but the argumentation stems from pragmatic knowledge not abstract conceptual issues. Furthermore, frequent negotiation of control and autonomy by 2-year-olds at home provides them with practical experience and an intrinsic interest in thinking.

We have argued that the episodic memory store built up by the routine social and semantic events encountered by young children provides a ready-made mechanism for relating information and drawing conclusions. In a rudimentary form we have tried to provide an alternative conceptual framework for *how* the deductive thinking of young children that we and other researchers have found, can develop. Scripts provide an interpretive system out of which logic can grow. No doubt the detailed perfecting of scripts goes on all our lives, but Schank is right to maintain that script building proceeds at a tremendous rate in young children. For this reason it is important to establish the ways in which script acquisition occurs. From our work it is clear that the process is not consciously educational or particularly taxing but can be seen as a by-product of mothering in the preschool years.

We have presented an impressive body of evidence to support the notion that very young children can reason successfully so long as the context of the problem is set within the child's own experience. We now turn to transitive inference questions; one type of the formal, disembodied, reasoning problems presented to children in Piaget's classic investigations, and consider first the conflicting evidence regarding children's ability to solve these problems, and second, the relationship between the cognitive demands of the task and the conceptual knowledge that children bring to the problem. In particular, we are interested to know if the ability to solve disembodied reasoning problems, as opposed to problems deliberately set within the child's understanding, also depends upon knowledge developed through real-world experience.

According to Piaget, preoperational children cannot make transitive inferences (Inhelder and Piaget, 1958). A transitive inference is made when the relationship between two items is found from the relationship between each of these items and a shared central term. Piaget for example used boxes of different weight, and after telling the children 'A is heavier than B, and C is lighter than B' asked 'which is heaviest?' or 'which is lightest?'. He believed that the children's difficulty arose because they lacked three essential mental operations: an inability to make judgements about comparative relationships which leads to statements such as 'Edith is fairer than Suzanne' being understood as Edith is fair and Suzanne is fair; an inability to reverse relationships; and an inability to integrate separate pieces of information.

Bryant and Trabasso (1971) however produced evidence which suggested that children as young as 4 years old could answer transitive inference questions correctly under certain circumstances. They trained children to learn the relationships between adjacent pairs of sticks taken from a series of five sticks: A, B, C, D, E. The sticks were presented in pairs with the size differences hidden. When all the pairs had been learned, the children were tested on the size relationship between sticks B and D on which no training had been given. Their ability to judge the BD relationship correctly was taken as evidence for the making of transitive inferences. On the basis of this result, Bryant and Trabasso (1971) and Bryant (1974) argued that children's failure in classic transitive inference questions arises from lapses in memory for the information given and that young children can make inferences about size relationships using a central term.

Memorizing and not-forgetting, however, are not necessarily the same thing. In two experiments using 8-year-old children, in which the information could not be forgotten, since it was written down, few children succeeded in answering the questions correctly to a level above chance: Exp. 1: 2/27 children, Exp. 2: 8/30 children (Funnell, 1978, unpublished). And in a further experiment, in which the information was again supplied in written form, ability to answer transitive inference questions was not related to short-term memory as measured by auditory-verbal digit span (Pearsons product moment $r = 0.09$). So, it does not appear that preventing the children from forgetting the information is sufficient to enable them to succeed in making transitive inferences.

Why, then, were the children in Bryant and Trabasso's experiment successful? The answer seems to lie in the use of both labels, *longer* and *shorter* being given for each stick. For example, the children were not only told that the blue stick was longer than the red stick, but also that the red stick was shorter than the blue stick. When Trabasso, Riley and Wilson (1974) repeated this experiment but using only one label, longer or shorter, two-thirds of the children in the group were unable to learn the pair relationships to criterion level. And of the small group who succeeded, the correct answers to the transitive inference BD comparison were not significantly above chance.

Bryant (1974) was particularly prepared to believe that young children might make transitive inferences since experiments had shown that children of 4 years could use 'relative' codes. In a series of presentations of pairs of shapes, children were able to learn to identify the smaller or larger shape, but not to identify a particular shape on the basis of its exact, physical dimensions (Graham, Ernhart, Craft and Berman, 1964; Lawrenson and Bryant, 1972). Since 4-year-olds could consistently choose the smaller or larger of different pairs of items, Bryant (1974) assumed that these children could understand relationships such as smaller or larger. However, a perceptual judgement between two items does not necessarily require the use of relative codes. Certainly the choice of one shape has to be made with *reference* to the other, but this reference may be made on the basis of contrast, such as choose the small one. An ability, therefore, to judge relative size is not the same as understanding relative terms, and this is clearly borne out in Bryant and Trabasso's study. The 4-year-old children in their study were unable to understood the words 'bigger' and 'smaller', so 'big' and 'small' had to be used instead.

This observation deals a double blow to Bryant and Trabasso's claims that young children can make transitive inferences. First of all it questions the evidence that young children can use relative codes. Second, since transitive inferences involve relationships between items, children who give the correct answers have apparently made relational decisions when in fact, no verbal information about relationships was ever given.

Subsequent experiments have clearly shown that most 5-year-olds, and many 8-year-olds make categorical judgements about size relationships (Funnell, 1978). In an experiment carried out to investigate how children understand statements such as 'A is bigger than B', children were asked to give legs to space creatures (called Jupes) according to the rules which the creatures had brought with them. The Jupes' bodies were different colours but all the same shape, while the seven different sizes of legs were all coloured silver. The rules were given in the form of the statements used in transitive inference problems, for example 'Red Jupe is taller than Blue Jupe. Green Jupe is shorter than Blue Jupe'. The sentences were spoken separately to the child and repeated several times; only when the children had responded to the first statement was the second statement given. Three main strategies emerged (see Table 7.1): First,

Table 7.1 Number of children in each age group consistently using each strategy

Performance strategy		*No. of children*	
Statement 1	*Statement 2*	*5 yrs (n = 20)*	*8 yrs (n = 20)*
1 Jupe	1 Jupe	5	4
2 Jupes	2 Jupes	8	3
2 Jupes	1 Jupe	1	8
No definite strategy		6	5

two Jupes were made, one in response to each statement, second, four Jupes were made, two to each statement, and third, three Jupes were made in the correct size relationships.

When the third strategy was used, the second Jupe made in the first statement was always given an intermediate size of legs. Using a middle leg size was clearly related to making only three Jupes and is a direct indication that these children understood the terms taller and shorter as relationships of size. Children who only made one Jupe, or who made both Jupes in each statement, used extreme leg sizes. For example, given the statement 'Red Jupe is taller than Blue Jupe, Green Jupe is shorter than Blue Jupe' children making one Jupe, made a tall Red Jupe, a short green Jupe and no blue Jupe at all. While children who made both Jupes to both statements made a tall red Jupe and a short blue Jupe and then made another blue Jupe with long legs, either by taking the red Jupe's legs away and giving them to the short blue Jupe, or by making an entirely new blue Jupe with long legs, placing it next to the short blue Jupe, and then going on to make a short green Jupe.

Obviously, those children who interpret the instructions in terms of relationships, also integrate the information in the two statements. It is also clear that children who make both Jupes to both statements understand relationships in terms of contrast, so that a statement such as red Jupe is taller than blue Jupe, means red Jupe is tall and blue Jupe is short. Children who interpret comparative terms as absolute sizes do not integrate the separate statements in the instructions.

How then is it that children in Bryant and Trabasso's study learnt the pair relationships and made correct answers to the transitive pair, when they could not understand relational adjectives such as bigger, and are unlikely to have been able to integrate the separate pieces of information? As we have already noted, the use of both relative terms was crucial to their experiment, since without it, most children could not learn the initial pairs. Trabasso, Riley and Wilson (1974) produced evidence which suggests that the training resulted in the children assembling a linear array from the separate pairs of sticks, and used this to make their judgements about the unlearnt BD pair. The children learnt the outer AE sticks first, then sticks B and D and finally stick C was learnt. They argue that this is evidence for internal representation in the form of linear order. In fact, Youniss and Furth (1973) had initially objected that Bryant and Trabasso had failed to establish a reasoning capacity that was independent of the use of memory rules. It now seems that the use of both labels and the memory training involved led to the integration of separate pieces of information that the children would normally leave as isolated components.

There is good evidence to suggest that separate pieces of information regarding one subject tend to become connected to other memories of that subject in long-term storage (Loftus and Palmer, 1974; Garrod and Sanford, 1977; Davis and Sinha, 1950). It is likely that in Bryant and Trabasso's experiment children began by thinking that the blue stick which is shorter than the red stick, was a different stick to the blue stick which is longer than the green stick. But the organization of the material in memory may well have resulted in the combination of the two separate pieces of information into one entity: the blue stick, which is longer than the green stick and shorter than the red stick.

As we have already observed, there is excellent evidence to show that children can integrate separate pieces of information and that Piaget was wrong in believing that this was one basic difficulty which prevented pre-operational children from making transitive inferences. Not only have the children in Bryant and Trabasso's study clearly learnt to integrate information, but Donaldson has provided many examples of such integration, even of quite contradictory material by nursery children (Donaldson, 1978).

Why don't the children who understand relational terms in categorical terms in the Jupe experiment, integrate the information? We would like to argue that only when children are forced to integrate the relationships between separate pairs of items do they begin to understand relative terms such as longer and shorter in terms of relationships. In most situations in which a child encounters judgements about size differences the child is not forced to integrate information and categorical judgements supply the right answer. For example, if asked to choose the smallest ball from a number, he is unlikely to then have to choose the same ball when asked to choose the biggest. Thus objects can be assigned to two classes big and small in any decision, and the fact that the object might be judged as both big and small does not arise.

However, when children have to make relationships between themselves and other items they are forced to realize that while physically they remain the same size, nevertheless they differ in size in relation to other items, and are sometimes bigger, sometimes smaller. Thus, faced with the contradiction 'Daddy is big and I am small, baby brother is small and I am big', the child learns that objects cannot be assigned to consistent groups of big and small, but vary in relation to other objects along a continuum, and that size is relative.

Good evidence that relationships to oneself are understood more easily than relationships between other items was obtained from a final transitive reference experiment using 8-year-old children (Funnell, unpublished). These children (sixty in number) were given two sets of problems in which the central term was either another person's name or a first person pronoun; for example,

(a) Richard is taller than David. Richard is shorter than Peter.

(b) I am taller than Michael. I am shorter than Brian.

When the personal pronoun problems were given before the third person problems, children were significantly better at both types of problems (t-test $p < 0.01$), but if the third person problems were given first, children were equally poor at both types. This suggests that when the personal relationships were given first, some children were given insight into the nature of the problem, and they were then able to apply the same reasoning to third person problems. But, without this help, children who met the third person problems first gave up the search for a reasoning strategy so that when the first person problems arrived, they failed to recognize the explicit relationships inherent in these problems.

It is not sensible to talk about children's ability to integrate information as if integration were a mental operation detached from the knowledge to which it is applied. Integration can only occur when the independent items of information are already related conceptually and is therefore itself a product of understanding.

Failure to answer classical transitive problems is therefore not the result of lack of abstract mental operations such as integration or reversibility, as Piaget suggests, but arises from insufficient experience with real-world situations in which the child learns to relate size along a continuum, rather than in terms of contrast. Piaget's own theory of horizontal decalage, developed to explain children's variability in reasoning according to the materials used, is in itself, clear recognition that apparently abstract reasoning is firmly rooted in the understanding of the materials to which it is applied.

Another area of development in which the role of experience should be scrutinized is the acquisition of reading and spelling skills. Here a unique set of translation processes from print to meaning and sound as in reading and from meaning and sound to orthography as in spelling, have to be built up in the primary school years almost from scratch. Children come to the task able to speak and understand oral language but with only a tacit and limited knowledge of the phonetic and articulatory constituents of English words (Read, 1971; Liberman, 1973) and totally ignorant of the complications of English orthography and its relationship to spoken language.

It has been argued that children will not read unless they achieve an operational understanding of certain key concepts (Marcel, 1980). We would agree that children must understand that reading should be for meaning; that meaning is represented by visual symbols; and that these symbols match onto speech. And we have already argued that fitting these concepts into the child's existing knowledge provides the necessary interface to 'operational understanding' and is the goal of pedagogy.

But these conditions are a necessary and not sufficient condition for proficient reading and for the proficient teaching of reading. We must understand what the cognitive processes involved in reading are and how these processes work together. How does the transition to literacy come about? How can we reliably diagnose the sources of difficulty in young readers before they are irrevocably switched off from the printed word, and offer successful remediation?

Education, with regard to the teaching of reading has been largely a 'suck it and see' approach, and has been bedevilled by a cyclical pedagogy based on theoretical extremes (ITA, Look-and-Say, etc.). There has been little evaluation of what a particular method achieves or fails to achieve in establishing the normal range of reading skills because until relatively recently there has been no systematic attempt to understand how the processes that have to be built up in reading relate and function. Without a plan of the reading system teachers have been working in the dark.

Now, however, reading processes are beginning to be understood, and a model, sufficiently detailed to be usefully applied to practice is emerging. Certainly, most of the evidence upon which the model is based originates from work with adults, both normal or brain-damaged after trauma, but the basic premise we wish to make is that the reading processes exposed through experiments with adults are the very processes that children have to establish when learning to read. Thus, in understanding how the literate adult reads, we have knowledge we can apply to the learner reader and use to pinpoint the locus of particular problems.

It is impossible here to refer to all the studies which have made significant contributions to our present understanding of reading processes: reading is a highly complex mental activity involving many functional components, and its study has spanned many years. Henderson (1982) and Coltheart, Patterson and Marshall (1980) provide comprehensive coverage of current theories and investigations into normal and pathological reading processes.

Understanding of the intricate processes that contribute to each of the major components of the reading system remains obscure; we do not yet know for example how exactly letters are identified, or how words are broken down into syllables or phonemes. While these are obviously essential parts of the whole process of reading, we will not discuss such issues here, but will concentrate instead upon the relationship between the major components (for example, between the processing of the orthographic and phonological form of a word) and the relevance of the interconnections for strategies in reading.

While there is some disagreement about the nature and number of the reading strategies available to the normal reader, the bulk of the evidence now supports the existence of three pathways from print to sound, which for clarity are illustrated in the flow diagram presented in Figure 7.1.

In this diagram, the pathways can be classified into lexical and non-lexical processes. The two lexical processes depend upon the identification of the whole letter string as a known word. This is accomplished by matching the letter string against records of familiar letter sequences held in the orthographic store (process 3). Once the letter string has been identified as a word, lexical pathways diverge. The *semantic lexical pathway* (route 1) first accesses the word meaning (process 4) and then retrieves the phonological form of the word (i.e. the sound) from the store of phonological codes (process 5). The *phonological lexical pathway* (route 2) retrieves the phonological word form directly (process 5), thus bypassing semantic mediation.

Non-lexical reading processes break the letter string into familiar letters and letter groups (process 1) and directly access the sounds appropriate to these letters from the phonological store (process 2).

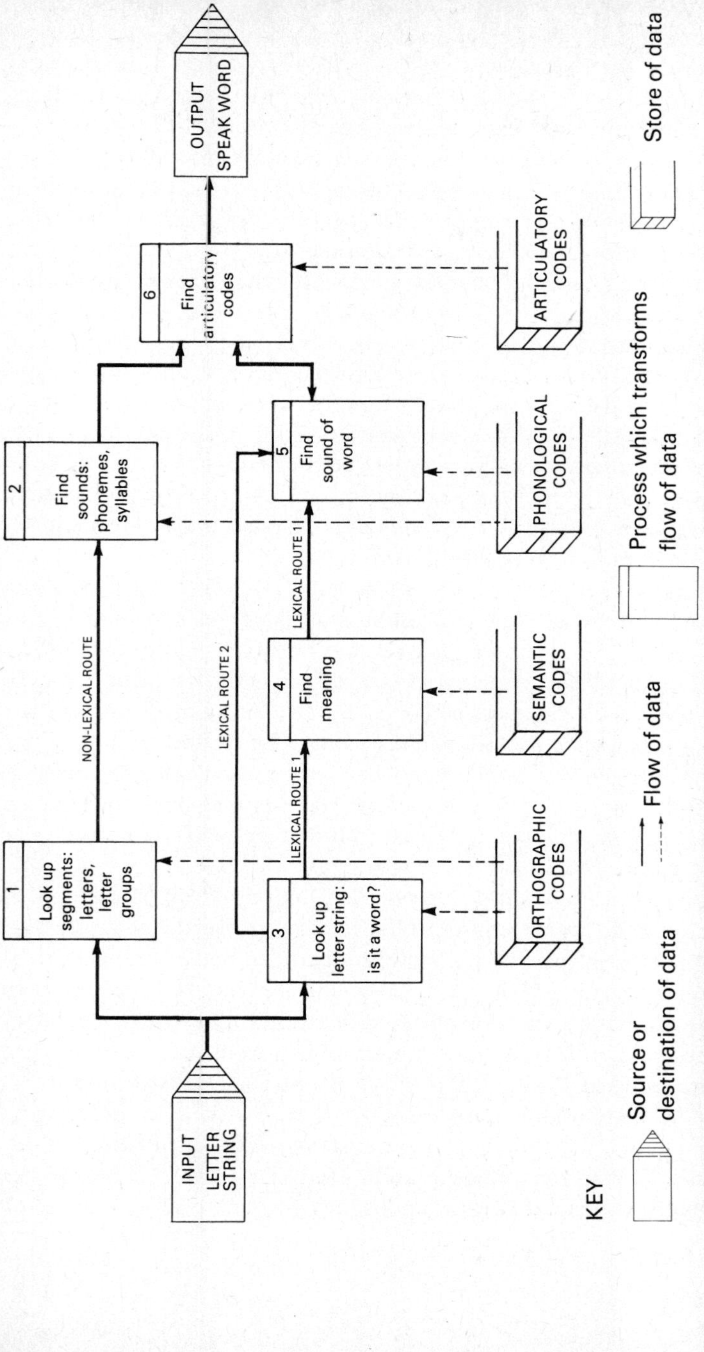

Figure 7.1 Logical data flow diagram of reading processes involved in word recognition.
Source: Funnell, in preparation.

These phonological segments are then blended together. One theory suggests that this blending takes place in the articulatory loop of working memory (Baddeley, 1977), but no attempt has been made to incorporate processes for blending into this model. At the final stage of reading, the words are spoken aloud after the articulatory codes for verbal production have been activated (process 6).

The competent reader requires use of both lexical and non-lexical reading strategies. The non-lexical route is essential for decoding new words into sound and also appears to act as a check against errors made by lexical strategies. Lexical strategies are necessary not only to allow direct access to lexical semantics, but also to prevent mispronunciation errors which arise when the non-lexical route operates in isolation. Since the English language does not have a regular or consistent correspondence between letters and sounds, irregular written words such as *island* are mispronounced e.g. **'izlənd** when non-lexical strategies function alone. So it is that the reading errors which a reader makes act as clues to the reading strategies employed, as the following mistakes made by children with severe reading difficulty show.

A 16-year-old developmental dyslexic (CD), when asked to define and then to read aloud the printed word *gauge* said 'a big dip . . . gorge', yet read out the letters g.a.u.g.e. correctly (Coltheart, 1982). She often failed to read irregular words correctly, and this error, in which the vowel di-graph is given its most frequent pronunciation (ɔ) indicates use of the non-lexical route. Her understanding of the word is erroneously based upon her own phonological rendering. Baffled by the production of incorrect words and non-words when reading aloud, this reader must rely on context to correct her understanding.

Another developmental dyslexic (AF) observed by Maggie Mills and similar in many ways to CD, is able to use the phonological lexical pathway (pathway 2) in reading since her pronunciation of irregular words is nearly always correct. She, like CD, has to reach meaning via the phonological representation of a word: access to semantics directly from the orthographic specification of the word appears to be impaired. Thus, if AF is given a single printed word, one of a homophone pair (*bare*, *bear*) and asked to define and pronounce it, then *bare* is pronounced correctly, but defined as 'an animal'. If given /**bɛə**/ orally and asked to spell it, AF first writes *bair* which is then defined as 'an animal' and then writes *bear* which is defined as 'no clothes on'.

Furthermore, if presented with a pseudohomophone to read (e.g. *frait*) AF judges it to be a word, pronounces it like *freight* and defines it as 'something on a lorry'. If *frate* is presented instead, the same responses occur. Only a direct link from the orthographic specification of the word to semantics can disambiguate homophones which share the same phonological structure. AF cannot reliably choose between the various spellings of *freight* to match the definition given, and while this seldom causes a problem when reading in context, written language performance is seriously impaired.

Many dyslexic children show a contrasting pattern of errors to CD and AF. These children have difficulty in reading aloud novel words or non-words. Unlike normal readers, the ability of the dyslexic children to decode novel words does not improve with an increase in reading age as measured by standard tests (Snowling, 1980). Only the vocabulary of familiar written words that can be read by lexical strategies improves. To read novel words, non-lexical processes are required and these do not appear to function.

The children reported so far have severe and possibly intractable problems in reading, but many readers who finally overcome these difficulties display early reading patterns similar to dyslexia, and we suspect in these cases that the teaching approach used may be responsible.

Clearly the processes we have described have implications for the teaching of reading. Two popular teaching schemes, Breakthrough to Literacy (BTL) and Traditional Phonic Instruction (TP) are theoretically appropriate to investigate in the light of the reading processes proposed. Briefly BTL uses written words volunteered from the beginner reader's vocabulary which are held in a sentence maker and dictionary from which the child can draw printed words to express his thoughts. No words are split into phonemes although morphemic chunks (ed, ing) are used. Children copy out and read their sentences to the teacher and draw pictures about them. Phonic awareness is taught later. TP is very different, phonic techniques are taught via colour and story codes so that particular sounds are associated with the beginning letter of a particular character's name and all similar sounds have the same colour or shape. Single letters or combinations change colour or shape when their sound changes, and letters having the same sound have the same colour or shape. Words are split up into constituent sounds and sound segments are blended according to associated visual codes such as shape and colour. See Figure 7.2 for example.

Figure 7.2

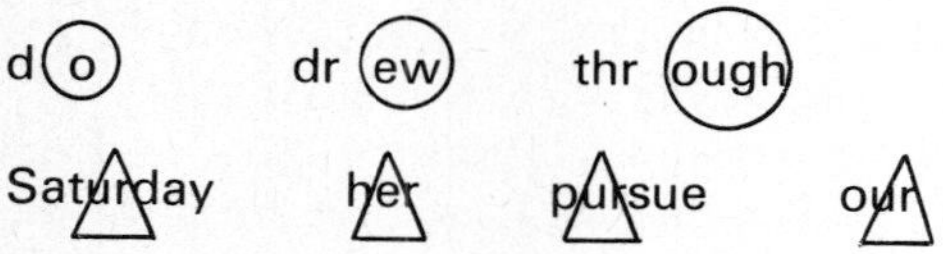

In a study by Rao (1982) twenty-four children (age range 6.5 to 7.4 months) equated for IQ (Raven's matrices), sex and reading age were given various reading tasks to establish the status of their reading strategies. Half were taught entirely by BTL and half by TP. Teachers were observed first to see that their teaching methods were actually as described. The main findings were first that BTL and TP groups were equally accurate in pronouncing high frequency irregular words (67 and 60 per cent correct respectively) and regular words (70 and 81 per cent for BTL and TP respectively) and second, that the children taught BTL relied on the initial part of a word to the virtual exclusion of any other information, while the TP group did not. Thus, when given a translation task where a single four-letter regular or irregular word spoken aloud has to be matched to one of a set of printed words from which was missing the initial, middle or end letter, the results in Table 7.2 were obtained. In this task the BTL children cannot perform above chance where initial or middle information in a word is missing. The same conclusion can be drawn by examining performance on a visual matching task of CVC non-words, or irregular words to see which letter position is most frequently matched when a choice is offered (*cug*: che; tuk; ilg, or *any*: all; one; spy). Table 7.3 indicates the performance.

Table 7.2

	Letter of word missing			
	Beginning	*Middle*	*Last*	
BTL	16%	55%	72%	*Percentage correctly matched*
TP	75%	100%	97%	

Table 7.3

	Letter of word missing				*No response*
	First	*Middle*	*Last*		
Non-words					
BTL	93%	5%	0%	Percentage correctly matched	2%
TP	40%	23%	33%		4%
Irregular words					
BTL	73%	3%	14%		10%
TP	23%	28%	48%		1%

For the BTL group attention is riveted to initial visual information, but the children taught by phonic methods attend fairly consistently to all the letters in the stimulus.

In a further experiment the groups of children were given single printed non-words that could be legitimately pronounced in more than one way. For example, the non-word *tave* can be pronounced using the regular pronunciation of the letter group *ave* to rhyme with *gave*, or an irregular pronunciation to rhyme with *have*. Since *have* is the most frequently occurring word containing the letter group *ave*, a lexical strategy in which the letter string is matched against known words is more likely to produce an irregular pronunciation, while the regular pronunciation is more likely to result from a non-lexical strategy. It was found that the BTL group gave a regular pronunciation on only 16 per cent of occasions in contrast to the TP group's 53 per cent. Responses reflecting irregular word pronunciation did not differ between the groups. The most striking result however was that real words, sharing at least the first and last letters of the non-word, were substituted on 46 per cent of occasions by the BTL group but not at all by the TP group.

Again, in a lexical decision task, in which non-words were derived from real words by changing one letter, the BTL group were three times as likely to judge an irregular non-word to be a word than were the TP group. When these same children were tested six months before the work described, only the TP group were able to match a pseudo-homophone *burd* to a picture of a bird and only they were able to perform rhyming judgements which depended on the end segments of regular words.

Thus, while the two groups are equally accurate in reading aloud words, the TP group in addition show evidence of non-lexical processing in segmenting phonemes, paying attention to all parts of a word, in rhyming and translating pseudohomophones to meaning, using more flexible chunking strategies, and choosing the most regular pronunciation of a letter string with which to interpret the sounds of non-words. These findings are broadly in line with those reported by Alegria (1980) for phonemic word segmentation skill in 7-year-olds; Barr (1978) for non-word or real word substitution errors in 6-year-olds' reading, and Peters (1967) for type of errors made by 8-year-olds in spelling to dictation.

We may conclude that the relative status of the developmental reading strategies we have described is at least at the early stage of reading markedly different as a function of reading exposure.

It is not surprising, perhaps, that the BTL group showed a lack of phonic strategies, since phonic techniques had not been taught, but it is disturbing that these children also know less about the letters that make up a word than the children taught to read by phonic methods, and this deficit is a potential cause of difficulty. The identification of the complete letter string as a known word depends, not upon recognition of the wholistic shape or pattern of the written word, as is still widely believed, but upon identification of letters and their relative position in the word (Snowling and Frith, 1981). Given a small vocabulary of orthographically dissimilar words, attention to the initial letter only, or to the relative length of each word, may be sufficient to distinguish one word from another. But as the vocabulary increases, detailed analysis of written words, particularly short words containing commonly occurring letters, is necessary for accurate identification: children who confuse such words as *was* and *saw*, seem to have processed the letters in the word, but have failed to attend to their order. While reading may proceed fairly well on the basis of incomplete orthographic representations, since context will help to disambiguate a word, detailed analysis of the specific physical characteristics and location of letters in words, would appear to be essential for efficient spelling; phonic methods of teaching appear to be superior for these purposes.

There is little evidence to suggest that phonic awareness in reading emerges spontaneously as a result of exposure to words through Look-and-Say methods. Many familiar words given to beginner readers are irregular; ten of the first 40 words in the BTL scheme are words whose mapping between letters and sounds cannot be generalized to other words (e.g. are, was, said, want). Letter to sound conversion rules implicitly derived from such words will result in confusion.

To develop non-lexical strategies, children must chunk print into segments bearing a specific sound representation (ng, she, oa) and also be able to blend sound segments into larger units. Here explicit teaching methods (e.g. traditional phonic instruction or the use of SRA work cards) seem to be absolutely necessary: firstly because the choice of letter groups into which the written word is segmented will greatly affect success; for example, a child might segment *boat* as b/o/a/t rather than b/oa/t; and secondly because children do not appear spontaneously to segment word sounds into phonemes. Liberman (1973) noted a rapid improvement from zero ability to 70 per cent success in phoneme segmentation during the first year of schooling, and also observed that good readers were much better at phoneme segmentation than poor readers.

Phonic segmentation and blending is thought to demand the use of short-term auditory memory and poor readers are frequently reported to make poor use of this process (Shankweiler, Liberman, Mark, Fowler and Fischer, 1979; Nelson, 1980; Hull, 1977). It is a moot point whether these poor readers fail to use auditory short-term memory processes because of some sort of developmental delay, or whether lack of training in phonic techniques is specifically to blame.

The diagnostic value of the model of reading processes we have described is clear enough, and since probably no amount of exposure to reading practice can rectify some of the developmental impairment in the most severely affected children we have described, the ever-recurring experience of failure for these readers could be avoided by the sensitive teacher, through concentration on those reading strategies that yield most success.

Proficiency in the translation processes required in reading normally results from practice at reading activities which failing readers have learnt very skilfully to avoid. Often secondary school children read like 8-year-olds because that effectively is when their reading experience stopped. The model we discuss at least gives us a chance to distinguish severe impairment from lack of exposure.

Does it matter how a child is taught to read? It is a bold assumption even that children learn what the teacher thinks he is teaching.

If the development of reading pathways is a function of instruction, as we have suggested it may be, then which techniques produce the best results, and how pervasive are the effects, are important questions to ask. No one knows whether the early differences found in children taught to read by different methods, persist: or what their long-term implication might be. How the reading system is developed within the framework we describe is an empirical matter. Ideally research involving detailed, longitudinal description of individual progress during the primary school years, should provide a data base from which we can provide answers to such vital questions as what should be taught, and how reading should best proceed in order to develop competent reading skills in all educable children.

The purpose of this chapter has been to consider children's thought and their acquisition of literacy in a conceptual framework that emphasizes the process of development and *how* cognitive skills get built up and changed. In concentrating on how children represent and use the real world knowledge acquired during early interaction at home, we sought to explain why the ubiquitous concept of 'context' has so often been found to facilitate thinking and problem solving in young children. We recommend an approach to the study of cognitive development which is, above all, practical. It asks, for instance, why one task using relational information turns out to be more difficult than another and how a particular teaching procedure affects reading strategies. If, as we believe, it is the possession of scripts and strategies, personal involvement and self-awareness that differentiates children's thought processes then it is surely time to ask *how* these differences come about.

References

Alegria, F. (1980) Cited in Marcel, A. H., Prerequisites for a more applicable psychology of reading. In H. Gruneberg, M. Morris and R. Sykes (eds) *Practical Aspects of Memory*. London: Academic Press.

Baddeley, A. D. (1977) Working memory and reading. In P. A. Kolers, M. E. Wrolstad and H. Bouma (eds) *Proceedings of the Conference on the Processing of Visible Language*. New York: Plenum.

Barr, R. (1978) Influence of instruction on early reading. In J. Chapman and P. Czerniewska (eds) *Reading from Process to Practice*. London: Routledge & Kegan Paul/Open University Press.

Bereiter, C. and Hidi, S. (1977) Biconditional versus factual measuring in children. Toronto: OISE. (ERIC Doc. Repro. Service Number ED 138381)

Booth, D. (1976) Language acquisition as the addition of verbal routines. In R. N. Campbell and P. Smith (eds) *Recent Advances in the Psychology of Language*. New York: Plenum.

Bowerman, M. (1978) The acquisition of word meaning: an investigation into some current conflict. In C. Snow and N. Waterson (eds) *The Development of Communication*. London: Wiley.

Bruner, J. (1975) From communication to language: a psychological perspective. *Cognition* **3**: 255–98.

Bryant, P. E. (1974) *Perception and Understanding in Young Children*. London: Methuen.

Bryant, P. E. and Trabasso, T. (1971) Transitive inference and memory in young children. *Nature* **232**: 456–8.

Clementson-Mohr, D. (1982) Towards a social-cognitive explanation of imitative development. In G. Butterworth and P. Light (eds) *Social Cognition*. Brighton: The Harvester Press.

Cole, M., Dore, J., Hall, W. S. and Dorby, G. (1978) Situation and task in young children's talk. *Discourse Processes* **1** (12): 119–76.

Coltheart, M. (1979) Disorders of reading and their implications for models of normal reading. In P. A. Kolers, M. E. Wrolstad and H. Bouma (eds) *The Processing of Visible Language*. New York: Plenum.

Coltheart, M. (1982) The psycholinguistic analysis of acquired dyslexia: some illustrations. *Phil. Trans. Roy. Soc. Lond.* **B298**: 151–64.

Coltheart, M., Patterson, K. and Marshall, J. C. (1980) *Deep Dyslexia*. London: Routledge & Kegan Paul.

Davis, D. R. and Sinha, D. (1950) The effect of one experience upon the recall of another. *Quarterly Journal of Experimental Psychology* **2** (2): 43–51.

Dockrell, J., Campbell, R. and Neilson, I. (1980) Conservation accidents revisited. *International Journal of Behavioural Developments* **3**: 423–40.

Donaldson, M. (1978) *Children's Minds*. London: Fontana.

Dore, J. (1977) Children's illocutionary acts. In R. Freedle (ed.) *Advances in Discourse Processes,* vol. I. Norwood, NJ: Ablex.

Dunn, J. and Wooding, C. (1976) In B. Tizard and D. Harvey (eds) *The Biology of Play*. London: Spastics International.

Ennis, R. H. (1975) Children's ability to handle Piaget's propositional logic. *Review of Educational Research* **45**: 1–42.

Funnell, E. (1978) *Children, Transitive Inferences and Relational Terms*. Unpublished B.A. thesis.

Garrod, A. and Sanford, A. J. (1977) Anaphora: a problem in text comprehension. *Journal of Verbal Learning and Verbal Behaviour* **16**: 77–90.

Graham, F. K., Ernhart, C. B., Craft, M. and Berman, B. W. (1964) Learning of relative and absolute size concepts in pre-school children. *Journal of Experimental Child Psychology* **1**: 26–36.

Henderson, L. (1982) *Orthography and Word Recognition in Reading*. London: Academic Press.

Hidi, S. G. and Hildyard, A. (1979) Four-year-olds' understanding of pretend and forget: no evidence for propositional reasoning. *Journal of Child Language* **6**: 493–510.

Hoogengraad, R., Grieve, R., Baldwin, P. and Campbell, R. (1978) Comprehension as an interacting process. In R. N. Campbell and P. T. Smith (eds) *Recent Advances in the Psychology of Language*. New York: Plenum.

Hughes, M. (1975) *Egocentrism in Preschool Children*. University of Edinburgh dissertation.

Hull, J. (1977) Cited in Baddeley, A. D., Working memory and reading. In P. A. Kolers, M. E. Wrolstad and H. Bouma (eds) *Proceedings of the Conference on the Processing of Visible Language*. New York: Plenum.

Inhelder, B. and Piaget, J. (1958) *The Growth of Logical Thinking From Childhood to Adolescence*. New York: Basic Books.

Lawrenson, W. and Bryant, P. E. (1972) Absolute and relative codes in young children. *Journal of Child Psychology and Psychiatry* **13**: 25–35.

Liberman, I. Y. (1973) Segmentation of the spoken word and reading acquisition. *Bulletin of the Orton Society* **23**: 63–77.

Liberman, I. Y., Shankweiler, D., Liberman, A. M., Fowler, C. and Fischer, F. W. (1977) Phonetic segmentation and recoding in the beginning reader. In A. S. Reber and D. L. Scarborough (eds) *Toward a Psychology of Reading*. Hillsdale, NJ: Lawrence Erlbaum Associates.

Light, P., Buckingham, N. and Robbins, A. (1979) The conservation task as an interactional setting. *British Journal of Educational Psychology* **49**: 304.

Loftus, E. F. and Palmer, J. C. (1974) Reconstruction of automobile destruction: an example of the interaction between language and memory. *Journal of Verbal Learning and Verbal Behaviour* **13**: 585–9.

McGarrigle, J. (1974) Conservation accidents. *Cognition* **3**: 341–50.

Marcel, A. H. (1978) Prerequisites for a more applicable psychology of reading. In H. Gruneberg, M. Morris and R. Sykes (eds) *Practical Aspects of Memory*. London: Academic Press.

Mills, M. and Puckering, C. (1982) Mother and child at home: the implications for early cognitive development. *Proceedings of Assoc. of Child Psychology and Psychiatry Congress*, Dublin, in press.

Nelson, H. (1980) Personal communication.

Omanson, R. C., Warren, W. H. and Trabasso, T. (1978) Goals, inferential comprehension and recall of stories by children. *Discourse Processes* **1**: 337–51.

Peters, M. L. (1967). The influence of reading methods on spelling. *British Journal of Educational Psychology* **37**: 47–52.

Piaget, J. (1928) *Judgement and Meaning in the Child*. London: Routledge & Kegan Paul.

Piaget, J. (1959) *The Language and Thought of the Child*. London: Routledge & Kegan Paul.

Piaget, J. and Inhelder, B. (1974) *The Child's Construction of Quantities*. London: Routledge & Kegan Paul.

Rao, S. (1982) *The Effect of Instruction on Pupil Reading Strategies*. Unpublished dissertation, University of Reading.

Read, C. (1971) Preschool children's knowledge of English phonology. *Harvard Educational Review* **41**; 1–35.

Rose, S. A. and Blank, M. (1974) The potency of context in children's cognition: an illustration through conservation. *Child Development* **45** (2): 499–502.

Schank, R. C. and Abelson, R. P. (1977) *Scripts, Plans, Goals and Understanding*. Hillsdale, NJ: Laurence Erlbaum Associates.

Shankweiler, D., Liberman, I. Y., Mark, L. S., Fowler, C. A., and Fischer, F. W. (1979) The speech code and learning to read. *Journal of Experimental Psychology: Human Learning and Memory* **5** (6): 531–44.

Slobin, D. and Welsh, C. (1973) Elicited imitation as a research tool in developmental linguistics. In C. A. Ferguson and D. Slobin (eds) *Studies in Child Language Development*. New York: Holt, Rinehart & Winston.

Snowling, M. (1980) The development of grapheme-phoneme correspondence in normal and dyslexic readers. *Journal of Experimental Child Psychology* **4** (29): 294–305.

Snowling, M. and Frith, U. (1981) The role of sound. Shape and orthographic cues in early reading. *British Journal of Psychology* **72**: 83–7.

Taplin, J. and Staudenmayer, H. (1973) Interpretation of abstract conditional sentences in deductive reasoning. *Journal of Verbal Learning and Verbal Behaviour* **12**: 530–42.

Tizard, B., Hughes, M., Pinkerton, G. and Carmichael, H. (1982) Adults' cognitive demands at home and at nursery school. *Journal of Child Psychology and Psychiatry* **23** (2): 108–17.

Trabasso, T., Riley, C. A. and Wilson, E. G. (1974) The representation of linear order and spatial strategies in reasoning: a developmental study. In K. Falmague (ed.) *Psychological Studies of Logic and Its Development*. Hillsdale, NJ: Lawrence Erlbaum Associates.

Wallington, B. A. (1974) *The Development of Reasoning in Preschool Children*. University of Edinburgh, dissertation.

Warren, W. H., Nicholas, D. W. and Trabasso, T. (1980) Event chains and inferences in understanding narratives. In R. Freedle (ed.) *Multidisciplinary Approaches to Discourse Comprehension*. Hillsdale, NJ: Lawrence Erlbaum Associates.

Wason, P. C. and Johnson-Laird, P. N. (1972) *Psychology of Reasoning: Structure and Content*. London: Batsford.

Weitz, L., Bynum, T., Thones, E. and Steger, J. (1974) Piaget's stystem of 16 binary operations. An empirical investigation. *Journal of Genetic Psychology*.

Wood, D., McMahon, L. and Cranstoun, Y. (1980) *Working with Under-fives*. Oxford: Grant McIntyre.

Youniss, J. and Furth, H. G. (1973) Reasoning and Piaget: A comment on Bryant and Trabasso. *Nature* **244**: 314–15.

8 An introduction to Soviet developmental psychology

Andrew Sutton

Our tardy discovery of Piaget and his school has had a substantial effect on the course of developmental psychology in the English-speaking world. It remains the case, however, that English-speaking psychology makes little effort to explore and accommodate psychological thinking outside its own linguistic community. With respect to Soviet developmental psychology, how much are we missing? The psychological output of a society is difficult to quantify. Some time ago Berlyne made the following comparative estimate:

> In many areas of psychology 80 or 90 per cent of the important work is probably in English, so that anybody who neglects the literature in foreign languages may be missing a few interesting studies, but will not be missing a great deal. In child psychology, however, this will not be the case. There are in the world today three bodies of work on child psychology, each of about equal volume as far as empirical data and theoretical ideas are concerned. These are the literature in English, the literature in Russian and the literature in French . . . if we confine ourselves to English-language literature in child psychology we are confining ourselves to about one-third of the literature of child psychology. If we further confine ourselves to English-language literature on intellectual processes in children we shall probably have access to considerably less than one-third of the significant work. (Berlyne, 1963, p. 165)

Twenty years later Berlyne's rough estimate on the relative quantity of psychological effort directed towards understanding child development in the Soviet Union still seems substantially to stand. One should add that in neglecting the Soviet literature we are probably restricting ourselves to a very small proportion indeed of the significant literature on how to *influence* the development of mental processes.

If, however, we address ourselves to Soviet psychology solely on the basis that it may provide us with 'more' data, analyses, theories etc. about child development, then we miss an important distinction and may fundamentally misunderstand what we find. Soviet psychology is as closely interwoven with its society and its history as ours is with our own. The Russian word *psikhologiya* is not coterminous in meaning with the English word 'psychology' and the Marxist concept of psychological *practice* cuts quite across our own distinction between 'pure' and 'applied' science. Superficial similarities should not obscure the fact that the practice of Soviet developmental psychology represents a quite different social endeavour than does much of the developmental psychology of the West. More fundamentally, however, Soviet psychologists assert that their science is qualitatively different from our own in a way that we may find hard to recognize or accept. The American philosopher of science, Stephen Toulmin (1978), is one of the few Westerners to have expressed this difference: that, following the enormous creativity of L. S. Vygotskii, Soviet developmental psychology differs from our own in having made a quantum leap to a higher stage of scientific development. It is therefore dealing with questions that we have not yet the integrative theory even to pose.

The present chapter seeks neither to substantiate nor to refute this claim but solely to introduce a few basic ideas to clarify the by now extensive English-language literature from and about Soviet developmental psychology.

Sources

Russian technical prose is often turgid and convoluted to our tastes but the quality of translation into English and editorship of English translations may often add to the problems of the reader. Some translators are linguistically competent but have trouble with psychological terminology in English – others are psychologists in their own right but have trouble with Russian. A few – most notably the late A. R. Luriya – are Soviet psychologists writing in English, at times with considerably less clarity than would a native English speaker. The only general advice one can offer the non-Russian speaker is to read widely and appreciate that implausibilities or ambiguities may represent translation problems rather than weaknesses in the original text. Wide reading in the field is the reader's only way round a further translation problem that affects all translators, whatever their relative competence. There is no agreed system of rendering Russian psychological terms into English and, while translator A and translator B ought to be internationally consistent in how they translate tricky words into English, it is unlikely that they will both translate them the same. Because of such translation difficulties, look for the overall sense in books or articles: *never* compare the works of two translators word with word, sentence with sentence. To do so runs the risk of creating conceptual similarities or differences that do not exist in the original Russian!

Editors of translations bear a heavy responsibility in selecting and presenting Russian work. The reader should be alert for good editorship and seek out editorial information on translation policy, original publication date, details of omissions or even interpolations – and be correspondingly alert for the lack of such information. Out of the reader's control, however, is the perhaps inevitable bias introduced by the original selection of material to be translated. For example, much Russian empirical material is published in monograph whilst much English translation appears in journals or anthologies. To the English reader, therefore, Soviet psychology may appear unduly 'theoretical'. At the same time, most editors are 'academics' and a large part of their market comprises other academics and their students – and almost everyone involved is probably a 'psychologist' (in our sense of the word). As a result, for example, Vygotskii has been presented in the English literature mainly as a theoretician, concerned chiefly with the relationship between speech and thinking – and perhaps a little lacking experimentally. All of these things he was: he was also a defectologist, a skilled clinician, a teacher, an innovator in the philosophy and methodology of science and a not inconsiderable figure in the development of Marxist thought.

Behind such production difficulties lies a linguistic problem for which there is no ultimate satisfactory solution other than a very considerable immersion in the field. Some important Russian words represent concepts with different boundaries from those evoked by their nearest English equivalent, for example:

obuchenie – may be translated as either 'learning' or 'teaching', the Russian word encompassing the whole process, the English words identifying its poles.

rech' – 'speech', not just the making of utterances but also certain features that we would categorize as 'language' and others (such as motivation) that we would regard as psychological.

The sense of a language depends in part upon associations that might be impossible to maintain in a literal translation, not least of which are historical and phonological similarities between certain words in the one language that do not exist in the other, for example:

znak – a 'sign' and *znachenie* – 'meaning'

obshchenie – 'socialization' and *obobshchenie* – 'generalization'.

Such relationships can lead to self-evident associations in the one language that demand far greater explanation or justification in the other.

With such caveats in mind the English-language reader has available a number of general guides to Soviet psychology (including Bauer, 1952, and Macleish, 1975), all unfortunately now rather out of date and none of them devoted specifically to developmental psychology. In the late fifties and sixties there were published a number of general anthologies (of which the longest and last was that by Cole and Maltzman, 1969) but this means of publication has been rendered superfluous by the regular appearance of the International Arts and Science Press (IASP) translation journals *Soviet Psychology* and *Soviet Education* which constitute an important source of current awareness of what is happening in Soviet psychology.

Specifically in developmental psychology there has been a recent spate of interest in the works of the *troika* of Vygotskii, Leont'ev and Luriya (see Luriya, 1976, 1979, 1982; Vygotskii, 1978; Wertsch, 1981). Perhaps in response to this the Russians themselves have begun to produce their own translations (most importantly Leont'ev, 1981).

History

Soviet psychology should be read and understood in the light of the political and intellectual life of its time. Its development may be conveniently considered in three periods.

(1) 1917 to 1936

There had been the beginnings of a small psychological establishment in pre-revolutionary Russia. The early years of the Revolution saw enormous intellectual excitement in the arts and sciences, when ideas and practices considered 'progressive' in the West were eagerly examined to see how they might contribute to remaking humanity, and Soviet psychology underwent rapid development with ideas inherited from the past intensively examined and discarded. Amongst these were psychoanalysis, found wanting very early on in the twenties because of its fundamentally idealistic and individualist nature. Luriya (1979) has recorded his own early flirtations with the works of Freud and Jung at the very outset of his career. Also influential for a while in the land of Pavlov were various behaviourisms though by the end of the twenties these had been dismissed as mechanistic. Pavlov himself, it should be noted, via the 'second signal system', adopted a far from mechanistic position towards the role of cognition in learning and living (see Razran, 1971). Psychometrics were also widely adopted, their use persisting into the thirties.

By the end of the twenties, however, the need to create a Marxist psychology was beginning to produce increasingly novel responses. Especially influential was 'paedology', an attempt to provide a 'unified science of childhood', purporting to relate to education much as do anatomy and physiology to medicine. Many notable figures were associated with this movement in its early days, including Krupskaya (Lenin's widow) and a young and intense psychologist called Vygotskii. Also associated with it were some rather dubious Western approaches, especially intelligence-testing and certain 'progressive' ideas in education.

Vygotskii soon turned away from the paedologists and, in the early thirties, was engaged with his collaborators and students in extensive clinical, practical and experimental work which included defectology (the study of handicapped children), neuropsychology, psychopathology and anthropology, as well as normal mental development. One of Vygotskii's earliest publications had been in English but, despite further English-language papers in the late twenties and early thirties, the work of Vygotskii and his group appears to have made no contemporary impact upon developmental psychology in the West (either our own or that of Piaget).

By the early thirties psychology and education were coming under increasingly critical official scrutiny and control as part of the growing centralization and authoritarianism of all social life under Stalin. When Vygotskii died in 1934 the psychological journals had already ceased publication, contacts with the West were closing down rapidly and his own writings were coming in increasingly for criticism. The passing of the 'Decree against Paedological Perversions' of 1936 is conventionally taken to mark the end of the first period of Soviet psychology – by then, however, a new quality was establishing itself in Soviet life, the decree marking only the final break with the past.

(2) 1936 to 1955

The new quality was Stalinism, under which psychology lived a tenuous existence. Initially it was dependent largely upon other disciplines (medicine and education) in which state it survived until after the Second World War. In the post-war period, however, its very existence, even at this level, came under strong attack. From 1949 the teachings of Pavlov were seized upon as a means whereby human nature might be directly controllable, as part of the wider 'transformationist' movement best known to us through the career of Lysenko. Pavlov himself had died in 1936, his views being considerably distorted in this 'neo-Pavlovian revolution'. Many Western impressions, both of Pavlov and of Soviet psychology, appear to have been formed over this period and the years that immediately followed it.

(3) 1955 to date

Stalin had died in 1953. Khruschev's denouncement of his rule came in 1956. Already the previous year *Voprosy psikhologii* (*Questions of Psychology*), the first psychology journal for over two decades, had commenced publication. 1956 saw the first edition of Vygotskii's works to appear since soon after his death whilst the next year, the year of Sputnik, found Luriya in London introducing his work on 'verbal regulation' (Vygotskian theory worked out experimentally within a neo-Pavlovian methodology!).

Since then Soviet psychology has increasingly established its own, separate identity and reopened its windows on the West. The seventies have seen a growing up-take of Western experimental methods, a rediscovery of the empirical and theoretical work of the twenties and thirties and latterly, even a liberal toying with ideas from sociobiology and psychoanalysis. So does stage negate stage.

Vygotskii's theoretical position has provided the most pervasive influence on the present Soviet understanding of the nature of human mental development. It has to be remembered that Vygotskii himself died a long time ago and that his ideas have been subject to further elaboration and development, by his two close associates, A. R. Luriya (died 1977) and A. N. Leont'ev (died 1980), as well as by second- and third-generation Vygotskians. Important aspects of this 'Troikan psychology' have included Vygotskii's 'socio-historical theory' and his notion of the 'zone of next development', the dialectical materialist theory of stages as applied to human mental development and Leont'ev's 'activity theory'.

The socio-historical theory

Vygotskii had set himself the awesome task of writing a *Kapital* of individual human development. He died without having achieved this but his 'socio-historical theory' (sometimes called the 'cultural-historical' or 'instrumental-historical' theory) has proved the foundation of present-day Soviet developmental psychology: materialist, dialectical and consistent with Marx's socio-historical principle that human mental characteristics have been formed in the process of historical and social development. It is materialist in that it founds mental processes firmly in the activity of the brain, rejecting the dualistic separation of psychological from physiological processes. At the same time it denies that human abilities, traits, voluntary actions, logical memory, etc. are 'natural', innate properties of the brain. Instead, it asserts that they are brought into being out of the dialectical interaction of the child and its social world, the world of adults in which it acquires and internalizes humanity's collective experience to create qualitatively new mental structures, the 'new functional organs' (Leont'ev, 1963) of human thinking.

The topic of psychology, therefore, the development of *human* mental characteristics, is qualitatively different from the thinking, behaviour, etc. of animals. In animals, behaviour depends directly upon inherited, biologically fixed experiences, consolidated in the unconditional reflexes, or upon creatures' own individual experiences, acquired ontogenetically as conditional reflexes. In both cases the behaviour has a direct (in Russian, an 'unmediated') origin, either in the organism itself or in its material environment. Human beings share these lower-order influences but, additionally, experience an indirect ('mediated') form of learning, one that takes an overriding or leading role in determining the structure and content of human mental life, culminating in the formation of human consciousness, the highest form of the organization of matter.

From the moment of birth the human infant experiences a *social* world in which experience is always mediated through relationships with adults. Of particular importance in this, both as a form of social intercourse and as a transmitter of culture, is the mediation of speech. The nature of the child's social intercourse, in particular speech, means that experience is not solely of the world's *actual* properties, propensities and relationships (as in Pavlov's first-signal system, on which animal learning depends) but upon such properties, propensities and relationships *detached from actual objects and experiences*, i.e. upon meaning (Pavlov's second-signal system).

The direction of human mental development is, therefore, from without to within, from external behaviours, social, semantic, between real people, to the complex internal forms of mental life. Consciousness, though biological in its base, is social in content and – contrary to widespread impressions in the West, largely gained during the neo-Pavlovian revolution – 'the heuristic value of the conditioned response [*sic*] is not in interpreting social behaviour biologically but in modifying biological behaviour socially' (Razran, 1935). Our mental characteristics have only an indirect (mediated) dependence upon our biological inheritance. Differing properties of the nervous system are merely internal conditions for mental development. How the individual child develops will depend upon its social, historical context and how well this is mastered in the course of upbringing and education.

Zone of next development

The Soviet concept 'potential' and of how it might best be evaluated, as part of the socio-historical theory, differs fundamentally from the dominant view of these matters in the West. In the Vygotskian view, children's potential is not something that they bring into the world, determined by unalterable properties of their physiological make-up and dependent upon life experiences only in that it may be 'fulfilled'.

Instead, potential is *created* in the process of upbringing and education. Individuals with differing physiological inheritances may be equally successful at the psychological level – though they will have achieved their success at differing rates and *via* different courses of development. In Vygotskii's view the most important index of a child's development was not what that child could presently do – an *intra*personal feature dependent upon the child's accumulated past experiences – but what that child might be brought to do in purposive interaction with adults – an *inter*personal feature dependent upon new social experiences. In Vygotskian psychology the prime focus is upon the *processes* involved in the second of these, rather than upon the *products* manifest in the first.

Vygotskii described two levels of development, existing simultaneously in the developing child:

(1) The 'actual' or 'present level of development', indicated by what the child can do on its own, without the collaboration of adults.

(2) The 'potential level of development', demonstrated by what the child can do in collaboration with adults, with the maximal, optimal help, guidance, explanation, demonstration, encouragement, reassurance, etc. that adults can give.

Vygotskii termed the gap between the actual and potential levels of development the 'zone of next development'. The zone of next development indicates what the child is ready to master next on the basis of present achievements, given the best possible adult attention. In the course of development new mental tools are created in social interaction and passed down from the zone of potential into the zone of present development. As this happens new potentialities are created and the zone of next development is pushed further ahead by the rising level of present development. Teaching and upbringing best assure development when directed towards the top of this zone.

An important innovation stemming from this notion has been the 'teaching experiment', considered by Soviet psychologists to represent the biggest step forward in mental testing since Binet. The teaching experiment differs from Western standardized testing in fundamental aspects. It does not seek to establish how much the child already knows or can do unaided but presupposes that, with help, the child will be able to solve a task beyond its present abilities. The object is to determine the amount and nature of the teaching (*obuchenie*) required to create a new, generalized skill. For example, the child might be first administered a task too hard for it to solve, taught to solve an analogous problem, then re-evaluated on the original task to trace the changes that have taken place in thinking processes under the influence of certain kinds of teaching. Or the child is presented with too hard a task, then is helped to a solution with the help carefully meted out to indicate how much and what kind is required, final mastery being indicated by the ability to use what has been taught to solve an analogous problem.

The teaching experiment has made no impact in the West. Perhaps methodologies from the cultural-historical tradition cannot be readily translated into our own work. Though this specific methodology dates from the recent stage of Soviet psychology its precursor, the 'natural experiment', tended to be similarly disregarded. One natural experiment, conducted in Vygotskii's lifetime, the classic twin study of Luriya and Yudovich (1959), has been frequently cited in Western texts and aspects of it have been replicated in Britain (Douglas and Sutton, 1978). It has not, however, provoked substantial consideration of the psychological principles and educational measures for the creation of human potential in social interactions with which it is associated in its country of origin.

Stages

Engels' laws of dialectics concern the mechanisms of discontinuity and change. Marx's theory of social history is one of changes in kind, from tribalism to slave society to feudalism to capitalism to socialism. To a Marxist the word 'development' has established implications which apply to the whole of nature and human life. Briefly, dialectical materialism distinguishes between two related types of change, changes in *amount* and changes in *kind*. Changes in amount, quantitative change, constitute growth: changes in kind, qualitative change, constitute development. The two are intimately connected: the processes of growth within a phenomenon generate internal 'contradictions' between its component parts, which become so strong as to create a 'crisis' which is resolved when the whole rearranges to incorporate new qualities, at a higher level or stage of being.

The child's physiological growth is for the large part just that, a quantitative increase in the size of organs. The child's mind also undergoes periods of growth in which the child increases the amount that it knows, can do, etc. in its participation in its material and social world. But this is interrupted over the course of childhood by a series of crises in which the *ways* that the child thinks, behaves, etc. change as altogether new qualities are created at successively higher mental stages. The word 'development' has a specific meaning for Soviet psychologists, invoking particular courses and forces altogether unfamiliar to most 'developmental' psychologists in the English-speaking world.

Charting the course of mental development and its underlying forces was a central concern of Vygotskii's at the close of his life. He and his successors have regarded the proper definition of the stages of child development to be a prerequisite for an effective approach to bringing up and educating children. One of his papers on this topic is quite well known in English (Vygotskii, 1967) though its purpose may be easily missed because of its (to us) unfamiliar intention and terminology. To the educator (and such Vygotskii was) important problems of stage development are, first, to determine the 'leading activity' for learning that defines each stage and, secondly, to understand the inner contradictions that bring about stage change and are thus essential to development. The conventional terminology of the Soviet stage system and its leading activities is outlined in Table 8.1. It is essential to the understanding of Soviet texts to recognize that terms such as 'early age' or 'preschool' refer to defined stages of development, qualitatively different one from the other and involving not only differences in the child's mental structures but also differences in the kinds of adult-child interactions best suited to bring about the development of new mental qualities.

English-language readers know this area best through Luriya's laboratory studies of the 'verbal regulation of behaviour' (better translated as the 'speech regulation of actions'), conducted in the fifties using a somewhat neo-Pavlovian methodology to illustrate the step-by-step process of mental development, adult to child and outer to inner. Zaporozhets and El'konin (1971) have provided a broader picture of Soviet studies of young children, in which the emphasis upon stage is clearly apparent.

Though the general stage structure of development has been broadly agreed by Soviet psychologists, the precise relative status and importance of the various developmental crises has been subject

Table 8.1 Conventional terminology, leading activities and age ranges of stages of development in Soviet psychology. (Note that the ages given are very approximate, and will vary considerably with the conditions of upbringing and education.)

18 years	Adulthood (work)
15–16 years	Youth (vocational interests)
11–12 years	Adolescence (personal relationships)
7 years	School age (formal teaching)
3 years	Preschool age (role play)
1 year	Early (or pre preschool) age (manipulation of objects)
Birth	Infancy (direct emotional contact)

to debate and there has not been exact agreement on what constitutes a 'period', what a 'stage' and what merely a 'phase'. El'konin (1972) has made a complex attempt at an inclusive theory, which will serve here to illustrate both the dialectical pattern that Soviet psychologists seek to discern in development and the Vygotskian concern to integrate the emotional sphere with the intellectual in understanding the development of mental life.

El'konin considered the separation of the intellectual from the emotional aspects of development – most clearly exemplified, he felt, in the ideas of Piaget – to constitute an unacceptable dualism within psychology. He proposed that this dualism could be overcome in a way that reconciled empirical data with dialectical theory by distinguishing two kinds of child activity. The first group consists of activities which occur within the interactional system, child-social adult: they involve an orientation towards the meaning of human activity and the learning of the objectives, motives and norms of human relationships. It is in these activities that the child's needs and motivations are formed. The second group consists of activities within the interactional system, child-social object: these involve socially evolved modes of action with objects and their various properties. It is in these activities that the child's mental powers are formed. Examination of the content of successive stages of development leads El'konin to propose that, at successively higher levels of organization, the two groups alternate in providing the leading activity for optimal mental development. It is the shift from one leading activity to the other that constitutes developmental crisis. El'konin identified two particularly sharp transitions over the course of childhood, at around 3 years of age and at the onset of adolescence, dividing childhood into three major periods separated by crises at both of which the child manifests a tendency towards independence and negative behaviour towards adults. Each period comprises two stages, the first lead by the learning (*obuchenie*) of the objectives, motives and norms of human activity, the second by mastery of the modes of actions with objects. El'konin's system is illustrated diagrammatically in Figure 8.1.

Figure 8.1 El'konin's proposal for a system of periods, stages and phases of childhood.
Source: El'konin (1972)

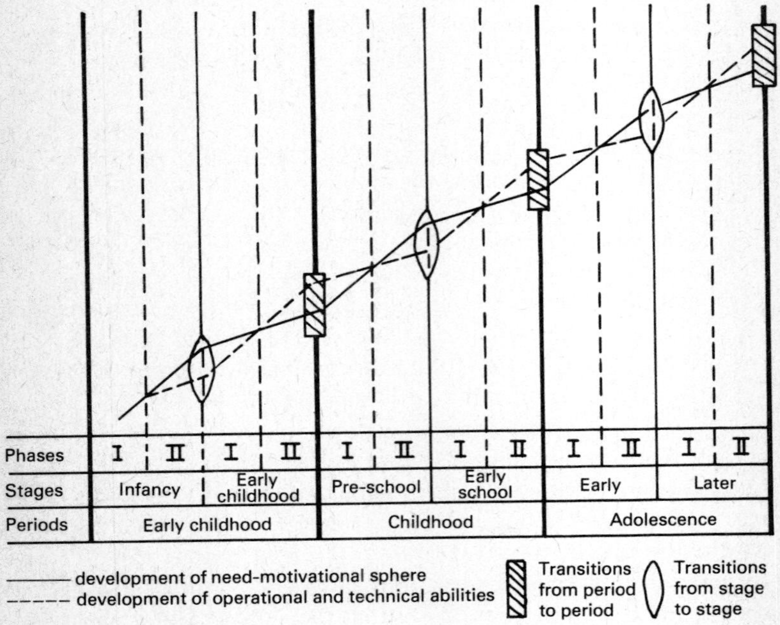

Such fascination with stage may appear irrelevant, even dysfunctional, to psychologists from the Anglo-Saxon tradition. Without an appreciation of this emphasis, however, and of its terminology and conceptual background, much Soviet child and educational psychology will remain unintelligible, whatever the quality of the linguistic translation. Taking it into account raises interesting questions. For example, at a specific level, the English-language reader might like to re-examine the familiar writings of Luriya upon 'verbal regulation' or of Vygotskii upon 'play'. More generally, there are important theoretical and empirical questions about how Vygotskian analyses apply to the more familiar stage systems of, say, Piaget and Kohlberg.

Activity

The English-language reader must remember that, although dialectical materialism provides an overarching unity to Soviet psychology that is lacking in our own, Soviet developmental psychology is not a single, monolithic whole. The theoretical line founded by Vygotskii has provided the broadest stream of ideas and findings but it has shown considerable development over fifty years and, at a given time, there are differences within it. There have, too, been other streams, the influence of which continues.

For all his founding genius, now widely acknowledged amongst Soviet psychologists, Vygotskii has not gone without criticism. In particular, it has been pointed out that his cultural-historical theory placed too much reliance upon the child's communications with its social world and upon meaning and the development of concepts in explaining the development of consciousness. Vygotskii offered a view of child development arising out of social communication rather than out of interactions with the real world. His general Marxist proposition about the social nature of human mental development is seen as correct but, instead of bringing out the essential role of labour activities *themselves* in linking children to their world, Vygotskii focused upon the instruments of labour. In this the cultural-historical theory is over-intellectual and, quite contrary to Vygotskii's firmly held intentions, it 'opens the door to idealism' (Leont'ev and Luriya, 1968). The theory of 'activity' (*deyatel'nost'*) attempts to redress this balance and is perhaps the most important theoretical position in present-day Soviet psychology. Activity theory is chiefly associated with the name of Vygotskii's colleague and friend Leont'ev (see Leont'ev 1981; Wertsch, 1981; Talysina, 1981), though Rubinštein made an important contribution from outside the main Vygotskian tradition (see Payne, 1968).

There is some present dispute in Soviet psychology about the relative status of Vygotskii's socio-historical theory and Leont'ev's activity theory. Was the former merely a precursor of the latter or is the latter no more than an off-shoot of the former? Whatever the answer to that question, English-language readers of Soviet psychology should bear in mind that Vygotskii worked half a century ago and that his writings, formative and influential as they have been, constitute the beginning rather than the totality of modern Soviet developmental psychology. Most particularly, they should beware of being lead through the door into idealism by his interest in meaning, concept formation and social interaction, redressing the balance by consideration of the activity theory that sites the origin of our mental life in our external, practical activities (our labour). For Vygotskii 'each higher mental function in the child's development appears twice upon the scene: first as a collective activity, a social activity, i.e. as an intermental function, second as an individual function, as the internal means of the child's thinking, as an intramental function' (Vygotskii, 1956, p.449). For Leont'ev, however, it is the child's own practical activities within that context that become internalized to assume a mental form (to become mental activities). Dualism is avoided by regarding internal and external activities as two forms of the same thing, related through mutual transformations. Both forms 'bind man to the external world, each in a different way. That external world is then reflected in the mind' (Leont'ev, 1947, p.313). The focus of psychology from this viewpoint is the actual process of the individual's interaction with the environment in the solution of specific tasks, processes which in the majority of cases jointly involve both mental and non-mental processes.

This orientation is very clearly a science of practice in the Marxist sense.

A Marxist science

Unfamiliar though the language, history, methodologies and conventions of Soviet psychology may appear to Anglo-Saxon psychologists, it is its explicit Marxism that for many proves its most mystifiying (and often its most alienating) feature. Marxism is a developing and diverse stance. The Marxism in question here is Soviet and Russian and the psychology of Vygotskii and his successors has been influenced accordingly – for example, the 'reflection' in the above quotation from Leont'ev is a philosophical concept of Lenin's. To understand Soviet psychology one must appreciate its philosophical basis.

One must also recognize its social role. Soviet psychology exists to advance the remaking of humanity: its concern with children is not simply to record and understand how they develop but to contribute to the mutability and transformation of that development. Soviet developmental psychology should not, therefore, be sought solely, or even chiefly, in the publications of university psychology departments and research institutes but in the work of the institutions involved in the education and upbringing of the new generation. The forms of such institutions may appear superficially familiar: their developmental-psychological theory is radically different from our own (see, e.g., Sutton, 1980). Despite shifts in emphasis over the years, the relative primacy of social practice remains a central point of difference between much of their psychology and much of our own.

Soviet psychology, like many other sectors of Soviet society, may often fail to realize this high practical ideal. For example, El'konin (1972) regards the stage structure built into the Soviet education system to have become so much in contradiction with the stages proposed by psychology as to constitute a crisis. An even more flagrant contradiction between psychology and pedagogy exists in the field of gender development. Soviet psychological theory provides a powerful model for arguing the social construction of male-female personality and intellectual differences, while Soviet educational practice runs on an implicit theory of their innate determination (see *Women in Eastern Europe*, no. 5, 1982–3, pp. 110–14). For Western psychologists, however, the immediate issue lies not in how the Soviet Union actually brings up its children (interesting empirical data though this might offer), nor in the ways in which Soviet society utilizes or restricts psychological knowledge (instructive, again, though this may be). Rather it is the structure of Soviet psychology itself, along with its content and findings, that immediately challenge the structure, theory and findings of our own psychology. Soviet psychologists are increasingly aware of Western psychologies and have become alert to the need to utilize (even though not, perhaps, to accommodate) the two bodies of work. There is now a considerable and rapidly expanding fund of material in English permitting us, in our turn, to examine their work – much of it admittedly 'difficult' but largely so in that it is unfamiliar.

It is still possible, however, to proceed right through a psychological education in the English-speaking world with no real awareness of Soviet psychology at all – or, what is worse, a distorted and unworthy impression. Increasingly, those who are willing to grasp the cultural and philosophical nettles involved may begin to benefit from Soviet work through English-language texts. Ultimately, though, we may have to recognize that a working ability to read Russian psychological texts may prove an important component of any proper education and career in developmental psychology.

References

Bauer, R. A. (1952) *The New Man in Soviet Psychology*. Cambridge, Mass: Harvard University Press.

Berlyne, D. E. (1963) Soviet research on intellectual processes in children. In J. C. Wright and J. Kagan (eds) *Basic Cognitive Processes in Children*, Research in Child Development Monographs 28 (2): 165–84.

Cole, M. and Maltzman, I. (eds) (1969) *A Handbook of Contemporary Soviet Psychology*. New York and London: Basic Books.

Douglas, J. and Sutton, A. (1978) The development of speech and mental processes in a pair of twins: a case study. *Journal of Child Psychology and Psychiatry* **19**: 49–56.

El'konin, D. B. (1972) Towards the problem of stages in the mental development of children. *Soviet Psychology* **10**: 225–51.

Leont'ev, A. N. (1947) *An Essay on the Development of the Mind*. Moscow (in Russian).

Leont'ev, A. N. (1963) Principles of mental development and the problem of intellectual backwardness. In B. Simon and J. Simon (eds) *Educational Psychology in the USSR*. London: Routledge & Kegan Paul.

Leont'ev, A. N. (1981) *Problems of the Development of the Mind*. Moscow: Progress.

Leont'ev, A. N. and Luriya, A. R. (1968) The psychological ideas of L. S. Vygotskii. In B. Wolman (ed.) *Historical Roots of Contemporary Psychology*. New York: Harper.

Luriya, A. R. (1976) *Cognitive Development: Its Cultural and Social Foundations*. Cambridge, Mass.: Harvard University Press.

Luriya, A. R. (1979) *The Making of Mind: A Personal Account of Soviet Psychology*. Cambridge, Mass.: Harvard University Press.

Luriya, A. R. (1982) *Language and Cognition*. New York: Wiley.

Luriya, A. R. and Yudovich, F. Ya. (1959) *Speech and the Development of Mental Processes*. London: Staples.

Macleish, J. (1975) *Soviet Psychology: History, Theory and Content*. London: Methuen.

Payne, J. R. (1968) *Rubinštein and the Philosophical Foundation of Soviet Psychology*. Basel/Stuttgart: Reidel.

Razran, G. (1935) Psychology in the USSR. *Journal of Philosophy* **32**: 19–24.

Razran, G. (1971) *Mind in Evolution*. Boston, Mass.: Houghton Mifflin.

Soviet Education (monthly) New York: M. E. Sharpe, Inc.

Soviet Psychology (quarterly) New York: M. E. Sharpe, Inc.

Sutton, A. (1980) Backward children in the USSR. In J. Brine, M. Perrie and A. Sutton (eds) *Home, School and Leisure in the Soviet Union*. London: Allen & Unwin.

Talysina, N. F. (1981) *The Psychology of Learning*. Moscow: Progress.

Toulmin, S. (1978) The Mozart of psychology. *New York Review of Books* 28 September: 51–7.

Vygotskii, L. S. (1956) *Selected Psychological Research*. Moscow: Academy of Pedagogic Sciences of USSR (in Russian).

Vygotskii, L. S. (1967) Play and its role in the mental development of the child. *Soviet Psychology* **5** (3): 6–18 (Vygotskii memorial issue).

Vygotskii, L. S. (1978) *Mind in Society*. Cambridge, Mass.: Harvard University Press.

Wertsch, J. (1981) *The Concept of Activity in Soviet Psychology*. New York: Sharpe.

Women in Eastern Europe. University of Birmingham: Centre for Russian and East European Studies.

Zaporozhets, A. V. and El'konin, D. B. (1971) *The Psychology of Preschool Children*. Cambridge, Mass.: MIT Press.

Name index

Figures in italics refer to bibliographical references

Subject index